The Natural Food Catalogue

The Natural Food Catalogue

Vicki Peterson

MACDONALD AND JANE'S LONDON

First published in Great Britain in 1978 by
Macdonald and Jane's Limited,
Paulton House,
8 Shepherdess Walk, London N1 7LW

ISBN 0 354 04303 X

This book was designed and produced by
George Rainbird Limited,
36 Park Street, London W1Y 4DE

Editor: Mary Anne Sanders
House Editor: Fiona Roxburgh
Designers: Juanita Grout and Christine Lloyd
Index: Ellen Crampton
Production: Bridget Walsh
Illustration Research: Karen Gunnell
Drawings: Lindsay Blow, Cheryl Clarke,
Ingrid Jacob, Angela Lewer

Printed by Butler and Tanner Limited, Frome,
Somerset.

Contents

The setting of words in CAPITAL LETTERS denotes that a fuller entry exists in the book and the reader is advised to turn to the index.

The conversions for the recipes have been done according to the advice given by the English Metrication Board, that is 1 ounce equals 25 grams, 16 ounces equal 450 grams. The cup measurement is based on the average American size of 8 fluid ounces. Awkward amounts have been rounded up or down to the nearest unit of 25 grams. For instance, where one cup of cooked, drained lima beans weighs 170 grams, this has been rounded up to 175 grams or 6 ounces.

Introduction

What are wholefoods?

I would describe a natural or wholefood as food free from chemical additives.

The Soil Association actually coined the word wholefood twenty years ago. Their definition is precise and explicit: 'Wholefood is exactly what the name implies. An unrefined food to which nothing has been added and nothing taken away.' Of course fruit and vegetables are wholefoods but one problem is to find them unsprayed and unwaxed and in this book the emphasis has been put on readily available dried foods. There is however a section dealing with how to create a healthy organic soil in our own gardens.

Until ten years ago the wholefood movement was evolving very slowly. A few independent thinkers such as George Bernard Shaw and Aldous Huxley were interested in natural foods but while the processing industry was rushing headlong towards chemical food only a few lone voices were raised in protest.

The very first advocate of natural foods was Dr T.R. Allinson. When the introduction of the steel-milling process took place in 1879 and eliminated the bran and wheat germ from bread, he realized that the population had been deprived, at one stroke, of a major source of vitamins and fibre. Dr Allinson warned that ill health and disease would follow and he was right. (See NUTRITION AND MEDICINE *page* 7).

The next pioneer to realize the importance of food was Dr Robert McCarrison. In the early years of the twentieth century he carried out the original research into the Hunzas, a people of the Himalayas famed for their longevity and remarkable health. Their diet was — and still is — wholemeal flour or millet, buttermilk, yoghurt, sprouted pulses, meat once a week, and plenty of fresh fruit and vegetables.

Dr McCarrison had a flair for research. He fed a colony of rats on the typical British diet of white bread, margarine, tinned meats, boiled cabbage, boiled potatoes, tinned jam, and strong tea with plenty of sugar. The result: the rats were nervous, stunted and liable to bite. Post mortems showed a high incidence of degenerative changes and a variety of infections and a similar test group fed on the Hunza diet stayed healthy and virile.

In 1930 Dr McCarrison became Director of Nutritional Research in India where he studied Sikh and Pathan diets and continued his research into the link between food and health. His tests subsequently became famous, but he was far ahead of his time, as was Dr Allinson.

In the middle 1950s a group of nutritionists in the U.S.A., led by Adelle Davis, began to warn that processed, additive-laden food would lead to ill health.

'The New Nutrition' spread rapidly and influential doctors such as Dr Roger Williams, the discoverer of pantothenic acid, added their weight to the cause. Dr Williams has stated quite emphatically that average supermarket produce is likely to be deficient in vitamin B6, magnesium, vitamin E, vitamin C, folic acid, and trace minerals. Regular use of such food, he believes, will lead to poor cell environment which could cause many so-called 'civilized diseases'.

The time was right for these ideas and it is astonishing to look back and see that only eight years ago a leading London specialist was treating diverticular patients with bran in secret as he feared the ridicule of his colleagues. Now, every medical authority in the world advocates fibre as an essential factor in the diet.

In the last five years growing disenchantment with the polluted society has created a climate of opinion in which ideas about wholefoods thrive. After all, it is a documented fact that the average man living in the Western hemisphere eats 2 kg (4 lb) of additives a year, the equivalent of 20 aspirin-sized tablets each day.

Wholefood is more than a mere definition. It is not only a way of thinking — but also a way of life, and easy to adopt.

Author's acknowledgments

I would like to thank the following people for their help with this book: Dr Carole Ashton-Jennings, Mr D. S. Backhouse of Höfels Pure Foods, Mrs J. Cameron of Wholefoods, Dr A.H. Dewar of the Royal Victoria Infirmary, Newcastle, Mr Lawrence D. Hills and Mr Alan Gear of the Henry Doubleday Research Association, Dr Gordon Latto and The McCarrison Society, Dr Alan Long, Nutritional Advisor to the Vegetarian Society, Mrs Daphne Neech, and Dr Shewell-Cooper; also, the following organizations: The Australian Honey Board, British Egg Information Service, The Cheese Bureau, The Flour Advisory Board, Harmony Foods, The Herb Society, The Lyon Playfair Library of Imperial College, London, Pasta Foods, and the U.S. Department of Agriculture. My thanks are due to the following friends who tested the recipes: Wendy King, Chris Liddiard, Irene McCartney, and Catherine Parry-Wingfield.

Nutrition and Medicine

'Of all the factors which make for human health the greatest single factor is perfectly constituted food.' So wrote Sir Robert McCarrison in his book *Nutrition and Health* in 1930. He was one of the pioneers who first saw the link between nutrition and medicine.

A great modern doctor, Dr Roger Williams of the University of Texas, U.S.A. discovered pantothenic acid and also named folic acid. He made the following report to the Secretary of Health, Education and Welfare in 1976: *'The sins of omission occasioned by modern industrialization of food production without adequate regard for nutritional value are many.*

Among the essential nutrient items likely to be deficient or out of balance in the supermarket produce commonly consumed are vitamin B6, magnesium, vitamin E, vitamin C, folic acid and trace minerals. This is not a complete list, but these items all appear to be involved in the heart disease problem. All these and other nutrient items are needed to keep the cells and tissues of hearts and blood vessels healthy.

Mental retardation, dental disease, arthritis, alcoholism and possibly even cancer, can be blamed on poor internal environments which the cells and tissues of our bodies have to live with. These . . . can be vastly improved by nutritional means. Because of decades of indoctrination, many physicians will automatically pooh-pooh the idea that nutrition can be so important for the prevention of disease. This is because they are so inexpert in the area of nutritional physiology. No physician worthy of the name, however, can take the position that ignorance about nutrition is preferable to understanding.'

Our modern diet

'The modern Western diet is a first class menu for disease', says Mr Denis Burkitt, Senior Research Fellow in Geographical Pathology at St Thomas's Hospital, London. Mr Burkitt was one of the first doctors to publicly warn against the lack of fibre in staple food. (*See* THE FIBRE FACTOR *page 8*)

The call for radical change in the civilized diet has also come from the influential voice of the U.S. Senate Select Committee on Nutrition and Human Needs, which opened its 1977 report with this sentence: 'The eating patterns of this century represent as critical a public health concern as any now before us.' The Select Committee laid down several major 'dietary goals' and a series of recommendations. The first goal may appear quite startling. In it the American people are urged to get far more of their calorie requirements from unrefined carbohydrates. This Select Committee recommendation is likely to stagger people who have

been brainwashed into believing that high protein diets are essential for health.

The Lancet reviewed the report with this comment: 'This first goal will surprise those — one hopes few of them are medical people — who still imagine that starchy foods are unhealthy or that bread and potatoes are especially fattening.' Before this is dismissed as another fad let us put the matter in perspective.

The U.S. Senate Select Committee's recommendations are endorsed by the Vegetarian Society in the U.K. who make similar suggestions for dietary change in their Green Plan report. The Society points out that vegetarians have traditionally eaten far more unrefined carbohydrates than the rest of the population. In fact, the American Academy of Pediatrics researched long-term vegetarians and found they 'demonstrated excellent health. There are some nutritional benefits of a well-balanced vegetarian diet, such as the rarity of obesity and a tendency towards lower serum cholesterol levels'. The Academy's report goes on to discuss 'concerns about agricultural practices and food processing which may have validity'. It lists hormones and residual antibiotics in meat and pesticide residues in dairy, fruit and vegetable products.

The U.S. Senate Select Committee voiced similar concern that highly processed foods are most likely to be high in saturated fat, sugar and salt. Also they are likely to contain unnecessary additives such as colouring. Children in particular consume large amounts of artificial colour in soft drinks. The Select Committee advised schools and colleges to serve unprocessed foods on the premises because they are cheaper and more nutritious.

Major dietary goals in the Select Committee's report

1. An increase in carbohydrate consumption to between 55% and 60% of caloric intake. At present it is about 46% in the U.S.A. and most western countries with half the amount represented by sugar.
2. Consumption of fat to be reduced to 30% of the caloric intake. In the average diet, fat provides 40% of the calories.
3. Cholesterol to be reduced to 300 mg a day — the average in the U.K. and U.S.A. is about 500 mg a day.
4. A reduction of sugar to 15% of the total caloric intake — 25% of the daily calories in an average American diet are provided by sugar.
5. A reduction in the salt intake to 3 g a day. The average modern, processed food leads to a salt intake of between 6-18 g.

Unrefined carbohydrates are foods such as wholemeal bread, GRAINS and brown RICE, fresh fruit and salads.

Getting the balance right

The best diet for health is all a question of balance. Protein and carbohydrate intake should be in balance. (See OUR MODERN DIET page 7). Vitamins and minerals should be adequately supplied. People who eat processed and convenience foods are most likely to be undersupplied. There is therefore a case for each one of us to work out our nutritional requirements according to expert opinion. Our modern diet could possibly be lacking in essential nutrients, and it is quite likely to be oversupplied in certain substances.

Take salt, for example. Health experts and the U.S. Senate Select Committee on Nutrition and Human Needs recommend a salt intake of less than 5 g a day. An average Western diet would contain between 6 g and 18 g. (See SALT page 107). Heavy consumption of salt overloads the system with sodium and disturbs the balance with potassium. This imbalance can lead among other things, to arthritis, and high blood pressure. Sugar, too, is likely to be eaten in huge quantities. The consumption of sugar has risen so much that an average 55 kg (120 lb) per head is consumed each year in the U.K., or about 142 g (5 oz) of sugar each day. How this overdosage can cause problems is explained by Dr Walter Yellowlees, a leading British doctor:

It is surely in keeping with what we know of the norms of physiology that an endocrine system, evolved to deal with the relatively slow absorption of glucose from sugars naturally diluted in fruit or root, should, when exposed to repeatedly massive doses of pure sucrose, become exhausted and bring yet another diabetic for treatment.

Many doctors now believe that overloading the system with sugar has a leading part to play in the so called 'civilized diseases'.

The fibre factor

The discovery that foods rich in roughage or fibre can help prevent the so-called affluent diseases has been hailed as one of the medical breakthroughs of the century. It is surprising to look back ten, or even five, years and see that doctors were advising patients with digestive and bowel diseases to take only refined food.

In the 1960s, one leading London specialist was treating patients on a high fibre diet in strict secret, for fear of ridicule from his colleagues. In 1974 Mr Denis Burkitt (See page 7), addressed a conference of British doctors. He strongly advocated natural fibre as a remedy for diverticulitis and other 'civilized diseases'. Next day, health food shops all over Britain sold out of bran. (See BRAN page 26). Books by Surgeon Captain Cleave and Dr Andrew Stanway, among others (see SOURCES page 157), brought the fibre subject before a wider public. Gradually the medical climate changed and the need for unrefined foods rich in fibre was adopted as a goal by the U.S. Senate Select Committee on Nutrition and Human Needs in 1977. The wheel had come full circle.

It is ironic to remember that in the 1880s Dr T. R. Allinson campaigned to stop the 'new' mill process removing the BRAN and WHEAT GERM from the flour. He was considered a crank and struck off the medical register. Leading doctors now agree that inadequate diets are responsible in part for many of the degenerative diseases so widespread in the twentieth century. One theory is that an 'incubation period' started in the 1880s with the devitalized diet and led to a rising graph of the so-called 'civilized diseases'.

Heart disease began to increase rapidly from 1911 — an 'incubation period' of 32 years. Diverticulitis (a balloon type blowout of the colon wall) was not even mentioned in medical text books until 1922 — an 'incubation period' of 43 years.

To support this theory it is interesting to note that diverticulitis generally only affects people over forty. So if a child was born in 1880 and brought up on refined bread as a staple food, by 1920 the 'incubation period' could leave him susceptible to a diverticulitis attack.

Heart disorders affect a much wider age group. This is reflected in the change in the Western diet and the corresponding rise of heart disease.

Why is fibre so important?

Fibre is the group of highly complex substances found in the cells of plants which the human digestive enzymes cannot break down. The latest medical knowledge indicates that our bodies are actually programmed to deal with this roughage. So highly refined foods without the essential fibre cause a definite chain of reactions which can result in the wide range of serious diseases we refer to as civilized diseases — from diverticulitis to obesity and dental decay.

One vital factor is the length of time that food residue takes to pass through the alimentary canal. This has become known as 'transit time' which is believed to be the clue to low fibre illness. Faeces need to be solid to pass through the colon and sometimes they are shunted back and forth to absorb more water. Fibre gives food the bulk it needs to pass along the bowel.

Not uncommonly, people of fibre-depleted diets retain food residues for five days or more. The inherent danger in this is pointed out clearly by Mr Burkitt. '*On a high fibre diet poisonous substances will be diluted and washed out every day. We believe that bowel cancer is caused by carcinogenous substances in the faeces acting in the gut.*' He says also that elderly people on low roughage diets in the U.K. often need two weeks for food to pass along their alimentary tracts.

In contrast, research with the Zulus in Africa shows that the longest 'transit time' is two days. It has been found that people who eat highly processed foods regularly develop unusually narrow colons, which can cause complications.

There is evidence to suppose that fibre can offer protection against heart disease. Dr Andrew Stanway in his book *Taking the Rough with the Smooth* (*See* BRAN page 26) says: 'We can say with some certainty that low fibre diets seem to alter the body's chemistry towards that associated with incidence of heart disease.' Research in the University of Washington, U.S.A., has shown that fibre also offers another valuable protection. Fibrous particles undigested by the body have the ability to absorb chemicals such as cyclamates, and other additives. Researchers in the U.K. have found that fibre can alter the bacteria in the bowel and render it less susceptible to disease.

Most people know that fibre prevents constipation. This is not a minor ailment but a serious symptom that the body is not functioning as it should do. Constipation is the first warning that fibre intake needs to be adjusted. Roughage in the diet is essential not only as a long term prevention, but also to maintain everyday health. According to Mr Burkitt, 'fibre can transform your life'.

How to put fibre in the diet

Mr Burkitt advises one tablespoonful of natural bran each day. An easy way to regularly eat bran is to put 100% wholemeal bread on the daily menu. Certain fruits and vegetables contain fibre although this is slightly different from cereal fibre. A combination of the two sources would be an excellent idea. Fibre rich plants are potatoes, carrots, apples, bananas, avocados, fresh blackberries, PAPAYA, dried dates (See DRIED FRUIT *page* 37) and figs, strawberries, and raspberries.

Food for healthy hearts

Heart disease, one of the major killers of our time, was practically unknown in 1900. Dr Paul Dudley White in his book *Heart Disease* writes:

When I graduated from medical school in 1911, I had never heard of coronary thrombosis, which is one of the chief threats to life in the United States and Canada today — an astonishing development in one's own lifetime! There can be no doubt that coronary heart disease has now reached epidemic proportions.

There is no possiblity whatever that doctors fifty years ago could not recognize or diagnose heart disease. Careful, well-documented records disprove this idea, for instance, in 1893 the distinguished Canadian doctor, Sir William Osler, recorded only five cases of angina amongst the 9000 patients in his hospital. Just thirteen years later, in 1906, he was able to describe 268 cases of heart disease in detail. Similar carefully noted rises in the numbers of heart patients occurred in Britain. By 1915 the level had reached 35 cases in each million; in 1931 it was 166 per million, and by 1969 it had soared to 2900 heart victims in each million.

Why has there been such a huge increase? Eminent doctors such as Wilfred E. Shute and his brother Evan Shute, believe that the heart disease epidemic is directly linked with the amount of vitamin E in the diet. Among the important properties of vitamin E, two are outstanding. First, this vitamin is a superb natural anti-thrombin and can prevent clots forming. Second, it is an anti-oxidant and can reduce the body's need for oxygen. Vitamin E has been shown to make a higher proportion of the oxygen taken into the body available to the tissues.

The Shute brothers are the leading proponents of vitamin E therapy. In their world famous Shute

Dr T.R. Allinson

Foundation for Medical Research in Ottawa, Canada, they have treated 35,000 patients with high doses of vitamin E. In his book *Vitamin E for Ailing and Healthy Hearts*, Dr Wilfred Shute describes how desperately ill patients are monitored on varying doses of vitamin E. He monitors not only the victims of heart diseases but also patients suffering from varicose veins, diabetes, kidney disease and burns.

'There is a dose appropriate to every patient', writes Dr Shute. 'It may require weeks or months to determine what his dose should be. Patience and skill are demanded by this type of treatment. There is no simple rule-of-thumb.' Levels of vitamin E are prescribed ranging from 150 I.U. to over 1000 I.U. Obviously it is unwise to take this sort of dose without medical supervision, particularly anyone with a tendency to high blood pressure.

There is a very good case, however, for each individual to naturally increase the amount of vitamin E in his diet. Dr Wilfred Shute makes the point that the epidemic in heart disease in this century can be traced back to the new milling process introduced in 1879 which removed the WHEAT GERM and the vitamin E from the bread. When the steel mills began to separate the germ from the wheat kernel, all the vitamin E and many other essential nutrients were lost from the staple food. The Western diet was thus deprived of its major source of vitamin E.

It has been estimated that paupers in a London poorhouse in 1870 were far richer in dietary vitamin E than the average person today. The U.S. Bureau of Research has found that a hundred years ago the average intake of vitamin E was 150 I.U. Today a 'reasonable diet' provides, on average 15 I.U. of vitamin E and a processed diet 7.4 I.U.

How to put vitamin E in the diet

The easiest way to redress the balance and put back vitamin E into the daily diet is to eat 100% wholemeal bread and wheatgerm cereal. The richest known source of vitamin E is wheatgerm oil. Other OILS, such as sunflower, sesame and safflower, are also rich in vitamin E. Heating the oils, or letting them become rancid destroys the vitamin. Other good sources of vitamin E are NUTS, watercress, spinach, lettuce and EGG yolk.

Other factors

It would be simplistic not to say that many factors are involved in a subject so complex as heart disease. Medical authorities throughout the world now generally agree that smoking, lack of exercise, and stress all make their contribution.

There is still some controversy about the exact role of animal fats or saturated fats. The Medical Research Council in the U.K., and the U.S. Senate Select Committee have both advised a reduction in the intake of saturated fats. It would obviously be sensible, and no hardship, to adjust this item in the diet. Foods like LECITHIN and vegetable oils play their part in creating a healthy environment. Both have powers to reduce the level of blood cholesterol. According to Adelle Davis in her book *Let's Eat Right to Keep Fit (See page* 157). *'It has become well known that vegetable oils, as sources of linoleic acid, are needed to decrease blood cholesterol, yet the equally essential cholin, inositol, vitamin B6, and magnesium are still largely ignored. If a person's diet is adequate, especially in these nutrients, he can produce all the lecithin his body needs'.* She goes on to describe how people with excessive blood cholesterol were given two tablespoons of granular lecithin each day. *'Their blood cholesterol levels fell remarkably within three months, although no other change had been made.'*

Ecological illness

Ecological illness is the term now being used to describe food and chemical allergies. Eminent doctors leading the research on the subject believe that a quite extraordinary range of illnesses can be caused directly by an allergy to certain foods.

The leading allergy specialist in the U.K. is Dr Richard Mackarness who, in his book *Not all in the Mind (See page* 157), lists the following illness which may be traced to food allergies:
Respiratory system — conjunctivitis, rhinitis, bronchitis, and asthma.
Skin — pruritus, urticaria, and dermatoses.
Digestive system — mouth ulcers, dyspepsia, peptic ulcer, regional ileitis, constipation, diarrhoea, and colitis.
Cardiovascular system — abnormal pulse rhythm (including slow or rapid heartbeat), anginal pain, high blood pressure, spasm of arteries in the extremities, and periodic fainting fits.
Musculo-skeletal system — fibrositis, aching joints, and certain forms of arthritis.
Central nervous system — headaches, migraine, neuralgia, pins and needles, numbness, convulsions, ringing in the ears, and vertigo.
Genito-urinary system — frequent urination, often incorrectly called cystitis, vaginal discharge, some cases of impotence, frigidity, and inability to conceive.
Mind and emotions — behaviour problems, inability to think clearly, neuroses, anxiety, panic attacks and lack of confidence and energy, depression, disorders of thought, including delusions and hallucinations, and some forms of schizophrenia.
Endocrine system — under and overactive thyroid gland, and menstrual disorders.

This list may seem astonishing, but doctors both in the U.S.A. and the U.K. have successfully treated every one of these ailments as allergic. Dr Mackarness has become convinced that of all the people needing their doctor's attention, no less than 30% have symptoms exclusively linked with food or chemical allergy. Of the remainder, he believes that another 30% have illnesses partly traceable to the same cause. What this actually means is that over half the patients treated by an average doctor endure pain, disease and surgical operations which they could avoid simply by not eating certain foods.

A neat illustration of this is given by Dr Blake Donaldson of New York in his book *Strong Medicine*. He describes how a patient came to his surgery saying she felt 'sick all over' and had severe headaches, abdominal pain and fatigue to the point of exhaustion. This woman had consulted many other doctors about these symptoms and had been operated on several times. Dr Donaldson listed his colleagues' diagnoses: slipped disc, fallen stomach, duodenal ulcer, low blood pressure, low blood sugar, calcium deficiency, vitamin deficiency, low thyroid, streptococcus infection, anaemia, and high cholesterol. When Dr Donaldson then tested the patient for food allergies he quickly found that she was sensitive to white flour. When this was taken out of her diet, all the symptoms cleared up in two weeks. (*See* GRAINS *page* 46).

Grains rate highly among the most common food allergies. A very severe reaction to gluten in wheat and other grains is now believed to be the cause of coeliac disease.

The great American allergy pioneer, Dr Arthur F. Coca, conducted an interesting survey among a hundred of his patients, described in his book *The Pulse Test — Easy Allergy Detection*. The results were surprising. Common foods eaten almost daily were the most usual allergens. Strawberries, often an allergic bugbear, came last on the list.

Food	No. of persons allergic	Food	No. of persons allergic
egg	33	pork	18
wheat	30	chocolate	17
white potato	30	lamb	17
cow's milk	29	coffee	15
orange	29	apple	15
beef	23	fowl	15
legume (pea and bean)	22	melon	14
fish	20	carrot	13
sugar cane	20	sweet potato	13
plum	21	grape	12
tomato	19	peanut	12
banana	19	pineapple	12
onion	19	beet, spinach	11
asparagus	19	maize (See CORN)	10
cabbage	18	yeast	9
		strawberry	6

From his vast experience of the subject, Dr Coca believes that 90% of the population is susceptible to food allergies. Other major allergens include tobacco, household dust, pollen, and chemical additives but reactions do vary with each individual. One of Dr Coca's patients was allergic to cow's milk, EGGS, corn (See GRAINS *page* 46) orange, olives, bananas, yeast, and beef. Her reactive symptoms were heart attacks, fainting, chronic cough, and outbreaks of hives.

Another patient was allergic to cow's milk, citrus fruit, carrot, beet, spinach, asparagus, onions, and NUTS. Her symptoms were constant common colds, indigestion, and neuralgia. Both patients recovered when the offending foods were taken out of their diets.

Find out your own allergies
If experts like Dr Mackarness and Dr Coca are right in their assumptions, many of you reading this page may be unsuspecting victims of allergies. According to Dr Mackarness there are five main clues:
- persistent fatigue, not helped by rest.
- over or under weight, or a history of fluctuating weight.
- occasional puffiness of face, hands, abdomen or ankles.
- palpitations, especially after eating food.
- excessive sweating, not related to exercise.

A person may easily be allergic to a food he is eating every day. Take CHEESE as an example. Mr Brown may be highly sensitive to cheese but he does not know this. In fact, Mr Brown loves cheese and eats it every day. What happens is that his body undergoes a curious adapting process to the food allergy and continues to do so until the adrenal glands are exhausted. This can take months or years. During this period Mr Brown may actually feel better immediately after a mouthful of cheese, although he might feel a bit tired a few hours later, or irritable the next day. In this way his system 'masks' the true allergic reaction. Any odd rashes, unusual fatigue or other symptoms will be put down to other causes.

However, if Mr Brown should come under any severe stress during his adaptive period, a violent reaction may occur. His system is already fully stretched adapting to and coping with the food allergy and cannot cope with another load. Mr Brown may then fall ill with any of the numerous diseases or ailments listed above, such as mental depression or heart disease. All depends on the particular weakness of the allergy victim.

It is interesting to note that until quite recently, a person who fell ill during a period of stress was thought to be reacting to the stress and referred to a psychiatrist. Dr Mackarness is now working in a psychiatric hospital where he operates an allergy clinic for mental patients.

Obviously it is a good idea for each one of us to find out our food sensitivities or allergies. There are two main ways: the abstention method or the pulse test.

Dr Mackarness uses the five day abstention system. His patients are put on a five-day fast with only MINERAL WATER to drink. Then foods are introduced gradually and the reactions noted most carefully.

In everyday life, the mineral-water fast is almost impossible to organize, so Dr Mackarness gives some everyday guidelines to follow. Try cutting out a whole group of foods commonly found to be allergenic such as sugars and cereal grains. Leave them out of the diet for at least one week and see if the symptoms improve. Then cut out another group, such as dairy foods, and so on. Keep a diary and note down reactions carefully.

Dr Mackarness finds that the main offenders usually are eggs, milk, processed foods, instant coffee and tea, (See BEVERAGES *page* 136) chocolate, cereals, sugars, beer, and whisky.

A period of abstinence is important because this is the way to stop the body adapting to any suspect food. After five or seven days, the system goes into a non-adaptive phase when the food allergy is 'unmasked' by causing an immediate reaction. During this time, it is quite possible to have a 'hangover' feeling if an allergic food has previously been eaten very frequently. At the end of the week introduce the avoided foods in the evening. You will then know straight away if you really are allergic to any food.

For instance, an egg-allergic subject may try eggs after a week of abstinence and find that his tongue becomes swollen, or his eyes run. There are a host of other reactions, some of them quite severe. American doctors prescribe a weak solution of bicarbonate of soda to cut down extreme reaction.

Dr Coca uses the pulse test method to discover allergies. There is some evidence to suggest that the pulse begins to race soon after the eating of a food allergen. To find the 'normal' pulse rate may be a difficult task for a highly allergic subject. The crucial figure is, according to Dr Coca, 84 pulse beats per minute. Anything over that, he says, must be suspected as an allergic reaction. The pulse must be taken immediately after waking up, and then in regular intervals throughout the day, especially after any food is eaten. Dr Coca advises each person to become sensitive to his pulse rhythms and quickenings. Some reactions are easy to detect. Mrs Coca's pulse raced to 120 after a meal of potatoes. 'The best thing any parent can do for a child is to learn about his pulse', writes Dr Coca.

Finally, persevere and find out your food allergies. As Dr Coca says, 'The most common comment from my patients is — "I feel like a new person"'.

How additives can affect the body

The ever increasing numbers of additives in our food present a growing threat to health.

Dr Richard Mackarness highlights the problem in his book *Not all in the Mind*:

I am sure that the sophistication and adulteration of food with chemical additives has increased enormously . . . and so has the consumption of processed starch and sugar (white bread, cakes, biscuits, sweets and soft drinks). It would be surprising if people were not allergic to pesticides put into the ground and sprayed on crops, to flour improvers, anti-staling agents, emulsifying compounds, artificial colourings, preservatives and the whole terrifying array of potentially toxic substances now being added to our food in order to improve its appearance, flavour, shelf-life and profitability.

Many other specialist doctors have discovered that patients can react quite violently to certain additives. Symptoms follow the general allergic pattern which may mimic the wide list of diseases from heart attacks to colic. (*See* ECOLOGICAL ILLNESSES *page* 11). For example, Dr Guy A. Settipane tested 38 patients who suffered from chronic urticaria (a skin complaint characterized by itchy swollen and sometimes weeping patches). He reported his findings in the American journal *Internal Medical News*. Thirteen of the patients reported immediate improvement when all chemicalized foods were taken out of their diets. Three of these patients were found to be highly sensitive to the yellow food dye tartrazine. Dr Settipane confirmed this by deliberately feeding them the additive and observing that the urticaria symptoms returned within three hours. Several other patients were mildly sensitive to tartrazine. It is recommended that anyone with possible sensitivity to this food dye should limit their foods to fresh meat and green vegetables. The artificial colour in some citrus fruits may also upset highly sensitive people.

Tartrazine is also known to cause asthma attacks in certain people. Yet the food colour is still being used in tablets prescribed for asthmatics. Identifiable conditions such as Kwok's Quease (or else known as Chinese restaurant syndrome) can be directly linked with a food additive. (*See* MONOSODIUM GLUTAMATE *page* 20).

What vitamins and minerals can do for you

Vitamins

Vitamin A

Vitamin A is a soft yellow substance which is soluble in fats but not in water. Lack of this vitamin can cause eye disorders, inability to see in the dark, and sore mouth and gums. Most important, a general shortage of it leads to susceptibility to disease and general ill health. Children who do not receive adequate amounts fail to grow properly. The pro-vitamin, carotene, occurs in carrots and all green plants.

The daily requirement for an adult is 5000 I.U. of vitamin A, but because it is stored by the liver and not affected by cooking, deficiencies of vitamin A are less likely to occur. However, mineral oil can cause the body to lose some fat-soluble vitamins. Dried fruits are often commercially sprayed with mineral oil. (*See page 37*).
Good sources of vitamin A are: Butter, milk, eggs, Brussels sprouts, carrots, peas, tomatoes, prunes, and dried apricots.

The B vitamin group

The B family group of vitamins has been the subject of intensive research, yet few experts agree on the amount needed for optimum health. Leading nutritionists such as Dr Henry Borsook and Adelle Davis are convinced that multiple B vitamin deficiencies are widespread in our moden diet, causing symptoms from fatigue to mental depression.

In his book '*Vitamins — What they are and how they can benefit you*' Dr Borsook comments on the difficulty of obtaining enough vitamin B: '*A good diet containing liberal amounts of salads, green vegetables, fresh fruit, milk and meat provides daily about 500 I.U. of B1 (thiamine). The 750 I.U. daily recommended are not obtained unless the matter is given some attention. The difficulty is that the foods commonly eaten do not contain high concentrations of B1 (thiamine). Another difficulty is the economic one. The tolerably palatable foods relatively rich in B1 (thiamine) — fresh vegetables and fruit — are expensive. Vitamin B concentrates are prohibitively expensive.*

The provision of large amounts of vitamin B at a price which the low-income classes can afford, and in a form palatable enough for them to take day in and day out, calls for expert knowledge of nutrition. It constitutes a major problem in nutritional engineering.' Adelle Davis, in *Let's Eat Right to Keep Fit* writes: '*The fifteen or more B vitamins are so meagerly supplied in our American diet that almost every person lacks them.*

Now that our breadstuffs are refined, no food rich in the B vitamins is ordinarily eaten daily. In fact, there are only four good sources of these vitamins: liver, brewer's yeast, wheat germ and rice polish. A few foods are high in one or two B vitamins, but to obtain our daily requirements of all of them from such foods is

Wheat germ

Brewer's yeast

Liver

Rice polish

impossible.' There are four major vitamins in the group:

B1 (thiamine), sometimes called aneurine, is soluble in water and easily destroyed in cooking especially with soda. The British Government advises an intake of 1 mg of thiamine a day. Lack of it can lead to depression, neuritis and beri-beri.

B2 (riboflavin) is also soluble in water and is not quite so easily destroyed by cooking. A severe deficiency causes cracks and sores at the corners of the mouth and sore or split tongues. Daily recommended requirement by the British Government is 1.5 mg.

Niacin (nicotinic acid), sometimes called B5 is water soluble but resistant to boiling water. Niacin is known as the 'mind vitamin' since a deficiency causes many mental symptoms. Quite a small lack of niacin can cause rough skin, sore tongue, and diarrhoea. Severe deprivations cause pellagra. Daily requirement is about 12 mg.

B1 (thiamine), B2 (riboflavin) and niacin are found in WHEAT GERM, BREWER'S YEAST, YEAST EXTRACTS, CHEESE, EGG, milk, wholemeal bread (see WHEAT *page* 56), OATMEAL, peas, beans, (See LEGUMES *page* 66), NUTS, potatoes and beer.

Vitamin B12 is the most recently discovered member of the B family group and the only one to contain a metal, in this case cobalt. The Vegetarian Nutritional Research Centre, in the U.K. has done a good deal of research, under the late Dr Frank Wokes, into body requirements for this vitamin. As B12 occurs mainly in milk, eggs and cheese, vegans were most susceptible to deficiencies. However, many foods such as plant milks, textured vegetable protein (TVP) and yeast extracts now contain added B12. There is some controversy about the B12 content of COMFREY and ALFALFA. Both these plants can, under certain circumstances, contain B12 but it depends on the nature of the soil. Only minute amounts of B12 are needed by the body.

Dr Wokes estimated the requirement at one millionth of a gram.

Vitamin C (ascorbic acid)

Vitamin C is soluble in water but not in fats. Lack of it can cause bleeding from the gums, slow healing of wounds, irritability, gloom, and fatigue. Severe deficiency leads to scurvy.

The American Government recommends a daily intake of 70 mg but views on this differ widely. Linus Pauling, the Nobel Prize winner, believes that upwards of 4 g of vitamin C a day should be taken at the beginning of a cold.

It is not as easy to get a good amount of vitamin C from ordinary food as many people imagine. Cooking can reduce the content by up to 75%. Fruit and vegetables start to lose their vitamin C the moment they are picked. Thus an orange, tabled as providing 50 mg, might well only contain a fraction of that amount by the time it has been carried halfway across the world and retailed.

Good sources of vitamin C are: oranges, peppers, tomatoes, potatoes, kohlrabi, cabbage, lemons, grapefruit, PAPAYAS, beet tops and spinach.

Vitamin D

Vitamin D is soluble in fats but not in water. It is the vital element which controls the absorption of calcium and phosphorus from the diet to form bones and teeth. Food and sunlight are the main sources of this vitamin. The ultra violet rays in sunlight turn the ergosterol beneath the skin into vitamin D. It can be stored in the body for several months. There is no recommended dietary goal for adults but children are recommended to have at least 400 I.U. daily.

Good sources of vitamin D are: EGGS, butter, CHEESE, milk and fortified margerine and other foods. Vitamin E is dealt with in NUTRITION AND MEDICINE.

Minerals

Potassium

Potassium is needed for muscle cells and blood corpuscles. We require about 3 g a day. It occurs in many common foods, especially vegetables, so there is little likelihood of a shortage.

Phosphorus

Phosphorus combines with calcium phosphate to form the major constituent of bone and teeth. It is found in EGGS, CHEESE, milk, OATMEAL, cabbage, and NUTS.

Iron

Iron is essential for hemoglobin and other pigments to carry oxygen to the tissues. Most authorities agree that adult males need about 10-12 mg of iron a day,

females about 15 mg, and children over nine 15 mg. It is found in liver, EGGS, baked beans (See KIDNEY BEAN *page* 56), wholemeal bread (See WHEAT *page* 72), RAISINS, watercress, OATMEAL, and many green vegetables.

Calcium

Calcium is needed for bone and tooth formation, and the complete functioning of the muscles. Vitamin D is required for calcium assimilation. We need about 800 mg of calcium a day, and growing children and expectant mothers need at least 1.3 g. It is found in milk, CHEESE, watercress, cabbage, EGGS, turnips, and wholemeal flour (See WHEAT *page* 56). White flour is generally fortified with calcium.

The healthy food guide

The following foods are worth dealing with separately as they have very special benefits.

Bran
The benefits of bran are now reaching a wider public than most other 'health foods'. This is because the link between a low-fibre diet and many degenerative diseases has now clearly been made. This is dealt with fully in THE FIBRE FACTOR *(See page* 8) and BRAN.

The easiest way to put fibre in the diet is to use 2 tablespoons of wheat bran each day; but foods of plant origin also have some fibre. Good sources are LEGUMES and LENTILS. Vegetables such as cabbage, potatoes, apples and bananas contain fair amounts of fibre.

What must be remembered is that meat, EGGS, fat, sugar, and alcoholic drinks contain no fibre at all. *See page* 26.

Lentils

Brewer's yeast
Brewer's yeast is now generally used as a nutritional booster or tonic. Its value lies in the very rich concentration of nutrients, especially the B complex vitamins. A small amount of dried brewer's yeast powder goes a long way to meeting the daily requirements of major B vitamins. 33 g (1 oz) or $\frac{1}{4}$ U.S. cup dried brewer's yeast contains 12.9 mg niacin, 1 mg B2 (riboflavin), and 5.2 mg B1 (thiamine). It is also a good source of phosphorus, potassium, calcium, and iron. However, any regular large amounts of brewer's yeast must be balanced with additional calcium and magnesium. *See page* 28.

Buckwheat
Buckwheat is the best natural source of rutic acid, a complex plant substance which has a beneficial effect on the circulation. Naturopathic and homeopathic doctors prescribe rutin for circulatory ailments and allied conditions such as high blood pressure, and chilblains.

Buckwheat is also rich in the B vitamin group. It is well worth putting on the menu regularly. *See page* 30.

Garlic
Garlic is a natural antiseptic that has been used as a medicine for 5000 years. Modern laboratories have identified its active constituents as allyl disulphate and sulphur compounds. Research by Drs R.C. Jain and D.B. Kowar at the University of Behghazi, Libya, showed that garlic oil effectively reduced serum cholesterol. The doctors noted that a dose of between 2-6 mg a day was also effective in reducing the incidence of atherosclerotic lesions in test animals by one third.

Naturopathic doctors prescribe garlic capsules for artery and blood vessel disorders and mucuous complaints, such as catarrh. The raw oil of garlic is more effective medicinally, but cooked garlic still has active constituents. *See page* 125.

Lecithin
Lecithin is a substance manufactured by the body that occurs naturally in certain foods. Various researches over the years have proved that it has an effect on lowering blood cholesterol levels and most authorities agree that high cholesterol levels have a link with heart disease. So it is obviously a good idea to seek those foods high in natural lecithin.

Soya beans. Much of the granular lecithin sold commercially is derived from soya beans. It has been found that soya substances have a good effect on intestinal flora, rather like YOGHURT. This research has been summed up by Dr Horvath in his book, *Some recent views about soya flour.*

It has been demonstrated . . . that the soy bean is of very great service in changing the intestinal flora, helping materially in driving out the offensive germs, which pollute our bodies, and give rise to colities and other acute and chronic infections besides headaches, skin troubles and a great variety of obstinate chronic maladies.

Soya beans have also been used in trials with allergic patients.

Buckwheat

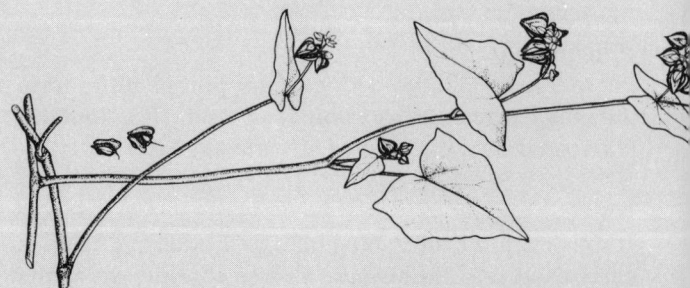

16

Papaya fruit

Oils

Vegetable oils are also good sources of LECITHIN. They are rich in linoleic acid which plays an important part in controlling cholesterol. The essential unsaturated fatty acids now appear to be necessary for the formation of certain body substances in the brain, lungs, and in the thymus and iris of the eye.

Everyone, even slimmers, should include essential oils in the diet. The following excerpt from the *New Scientist* (November 4th, 1965) outlines the functions of these fatty substances.

In recent experiments, they have been shown capable of influencing muscle activity in the female reproductive tract and in the air tubes of the lungs; they can alter the function of the brain, and also the level of the fat in the blood. From these findings it seems possible that . . . (essential fats) may be involved in such diverse disorders as infertility, asthma, schizophrenia and coronary thrombosis.

The beneficial oils are sunflower, safflower, wheat germ, olive and corn oil. Safflower and sunflower are particularly high in linoleic acid. *See page* 97.

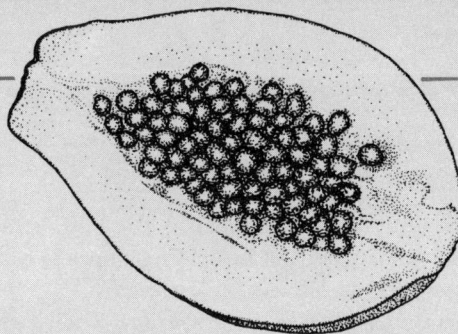
Sunflower

Onion

The old folk cures based on onions may have solid scientific facts to back them. Onions, like garlic, contain the natural antiseptic oils, allyl disulphate and cycloalliin. This natural constituent of onions was the subject of interesting research at the Royal Victoria Infirmary, Newcastle, England, by Dr H.A. Dewar, Dr R.K. Agarwall, and others. They found that cycloalliin had the ability to help the walls of the blood vessels, especially the veins, to dissolve the clots which tend to form inside them. This action, called fibrinolysis, was increased by this constituent in onion. The tests showed that boiling or frying the onions did not reduce their benefits.

This research is of particular interest to people suffering from heart disorder and may also possibly lead to additional research into onion and arthritis. Dr Dewar comments: 'The hypothesis upon which (cycloalliin) might be used for sufferers from arthritis would be that it might similarly help to dissolve the fibrin which form in inflamed joints as part of the inflammatory process.'

Papaya

The papaya fruit made the headlines in April 1977 when doctors at London's Guy's Hospital prescribed a papaya dressing for a kidney transplant patient. Modern drugs could not heal his wound, but fresh papaya pulp did.

Dr Malcolm Stuart, director of the English Herb Society, described how papaya was successful: 'The fruit contains papain, an enzyme which breaks down protein; we don't known how it works, but it may be that the enzyme breaks down the bacteria.'

This same enzyme has a beneficial effect on the digestion. It is only found in the *unripe* fruit. In the tropics, papaya has been used as a food and a medicine for centuries and both Columbus and Marco Polo were deeply impressed with its effects. *See page* 100.

Pineapple

Pineapple contains the enzyme bromelin, which has a powerful action on protein and so aids the digestion. It is bromelin that prevents pineapple from 'jelling'. In folk medicine pineapple juice is used for sore throats and colds.

Yoghurt

The virtues of yoghurt have become well known in the last few years. Most people have a vague idea that it is 'good'. The facts are less well known.

Yoghurt is very powerful indeed and contains a form of natural antibiotic. Dr David B. Sabine of the U.S. Vitamin and Pharmaceutical Corporation did a series of controlled tests in 1975. He grew harmful bacteria such as *E. coli* and added *acidophilus* yoghurt bacteria. The harmful bacteria began gradually to disappear, defeated by the 'friendly' bacteria of the yoghurt.

Dr Harry Seneca conducted tests at Columbia University, U.S.A., and found that when yoghurt is eaten regularly over a long period no other bacteria except the 'friendly' ones appear in the stools. His research indicated that yogurt needs to be eaten at least every two days to achieve this beneficial effect.

Yoghurt can also help the body to manufacture the B vitamins. Some modern drugs, such as penicillin and sulphur, can also destroy valuable intestinal flora. Yoghurt helps prevent this and is even prescribed by some Italian doctors along with antibiotics.

Yoghurt rates very highly as a food for positive health. It is easy to make at home therefore do not be tempted to buy the artificially flavoured variety. *See page* 119.

Additives

People of the Western World, headed by the U.S.A., are eating in their daily food an increasing amount of chemical preservatives, stabilizers, colourings, flavourings and other additives. The average American according to government statistics consumes well over 1.8 kg (4 lb) of additives each year; and the average Briton eats just over 1.4 kg (3 lb) of additives a year. That is the equivalent of 20 to 30 aspirin-size tablets of chemicals a day. To put the complex field of additives into perspective, it is as well to start with the food an average family might eat on an ordinary day.

For millions of people breakfast consists of coffee or tea, eggs boiled or fried, sliced white bread toasted with butter or margarine, plus a bowl of cereal. Lunch has many mothers reaching for fish fingers, instant mashed potatoes, and canned or frozen peas. Fresh fruit may finish off the meal. A more leisurely dinner could come from a packet of beef goulash with white rice, tossed green salad, followed by cheese or fruit.

Few nutritionists would criticize Mrs Average for ill-feeding her family. She has also taken advantage of the modern minimum preparation and convenience foods and balanced them with fruit and vegetables. Yet a closer look will reveal exactly what her family are ingesting with their food.

People who deliberately avoid packaged food because of the additive content may care to know that a recent World Health Organisation (WHO) check found unacceptable levels of paraquat (weed killer) in potatoes, milk, fresh olives, sorghum and maize (corn). A British government spot-check in 1976 found 70% of tested lettuces 'seriously contaminated' with insecticide residues. The American Academy of Pediatrics reported in 1977 that levels of hormones and residual antibiotcs in meat, pesticide residues in dairy, fruit and vegetables have now reached 'a level of concern'.

Surely additives are safe?

It is a very reasonable reaction to assume that the arm of our governments concerned with food standards such as the Food and Drug Administration in the U.S.A. and the Food Additives and Contaminants Committee in the U.K. would not allow unsafe substances to be added to food.

Unfortunately there is no comfort in this view. Governments throughout the world disagree on what

Butter
Permitted colour

White bread
Added nutrients, bleaches, improvers, emulsifiers and preservatives, plus sodium diacetate, aluminium phosphate and potassium bromate

Battery eggs
residues of hormones and antibiotics in poultry feedstuffs

Coffee
Caffeine (naturally occurring)

Fish fingers
sodium polyphosphates food starches, monosodium glutamate, colour

chemicals are safe enough to be added to food. It is only when a substance is the subject of popular outcry in many countries that the regulatory authorities are forced to act, as they did in the cyclamate controversy. When the U.S.A. banned cyclamate, the U.K. and other countries quickly followed.

Another example is butylated hydroroxytoluene (BHT), an antioxidant widely used in potato flakes, chewing gum, dry breakfast cereals, enriched rice, freeze-dried meats, and commercial cooking fats. BHT is not permitted in Australia or Sweden. The U.K. Food Standards Committee recommended a ban on all uses of BHT, but an outright ban was never carried out. In 1958 the Committee was appealed to by the food industry who wished to extend the use of BHT. They refused and expressed concern and in 1963 the Committee again reviewed the subject. Two years later a recommendation to ban BHT entirely was turned down. In 1972 researchers reported on BHT and BHA (butylated hydroxyanisole). 'These antioxidants can no longer be viewed as innocuous substances.' This is an indication of the time taken by one government to remove a potentially dangerous additive from the grocery shelves.

It is as well to remember the highly emotive issue of thalidomide which painfully illustrates that a permitted chemical distributed worldwide can be dangerous.

The complex problem of additives and safety has been summed up by Senator Ribicoff, Chairman of a U.S. Senate Committee looking into 'Chemicals and the Future of Man' in April 1971. He asked three questions:
1. How much do we know about the hazards to human health from these chemicals?
2. How much assurance of chemical safety do we require?
3. What must . . . (governments) . . . do to assure that the chemicals we absorb are safe?

These questions have still not been answered, and reveal that additive testing remains an inexact science. It is very difficult to find out all the effects of small amounts of substances taken regularly over a long period on the health of an individual and on future generations yet unborn.

Additives are checked for direct toxic effects. However, scientists are now aware that there can be other slight, delayed or indirect effects at basic cellular levels that are also hazards to human health. (*See* ECOLOGIAL ILLNESS *page* 11).

Most testing for safety is carried out on animals, but it has been proved that they do not always react to substances in the same way as humans. For example, rabbits can eat deadly nightshade without ill effects

Oranges	**Instant potatoes**	**Processed peas**	**Cheese**	**Lettuce**	**Beef Goulash**	**Rice**
permitted orange dye, wax, inhibitors, ripeners	salt, vegetable oil with anti-oxidant, emulsifier with emulsifying salt, colouring, flavouring, preservatives	sugar, salt, colour, flavouring	may contain mould inhibitors	insecticide, residues	Hydrolised vegetable protein, food starch, MSG, sodium alginate, colour, preservative, anti-oxidant	(white polished) talc and glucose residues from polishing. Talc contains asbestos which is a carcinogen

and penicillin is toxic to guinea pigs.

One vital point to remember is that additives are not tested in the possible combinations that can occur when Mr and Mrs Average sit down to eat an ordinary meal.

Synergism is a mechanism whereby the toxicity of one substance is increased by interaction with another. An example is the sometimes fatal combination of alcohol and barbiturates. It is impossible to test all combinations of food additives for synergistic effects.

Many additives are compounds of sodium and the preservative effects of vinegar, for example, are more conveniently obtained in certain food processes by sodium diacetate. The consumption of these additives in food may increase the intake of sodium to well above the recommended levels. (*See* SALT *page* 107). In addition the manufacturer can also bring out a special product for those on low salt diets.

What about food colours?

Food colours were of natural origin until about a hundred years ago when coal-tar dyes were first made. Now more than 90% of all food colours used are synthetic. The recent history of food colours in the U.K. is very revealing.

Up to 1957, the only restriction on the use of food colourings was a short list of prohibited substances but it was then realized that many colours were potentially hazardous substances and the list was reversed permitting thirty colours only. This list is gradually being whittled down and of the original thirty, only nine are still permitted. However, other substances have been added to the list as a result of the U.K. Entry to the E.E.C. In 1973 the U.K. had 23 colours on its permitted list, the E.E.C. had 19 and the U.S.A. had 11. There were ten common colours between the U.K. and E.E.C. lists and only four appear on each of the three lists. As a result of E.E.C. pressure five colours were removed from the U.K. list in 1977. Ten more colours on the U.K. and E.E.C. lists are due to be deleted in 1979 if more proof of safety cannot be produced.

One of the colours is amaranth or Red Dye No. 2 as it was called in the U.S.A. Amaranth had been classified by the Joint Food and Agriculture Organization and World Health Organization Expert Committee on Food Additives, an advisory body set up by the United Nations, as a colour 'acceptable for use in foods'. Long term tests on amaranth with rats, mice and dogs failed to reveal any cancer-inciting properties.

However in 1968 Soviet researchers reported carcinogenic properties on tests with rats and recommended that the use of amaranth in food be discontinued. In the U.S.A. the Federal Drug Authority took several actions as a result of the Soviet findings. It recommended a reduction in the use of the colour and carried out its own tests which confirmed the Soviet findings. It did not, however, ban the colour

immediately but requested a review of the data by an independent scientific body — the National Research Committee of the National Academy of Sciences in the U.S.A.

Amaranth was removed from the permitted food colourings list in the U.S.A. in 1976, eight years after the Soviet report was published. Amaranth is still permitted in E.E.C. countries but is due to be removed in 1979 along with the nine other colours. A body representing sections of the British food industry is attempting to keep amaranth and some other suspect colours on the U.K. list. Where it is not banned, amaranth is used mainly to colour soft drinks and sweets.

What about MSG?

MSG or monosodium glutamate (sometimes called monosodium glutenate) is a naturally occurring amino acid and is the 'star' food additive of the 1970s. It has a long history of use as a flavour enhancer in the Far East. MSG is now used to give a 'meaty' flavour to proteinaceous foods, and has become so popular among manufacturers that it is almost impossible to avoid in any processed soup or meat product. It also has the advantage of being 'natural', as it is manufactured from wheat or corn gluten or else from soya or sugar beet wastes.

The enthusiasm of the food industry for MSG can be appreciated by the following extracts from trade releases: 'much used to step up the indifferent or undistinguished flavour of many canned and processed foods'; 'helps to maintain the fresh cooked qualities of canned food'; 'suppresses oxidized flavour which may develop through storage'.

In 1968 Dr Robert Kwok published a description of his experience after a meal in a Chinese restaurant when he was seized with a frightful gripping pain in his chest and he more or less collapsed across the table. The attack subsided after a few minutes. After much research with interested colleagues he traced the cause to MSG and the condition is now referred to as Kwok's Quease or the Chinese Restaurant Syndrome.

Tests on animals with MSG have produced eye and brain damage in newborn mice, rats, rabbits and monkeys. As a result of these tests, manufacturers of baby foods have voluntarily withdrawn MSG from their products.

A substance closely related to MSG called hydrolyzed vegetable protein is now used following the adverse publicity for MSG. Hydrolyzed vegetable protein (HVP), also called protein hydrolysate, has undergone a process whereby individual amino acids, one of which is MSG, are released in free form. HVP — like MSG — has been shown to cause brain damage in newborn mice.

Why additives at all?

The basic problem with food is that it is plentiful in some seasons, such as harvest time, and scarce in others.

A highly urbanized population is only possible when there is a reliable food supply. The official justification for additives is that they ensure that food reaches the consumer in the best possible condition whatever the time of year, and they make it possible to provide everyone with adequate nourishment in a time of fluctuation and overall decrease in world food supplies.

A point not to be missed is that the food industry derives a lot of benefit from the artificially prolonged shelf life of many foods and manufacturers have always added things to their products for this purpose.

What are additives?

The following list describes the types of additives in common use. A welcome development in the E.E.C. countries is the requirement that all intentional additives in processed foods must soon be listed on the packet under a code number.

A manufacturer will no longer be able to state, for example, 'permitted preservative' in the list of ingredients and he must list the code number of the preservative used. The informed consumer, knowing the code, may then avoid the substances which he does not wish to consume.

Intentional food additives

Preservatives (also *see* sequestrants) are substances added to foods to delay or prevent undesirable changes. Some preservatives delay food spoilage caused by bacteria and enzymes. Others inhibit rancidity of oils and fats, some prevent changes of colour, flavour, texture, or appearance. Traditional preservatives include salt, vinegar, spices, wood, smoke, sugar. Present day preservatives include sodium nitrite, sodium and calcium propionate, sulphur dioxide, sorbic acid, sodium diacetate, sodium benzoate, methyl formate, diphenyl methyl bromide.

Many preservatives are toxic substances used well below established safety limits. However, the substances may be added to a wide variety of foods and overall the established safety limits may well be exceeded.

Sequestrants are substances which bind and de-activate metallicions such as iron and copper which are present in some foods and can cause spoilage. However, sequestrants may interfere with the absorption of minerals important for the diet. Sequestrants include tartaric acid, citric acid, phytic acid, calcium disodium EDTA. Phytic acid occurs naturally in wholemeal bread and grains but its effect is reduced by the enzyme action of yeast.

Some unusual sources of additives

Carrots
enzyme inhibitors used to prevent further growth

Potatoes and Onions
may be treated with anti-sprouting agents

Dried fruits
may be sprayed with mineral oil

Butter, margarine
may contain permitted colour

Lemons and other fruits
may be washed with retarding agents in their countries of origin. Many fruits are permitted to be detergent washed, waxed and dyed

Grapes and strawberries
may be sprayed with hormone mixtures to promote growth

Oranges
may be sprayed with orange food dye. The wrappers may possibly be treated with the chemical thiabendazole

Cheese
mould inhibitors, colouring, wax

Colourings are used to make food look more appealing as we have become conditioned to accept how they should look. They may be natural or synthetic substances. Regulations vary from country to country and colours permitted in one country may be banned in another. The trend is to reduce the number of permitted colourings as more research into their safety is carried out.

Flavourings are added to foodstuffs to provide or modify flavour and are commonly used to replace original flavourings lost by processing. They form the largest category of food additives and there are about 1600 in use in the U.S.A. Most flavourings presently in use are synthetic for reasons of cost and availability. It has been said that the world crop of vanilla is insufficient even to flavour the ice cream sold in the U.S.A., let alone the rest of the world.

The sheer volume of flavouring substances and their complexity has meant that the results of comprehensive long term scientific studies on the safety of many are still far from completion.

One of the difficulties is that flavours can be valuable trade secrets and the results of safety studies are treated as privileged material and are not made available to the public and for independent scientific review.

The results of safety studies to date do not give assurance of the overall safety of many flavourings currently in use. France is one country with a much more restrictive approach to the use of food flavours. Only seven synthetic flavours are permitted in French foodstuffs.

Flavour enhancers emphasize the flavour of a food. Traditional flavour enhancers are salt, spices, vinegar, and, in the East, MSG. MSG manufactured from vegetable protein has now become an almost universal flavour enhancer in processed proteinaceous foods.

Emulsifiers disperse one liquid into another, usually oil in water, and therefore make smooth creams. Some emulsifiers commonly used are lecithin, alginates, carrageenan (extracts from seaweeds), tragacanth, plant gums, and glyceryl monostearate.

Stabilizers impart a smooth texture and prevent the separation of an emulsion into its component liquids. Some stabilizers are gum arabic, guar gum, pectin, and sodium carboxymethylcellulose.

Humectants control the moistness of foods and prevent drying out. Liquid paraffin (food grade mineral oil) is applied to dried fruits to give a moist appearance.

Supplementary nutrients. Certain foods, such as white bread and breakfast cereals, have nutrients added to make up for those lost during processing. Some food scientists consider that the form of iron added to bread by law in the U.K. is in a form which is of doubtful value in human nutrition. Vitamins A and D are added to margarine and baby foods.

Extenders and fillers are substances added to foods to dilute, modify, or increase the bulk or weight of the product. They are usually much cheaper than the main ingredients and frequently consist of soya bean protein, starch, glucose, or casein.

Improvers are substances which improve the dough-making characteristics of flour for bread and other baking goods. Some improvers are ascorbic acid, calcium phosphate, ammonium bromate, sulphur dioxide, potassium bromate, chlorine dioxide.

Bleaches are used in several food processes. White flour of 70% extraction is yellowish when milled and oxidizes naturally in storage to the expected white colour over a period of months. The process is hastened by bleaching. A one-time flour bleach, nitrogen trichloride or agene was used for 25 years until it was shown to cause hysteria in dogs. It was then banned. Certain cheeses are traditionally made from goat's milk and are white in colour. Nowadays they are also made from cow's milk and naturally have a yellow colour. The yellow cheeses are bleached to the traditional colour. Some bleaches are nitrogen peroxide, chlorine dioxide, and benzoyl peroxide.

Unintentional additives and migrant additives

These substances find their way into food either during processing or packaging.

The materials for packaging food, for example, tin plate, gold linings in certain tins, PVC, paper, printing inks, and waxes may introduce unintended additives to food.

Gold lining in food cans, especially soup cans, is an established allergen. Recently questions have been raised about the safety of PVC wrappings because of the possibility of residues from a toxic gas which is sometimes used in the manufacturing process for PVC.

Residues in food may arise from agricultural and storage processes before the food is distributed for sale or for processing. Examples are residues of pesticides and fertilizers applied to the growing crop, and fumigants applied to the stored harvest, of antibiotics, and hormones fed to animals in modern farming, and radioactive and other substances in fish caught in polluted seas.

Governments are aware of the problems caused by residues as the widespread banning of DDT shows. Unfortunately, the same strictures that apply to the safety of the intentional food additives also apply to the safety of pesticide and other residues. There is also the problem that many farmers and their pesticide salesmen do not understand the meaning of the stream of regulations, explanatory bulletins, and notices, with which they are bombarded by government departments. In 1977 the Farmworkers' Unions in the U.K. protested against the indiscriminate use of sprays and chemicals which were harmful to their members.

Alfalfa

Known also as lucerne or buffalo herb, alfalfa is one of the oldest cultivated plants. The Arabs, who called it 'Father of all Foods', used it first as a cover crop and then as a feed for their magnificent horses. When they noticed that the animals eating it grew stronger and ran faster than the others, they began to eat the crop themselves with beneficial results.

Alfalfa has extraordinarily long roots, which regularly grow to 12 m (40 ft) under the ground and the U.S. Department of Agricultural Research has recorded roots 20 m (66 ft) long. The plant itself grows to about 90 cm (3 feet).

Experts believe that deep-rooted plants are a very valuable source of nutrition. They reach right down into the subsoil and gain minerals that shallow-growing plants cannot reach. Normally, only trees could tap these nutrients.

Nutritional content
Alfalfa contains vitamins A, B, D, E, K, and U. It is one of the rare sources of vitamin B12 (the only two known land plants which can contain B12 are COMFREY and alfalfa). The unusual vitamins K and U occur richly in this plant.

Protein content is high — 19% as compared to 16% in beef, and 3% in milk. Alfalfa is also rich in calcium with good amounts of iron, potassium, chlorine, sodium, silicon, magnesium, and trace elements. It also contains eight known enzymes.

Particular value
Nutritional experts in the U.S.A. rate this plant as one of the most important single food supplements and alfalfa powder is being sent to the Third World as an important item in the anti-malnutrition programme. Scientists at the U.S. Department of Agriculture are

above: enlarged section of the deep-reaching roots of alfalfa
below: above the ground, alfalfa sends up delicate leaves

now working on a pilot project in Berkeley, California and have managed to produce a bland, whitish, powder from alfalfa containing 90% protein. The rather powerful taste of alfalfa has always been a drawback up until now but the signs are that the Berkeley powder could become commercially available in the near future. Methods of obtaining alfalfa are:

Alfalfa powder Most of the powders now available have a fairly strong flavour but this can easily be disguised in soups and stews.

Alfalfa cereal The manufacturers have combined alfalfa with other ingredients, the result being a palatable cereal of very high nutritional content, marketed as Pablum.

Alfalfa flour can be added to other flours in small quantities and used in any normal recipe.

Alfalfa tea The leaves of the plant are rich in manganese and make a very beneficial tea. See HERB TEAS *page* 137

Alfalfa sprouts See SPROUTING SEEDS *page* 113

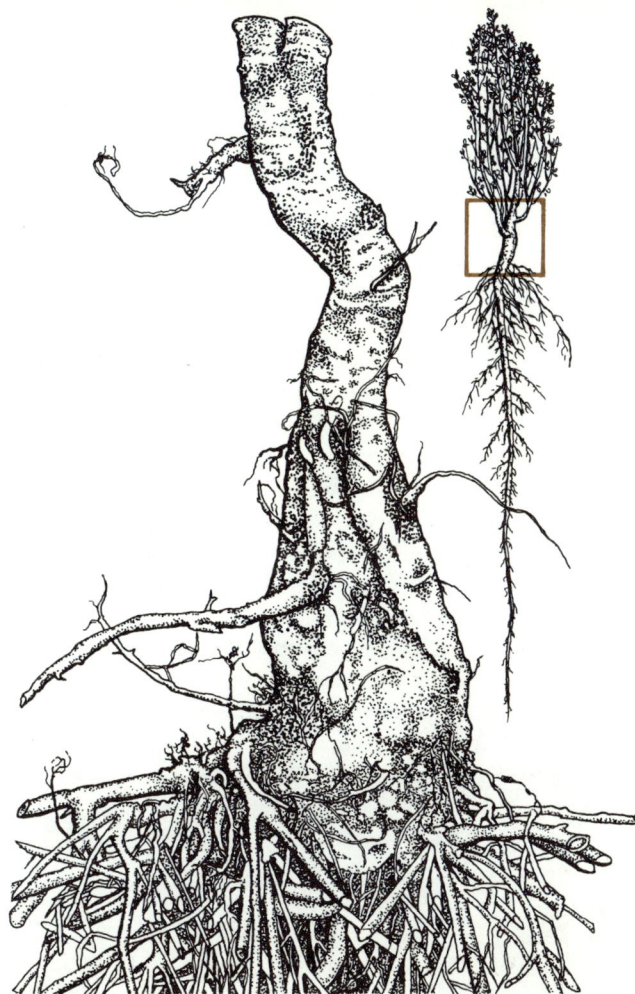

Apple-cider vinegar

Vinegar was invented when the first Stone Age man let his beer go sour and started to use the acid liquid instead of tossing it out. When aerobacter bacteria attack alcohol it turns into vinegar. Stone Age man discovered the special properties of vinegar: it was good for preserving many things from herbs to hides, made his tough meat tender, and had the ability to kill germs.

In addition to these qualities, apple-cider vinegar has further advantages over other kinds of vinegars. It is one of the great polychrests of naturopathic medicine and is used to heal a wide variety of illnesses and complaints.

Dr D.C. Jarvis of Vermont, U.S.A., has done more than anyone else to describe the virtues of apple-cider vinegar and in his book *Folk Medicine* (*See page* 157) he describes in detail how he used it to treat patients suffering from arthritis, skin complaints, overweight, dizziness, and food poisoning.

Strangely enough, research into the subject has not been done so far by orthodox medical men, but by veterinary scientists. Research has been done at Oslo University that proves that the bacteria that causes mastitis in cows can be killed by a solution of cider vinegar.

Nutritional content

Apple-cider vinegar is very rich in potassium, phosphorus, and calcium, with amounts of iron, chlorine, sodium, magnesium, sulphur, fluoride, silicon, and other trace minerals. An analysis of one brand proved it had 120 mg of potassium in each 100 ml.

Particular value

Exactly why apple-cider vinegar should be so efficacious is hard to say. Dr Jarvis' investigations led him to believe that this vinegar helped maintain the balance between the acids and alkalis of the body chemistry, a balance that is easily upset and vital for full health. He also noted that it associated minerals with potassium. It is a particularly good element of potassium which is essential for the working of the nervous system.

Types of apple-cider vinegar

There is a great variety of colours in cider vinegars ranging from light yellow to dark amber. This is due to differences in production methods and some firms add a small amount of burnt sugar caramel to make a brown colour. There is no rule of thumb to say that one has more value than another. It is true to say that certain brands definitely suit some people more than others and it is a question of trial and error. The actual content is bound to vary according to the type of apple used. Always buy cider vinegar that states quite clearly that it is made from the whole apple.

Apple-cider vinegar with honey is marketed as 'honeygar', and is quite simple to make yourself with equal amounts of HONEY and cider vinegar. Dr Jarvis recommends this mixture for many complaints. It is thought that the honey aids the absorption of the cider vinegar.

Apple-cider vinegar and health

Maurice Hanssen has described in his book *Cider Vinegar* how he conducted a survey of over 1000 people with the help of Applefords Cider Vinegar Ltd U.K. Over 400 people said they had noticed an improvement in their general health when regularly taking apple-cider vinegar, 39 felt that it helped rheumatism, 39 took it for arthritis, 14 for hay fever, 34 for stomach upsets, and 12 for high blood pressure.

How to take it

The general rule is two teaspoons of cider vinegar in one glass of water. Add more or less if you like, and mix in some honey. Dr Jarvis advises taking this first thing in the morning, and also sipping a glass of the mixture throughout each meal of the day.

As a gargle For a sore throat, put one teaspoon in a glass of water and gargle two mouthfuls of the solution every hour. Swallow the liquid after gargling. Dr Jarvis says that this treatment can cure a streptococcic sore throat in 24 hours.

Apple-cider vinegar and skin complaints

Half a cup of cider vinegar added to the bath water brings great relief to sufferers from skin disorders and itchy skin. Stay in the bath for at least 15 minutes and rub yourself dry with both hands, but do not use a towel.

Bran

Bran is the tough, outer pericarp layer of the wheat grain (*See* GRAINS *page* 46) and is removed together with the germ during milling to produce white flour. It is a rich source of high-quality protein, B vitamins and phosphorus and has always been valued highly as an animal foodstuff.

It is composed mainly of fibre and there is increasing evidence that the lack of fibre in the diet of Western man is linked with the growing incidence of degenerative disease. (*See* NUTRITION AND MEDICINE *page* 7).

The history of bran over the last hundred years provides a fascinating picture of a complete about turn in medical opinion. In London in the 1880s, Dr T.R. Allinson found that his patients recovered from their illnesses faster on an improved diet containing bran than if they had been treated with drugs. He urged that a law should be passed to forbid the separation of bran from the flour. In the face of mounting opposition he published many articles and books supporting a dietary rather than a pharmaceutical way to health. Dr Allinson was labelled a crank and struck off the medical register.

Forty years later, eminent doctors like Sir Robert McCarrison wrote about the influence of diet on diseases and health. The Kellogg Company sponsored detailed studies at Michigan State College, U.S.A., into the effects of their product All-Bran. This research showed that bran had a profound laxative effect and that fibre was essential in preventing constipation. However, at that stage, the medical profession was not interested in developing this thesis.

In Britain during the Second World War, the

Bran muffins

125 g (5 oz) or 1 U.S. cup wholemeal flour
2 teaspoons double-acting baking powder
225-350 g (8-12 oz) or 1 to 1½ U.S. cups yoghurt
2 eggs
pinch salt
75 g (3 oz) or 1 U.S. cup bran
2 tablespoons honey
2 tablespoons sunflower (or any vegetable) oil
2 tablespoons soya flour

Sieve the flour and add the beaten eggs. Mix in the yoghurt gradually and add all the other ingredients, blending well. The mixture should just drop off a spoon. Scoop into an oiled muffin tin and bake at 200°C (400°F, Gas Mark 6) for about 20 minutes.

Bran chaser
(Serves 1)

275 ml (½ pint) or 1¼ U.S. cups tomato or orange juice
2 teaspoons natural unprocessed bran — the finely powdered form of bran is best for liquids.
25 g (1 oz) yoghurt

Mix the bran in the yoghurt, pour into the tomato or orange juice and blend until smooth.

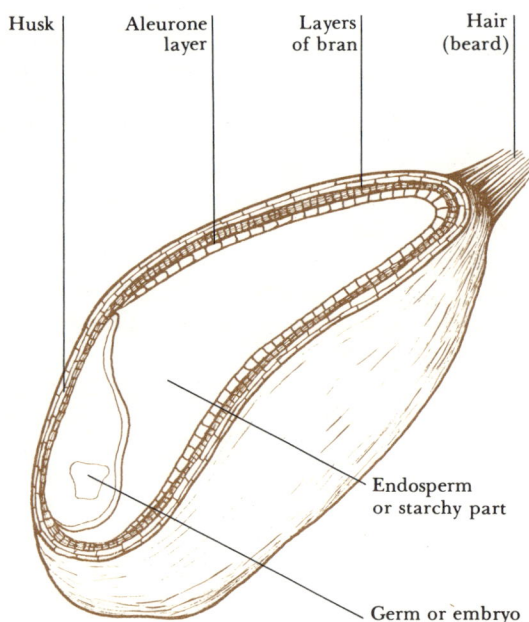

Husk | Aleurone layer | Layers of bran | Hair (beard)

Endosperm or starchy part

Germ or embryo

Government introduced National Flour with the dual purpose of reducing the wastage of wheat and increasing the nutritional content of a staple wartime food. The fibre content was five times higher than that of pre-war white flour. Records show that the British people have never been so healthy over the past seventy years than they were during this war.

The need for fibre

The dietary significance of the work of the bran pioneers is only now being fully understood and the debate is still being fuelled by continuing research into the benefits of bran. Surgeon Captain Cleave of the Royal Navy and formerly Director of Institute of Naval Medicine, U.K., did outstanding research into the significance of bran. Important work has also been done by Dr Denis Burkitt, Senior Research Fellow at St Thomas's Hospital, London (*See page* 7). A good introduction to the subject is Dr Andrew Stanway's book *Taking the Rough with the Smooth*.

What is fibre?

Plant fibre lies in the walls of the cells. It is now known to be a highly complex substance made up of polysaccharides, the major ones being cellulose, pectin, hemicelluloses, and lignins. Fibre is made up of a group of substances in the cells of plants and vegetables which cannot be broken down by the human digestive enzymes.

Fibre absorbs large amounts of water. This water-absorbing property is important since it gives the food the bulk it needs to pass along the bowel.

Researchers in the U.S.A. have found that fibre actually absorbs noxious chemicals, such as additives, in the colon, and has the ability to alter the bacteria in the bowel and make it less susceptible to certain diseases.

Nutritional content

25 g (1 oz) bran flakes contain: 3 g protein, 117 calories, 2 mg iron, 25 mg calcium, 248 mg phosphorus, 480 mg potassium, 960 mg sodium, 3.4 mg niacin, plus good traces of B1 (thiamine) and B2 (riboflavin).

How to get fibre in the daily diet

Many fruits, vegetables and pulses contain fibre. Bran was the traditional source of most fibre in Western diets until the introduction of roller mills nearly one hundred years ago. At the end of the eighteenth century, the average person ate about 450 g (1 lb) of bread a day giving 30 g of fibre. Today, a refined, processed diet could provide less than 5 g of fibre daily.

Fish, eggs, milk, meat, and sugar contain no dietary fibre. Though not a substitute for cereal fibre, good examples of fibrous fruits are apples, bananas, avocados, fresh blackberries, papaya, dried dates and figs, strawberries, and raspberries.

This should dispel the modern idea that fibre is often tough and nasty to eat. Think of the smooth blackberries that provide 6.6 g of fibre for every 144 g or 1 average cupful.

Most vegetables contain fibre. Peas, spinach, carrots, turnips, tomatoes, and sweet potatoes are good sources. Burkitt and Trowel in their book *Carbohydrate, Food and Disease* suggest that the diet should contain 2 g of wheat-bran fibre per day. Try and forget the idea that bran flakes or granules have to be endured each breakfast as it is simple to add them to soups, casseroles, minced meat, bread or cake cookery.

Does it matter what sort of bran?

Recent research in the U.K. by Dr K.W. Heaton supported by the McCarrison Society (*See* ORGANIZATION *page* 150) has proved that unprocessed, natural bran is better than refined bran cereal. Dr Heaton and his colleague Dr Wyman published their findings in the December 1976 issue of the American Journal of Clinical Nutrition.

As expected, unprocessed bran increased stool weight and reduced transit times. It also diluted the faecal bile acids. In contrast, All-Bran did not significantly alter any of these measurements although there was a trend in the same direction. Thus this study confirms the superiority of natural bran over the processed variety.

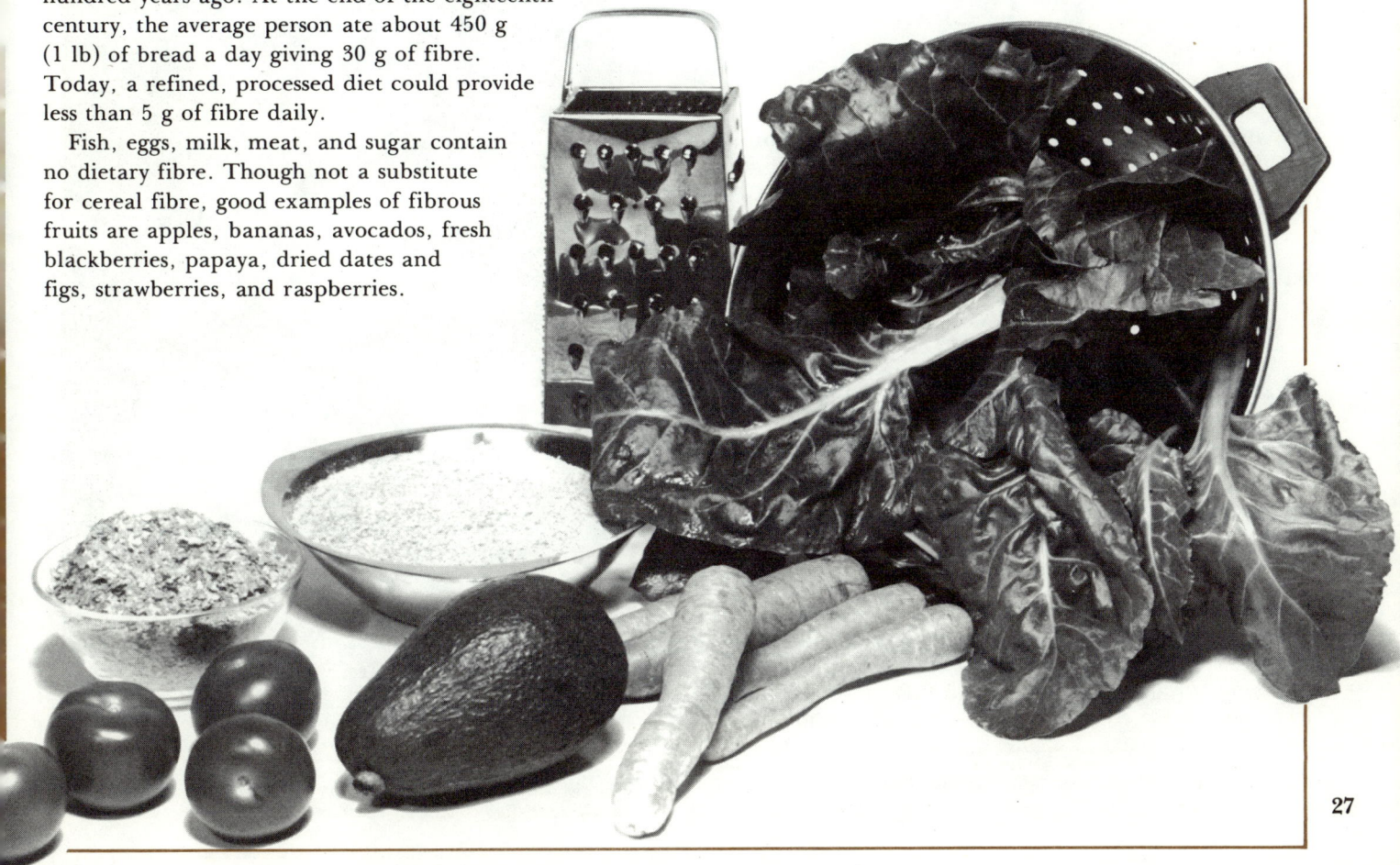

Brewer's yeast

Brewer's yeast is a by-product of the brewing process. Yeasts are tiny living plants that are present in the air around us and that congregate on fruits and grains ready to help convert the various types of sugar to alcohol in one of the great food chain cycles of Nature.

The earliest recorded use of yeast as a medicine was in 1550 B.C. in Eber's Papyrus during the eighteenth dynasty of Egypt. But it is only during the last few decades that the outstanding nutritional qualities of brewer's yeast have been researched.

An Egyptian woman pounding dough at the time of the 5th dynasty c. 2650 B.C.

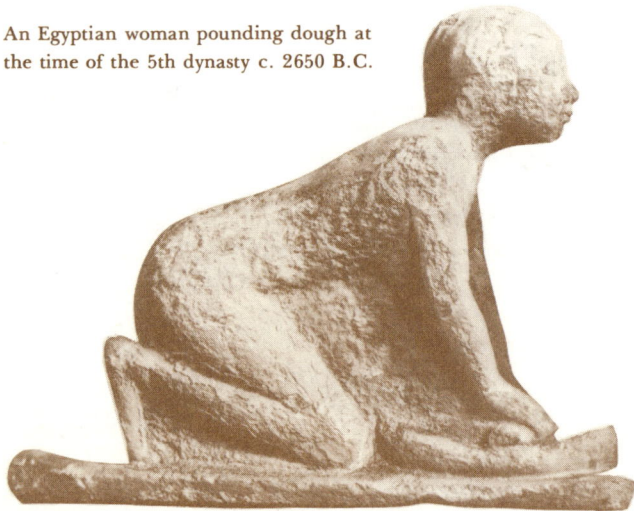

Nutritional content

Brewer's yeast contains sixteen of the twenty amino acids and the whole range of B complex vitamins. It is particularly rich in vitamins B1 (known as thiamine or aneurin) and B2 (riboflavin). It is a source of niacinamide, pantothenic acid, biotin, cholin, vitamin B6 (pyridoxine), folic acid, vitamin B12 and inositol. Yeast has large amounts of phosphorus, iron and calcium. Two of its important trace elements are chromium and selenium.

One g of brewer's yeast contains: 1.5 mg B1 (thiamine), 0.5 mg B2 (riboflavin), 4 mg B3, 0.4 mg B6, trace of biotin, 4.4 mg inositol, 0.1 mg pantothenic acid, 3.3 mg cholin, 0.05 mg folic acid and three calories.

Particular value

Brewer's yeast is especially rich in the vitamin B complex group. There are, in fact, only four good sources of the B family as a group: brewer's yeast, WHEAT GERM, RICE polish, and liver. Several foods are high in one or two B vitamins, but not in the B complex family as they occur in yeast.

It is perhaps easier to become deficient in the B vitamins than any others. This is because they are water soluble and can largely be destroyed by cooking and many of them cannot be stored by the body. People with little nutritional knowledge would be unlikely to eat one of the few sources of B complex daily, and might develop a deficiency.

A good guide to your intake of B vitamins is your tongue. It should be an even pink in colour and smooth round the edges. If B vitamins are undersupplied, grooves will start to appear. A large or 'beefy' tongue indicates a need for pantothenic acid. A magenta colour shows vitamin B2 (riboflavin) deficiency. A sore red tongue indicates the need for niacin.

Really severe vitamin B deficiencies cause diseases such as beri-beri and pellagra. Other symptoms of B deficiency include depression, fatigue, skin irritations, sores of the mouth and palpitations. Brewer's yeast's value to nervous illness has been well documented; one hospital group in Sweden gives large supplements to mental patients. The American nutritionist Dr Tom Spies treated the pellagra which was prevalent in the Southern States with up to 250 g (9 oz) of brewer's yeast daily.

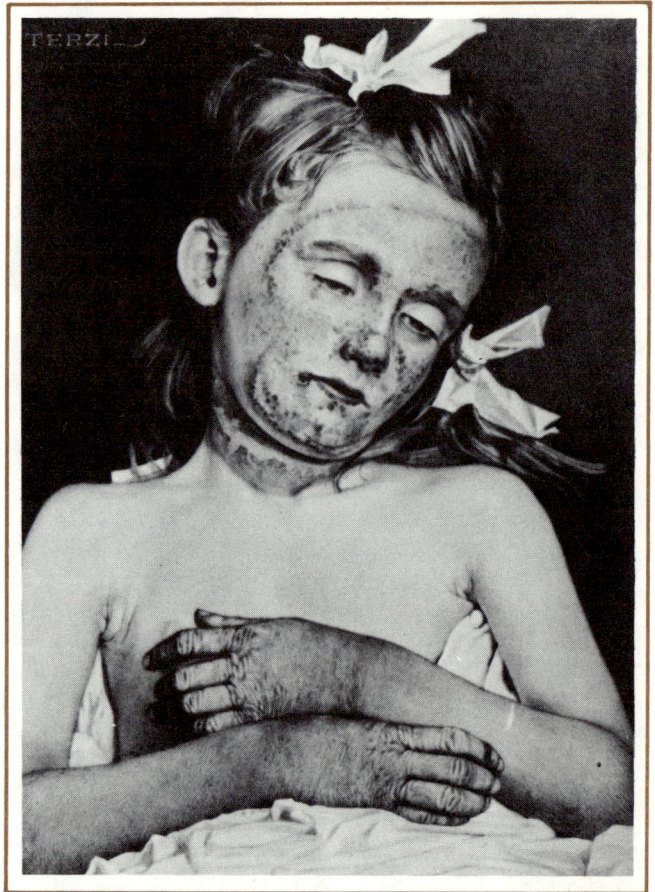

This girl with pellagra was treated as a mental patient in the 1920s, a few years before treatment was found for this vitamin B deficiency

Treatments by yeast

One element of yeast has the trace mineral chromium in its chemical structure and is known as the Glucose Tolerance Factor (GTF). This is necessary to regulate blood sugar and is important for diabetics and people with a tendency to low blood sugar.

Although it is possible to have deficiencies of a single B vitamin, it is rarely a good idea to buy, say tablets of B1 (thiamine) or B6. This is because the B vitamins work synergistically, or in concert with each other. Prolonged taking of one of the B family could cause deficiencies of the others. That is why brewer's yeast with its round balance of the B complex group is so valuable.

Types of yeast

Yeast varies according to the medium in which it is grown. Scientists in the U.S.A. have improved a strain of brewer's yeast which contains B12. Not all brewer's yeast has this vitamin, so non-meat eaters should study the label carefully. Also available are several types of de-bittered brewer's yeast which improve the taste.
Torula yeast (Candida yeast) has caused a certain amount of controversy. Some, but by no means all, of this strain of yeast, is grown on waste sulphite liquor from wood pulp. This source has been known to upset some people. Other torula yeasts are excellent, including those in liquid forms in certain tonics such as Bio-Strath available world wide. It is a question of trial and error, or perhaps asking the manufacturer his sources.

How to take brewer's yeast

It is fair to say that some people have to persevere with several brands of nutritional yeasts before finding one whose taste and composition suits them. Brewer's yeast is available in tablet form, but perhaps the easiest way to put it on the menu is in the form of dried powder. This can be stirred into a high-powered nutritional drink called 'Pep up' devised by Adelle Davis. (*See* RECIPE) Others find it more palatable in fruit juice. It is a good idea to keep a packet of the brewer's yeast powder handy in the kitchen and simply add it to soups, gravies and casseroles.

When first taking brewer's yeast some people experience flatulence or gas. Adelle Davis describes the problem succinctly in *Let's Eat Right to Keep Fit:*

Since faulty digestion is usually the result of inadequate B vitamins, the more gas you get from yeast, the more deficient you can know that you are in the B vitamins, and the more you need the yeast . . . If you lack hydrochloric acid in your stomach or produce too few digestive enzymes, much of the yeast remains undigested and your intestinal bacteria have a feast; they form gas. The healthy person digests yeast completely and has no gas or feeling of fullness from taking it.

It is wise to start taking brewer's yeast gradually, beginning with half a teaspoon. Most people find they can cope with it well in a few weeks.
A word of warning Never use baker's yeast, or any other live yeast. Research in the University of Wisconsin, U.S.A. has shown that live yeast goes on growing in the intestine and actually uses up the vitamin B in the body. This includes yeast supplied for brewing purposes. Home brewers wishing to make use of spent yeast should rinse it in fresh water, dry it, and de-activate the yeast by heating it to above 50°C, (95°F, Gas Mark 2), in the oven for 20 minutes depending on quantity.

Adelle Davis' Pep up
900 ml (32 fl. oz) or 4 U.S. cups
skimmed low fat, or whole milk
1 teaspoon to ½ cup yeast, depending on whether you are a beginner or a veteran.
100-125 g (4-5 oz) or 1 U.S. cup
non-instant powdered milk
1 tablespoon soy, safflower or mixed vegetable oils
100 ml (4 fl. oz) or ½ U.S. cup frozen, undiluted orange juice, or grape juice

A number of other ingredients can be added, such as granular lecithin, bone meal, calcium lactate or wheat germ.

Adelle Davis states that the aim with this fortified milk is to provide most of the essentials at one time: amino acids from complete protein, linoleic acid, all the B vitamins, vitamin C, and calcium and magnesium.

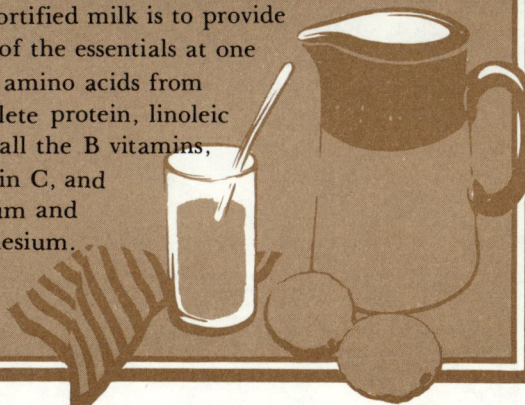

Buckwheat

Buckwheat is sometimes called saracen corn because it was brought to Europe from Asia by the Crusaders. It is not a grain in the botanical sense as it is related to dock and rhubarb, although most cookbooks classify it as such.

The 60-cm (2-ft) high plant has the most attractive heart-shaped leaves and pale pink, scented flowers. It is popular in the U.K. as an annual and used in some original flower arrangements. Buckwheat is widely used as a food and cover for pheasants and other reared game. Buckwheat cakes are very popular in the U.S.A. and northern Europe. (*See* RECIPE) The Germans use the grain for brewing beer and other drinks and they also make a fine buckwheat pottage. Buckwheat honey is very popular in Russia.

Nutritional content

Buckwheat is 11% protein. It is rich in iron and contains almost all the entire range of B complex vitamins. 98 g (3½ oz) of dark sifted buckwheat flour contains 11.5 g protein, 326 calories, 32 mg calcium, 340 mg phosphorus, 2.7 mg iron, 0.57 mg B1 (thiamine), 0.15 mg B2 (riboflavin) and 2.8 mg

Particular value

The rutic acid content of buckwheat places it high on the list of curative plants. Rutic acid has a powerful effect on the arteries and circulatory system. Many homeopathic doctors prescribe buckwheat for certain heart conditions, hardening of the arteries, varicose veins, and many circulatory problems.
Rutin tablets are available from Health Food stores.
Buckwheat flour can be more expensive than other flours because of the difficulty in removing the sheathlike husk. The flour can be used in muffins, pancakes and biscuit recipes. It is perhaps most successful in recipes that call for a heavier flour. Many recipes advise mixing buckwheat flour with other flours such as RICE or WHEAT to lighten it.
Buckwheat groats are the crushed and hulled seeds of the plant. They look rather like a beechnut. The groats may be cooked just like rice, simmering gently in water until soft; or their crunchiness may be used to good effect in biscuits or buckwheat brittle.

Buckwheat cake (quick method)

150 mg (5 oz) or 1½ U.S. cups buckwheat flour
1 tablespoon baking powder
Put these in a mixing bowl, and put the following ingredients in a blender:
3 eggs
225 ml (8 fl oz) or 1 U.S. cup runny honey
1 teaspoon vanilla
225 ml (8 fl oz) or 1 U.S. cup soya or sunflower oil
Blend well; pour over flour and mix thoroughly. Mould the mixture into a cake tin and cook at 190°C (375°F, Gas Mark 5) for about ½ hour.

Kasha loaf

Roast the kasha as described. Mix it with sautéed onion and mixed herbs; add an egg to bind and a dash of tamari soy sauce to flavour. The mixture should be quite stiff, and if it is too soft, add a sprinkling of wholemeal flour. Pour into a greased baking dish and bake at 200°C (400°F, Gas Mark 6) for 45 minutes. It can be served hot or cold in slices with vegetables.

Kasha is the name given to roasted buckwheat, traditionally found in Asia.

To roast buckwheat

Place a tablespoon of oil in a heavy pan and heat gently until quite hot. Add the buckwheat and keep stirring all the time until it is crisp and nutty.

How to cook it

Buckwheat needs three or four times as much water as does rice. Allow 4 cups of water to 1 cup of buckwheat. Bring the water to the boil and add salt. Add the buckwheat and immediately put on a tight-fitting lid and lower the heat. It should be ready in 30 minutes.

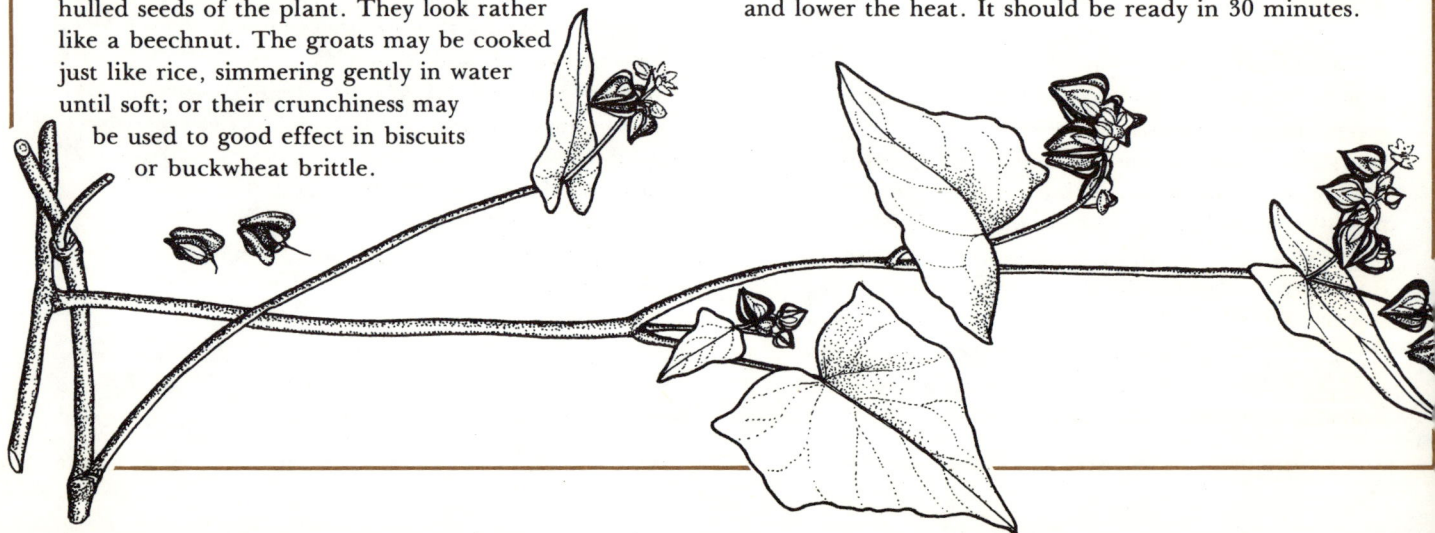

Carob

Carob is a legume belonging to the locust family. The beans grow on a fairly tall, evergreen tree which is also known as the locust tree. The edible pods and beans are sometimes called St John's Bread. The Bible tells us that St John the Baptist lived in the wilderness on locusts and wild honey. It was the carob or locust bean that gave him nourishment, not, as many modern readers suppose, the locust insect.

The carob tree has been valued for thousands of years as a source of nutrients both for humans and animals. Carob seeds were actually used to buy goods in Middle Eastern countries and it is from this trading that we get the word 'carat' used by jewellers today.

Nutritional content
Carob flour and powder is 8% protein and 72% natural carbohydrate. 140 g (5 oz) of carob flour contain 6.3 g protein, 252 calories, 493 mg calcium, and 113 mg phosphorus.

How to use carob
Carob beans are dried and ground into flour or powder which is easily used in milk shakes and many other recipes. (*See* RECIPES)

Many people regard carob as directly interchangeable with chocolate and simply substitute it in recipes.

Carob milk shake
In the blender put:
425 ml ($\frac{3}{4}$ pint) or 2 U.S. cups milk
1 or 2 tablespoons carob flour or powder
1 tablespoon honey
1 teaspoon brewer's yeast (optional)
half a ripe banana (optional)

Instant carob pudding
225 ml (8 fl oz) or 1 U.S. cup warm water
1 teaspoon of gelatine
3 tablespoons of honey
2 tablespoons of carob
100 ml (4 fl oz) or $\frac{1}{2}$ U.S. cup vegetable oil
1 teaspoon vanilla
2 eggs (optional)

This is very quick and easy to do in a blender but can also be done by hand. Blend the warm water with the gelatine. Buzz or whisk until it dissolves. Add the honey, carob, oil and egg. Blend well until smooth and pour into a mould. Chill in the refrigerator. Serves 4.

The advantages of carob over chocolate Chocolate, like all the cocoa bean products, contains caffeine. It needs to be artificially sweetened with sugar which carob does not. Cocoa beans are high in oxalic acid which is known to have the ability to 'lock in' calcium and make it unavailable to the body.

Carob contains pectin, the natural jelling substance. Much research has been done in the last decade on the treatment of diarrhoea and stomach upsets with pectin products. Many successful experiments with carob have been reported in *The U.S. Journal of Pediatrics* and the *Canadian Medical Association Journal* in which several doctors have recommended carob for straightforward digestive upsets. It is prescribed in a 5% solution, that is, one tablespoon to 225 ml (8 fl oz).

Cheese

There is a nice legend that an impatient Arab prince put some milk into his travelling pouch, slung it over the camel's hump, and set off riding hard across the desert. When thirst forced him to stop he found that the milk had turned into curds and whey, in other words, cheese. It is believed that the first cheese was made in this way by the nomadic tribes who wandered over eastern Europe and western Asia who used pouches made from the stomachs of goats, sheep or cows which contained rennin, a substance that causes milk to clot. The heat, rennin, and the motion of the camel provided an ideal situation for cheese making.

The Greeks valued cheese highly as did the Romans who introduced methods of making it into Britain, from where it was sent to other provinces throughout the Roman Empire.

Nutritional content

Cheese is rich in calcium, phosphorus, vitamins A, B2 (riboflavin), and the essential amino acids. 56 g (2 oz) of grated cheddar cheese contains: 226 calories, 14 g protein, 1 g carbohydrate, 19 g fat, 0.6 mg iron, 435 mg calcium, 390 mg phosphorus, 90 mg potassium, 540 mg sodium, 700 I.U. vitamin A, 0.2 mg vitamin B2 (riboflavin), with small amounts of vitamin D, niacin, vitamin B1 (thiamine) and B12.

Creamed cottage cheese

This is sometimes known as pot cheese or schmierkase in the United States. Its main advantage is its lower number of calories. 112 g (4 oz) creamed cottage cheese contain: 120 calories, 15 g protein, 3 g carbohydrate, 0.45 mg iron, 102 mg calcium, 280 mg phosphorus, 85 mg potassium, 312 mg sodium, 215 I.U. vitamin A, 0.3 mg B2 (riboflavin), 0.1 mg niacin.

Particular value

Cheese is a complete protein as it contains the eight essential amino acids which the body cannot manufacture itself. It is perhaps the least expensive way of obtaining a supply of complete proteins and so rates very highly in the daily diet. Added to this, cheese is very flexible and can be used in thousands of ways.

Types of cheese

There are over 400 known types of cheese, many of them the exotic specialities of various countries. Generally speaking, hard cheeses such as Cheddar and Gloucester are of higher nutritive value than softer ones like Camembert because they contain less moisture. Processed cheese is considered by some nutritionists to be inferior and also may contain additives.

1 Tôme au raisin 2 Burrino 3 Dolcelatte 4 Jarlesberg 5 Stilton 6 Epoisses 7 Red Windsor 8 Provolone 9 Sage Derby 10 Edam 11 Gaperon 12 Emmenthal 13 Blue Cheshire 14 Brie 15 Walnut cream cheese 16 Log chèvre 17 Fromage de monsieur 18 Neufchâtel 19 Parmesan 20 English goat cheese

How to make your own cheese

The English Cheese Bureau gives these easy instructions to make
a delicious fresh cheese that must be eaten within two days.
Ingredients 575 ml (1 pint) or 2½ U.S. cups pasteurized milk 1 lemon pinch salt
Utensils sterilizing solution lemon squeezer saucepan thermometer
large bowl colander butter muslin cloths shallow dish
perforated ladle string spoon greaseproof paper

Sterilize all equipment by plunging
in bowl of sterilizing solution.
Squeeze juice from lemon. Heat milk
to 38°C (100°F) and pour into bowl. Add
lemon juice to milk and leave for 15 minutes.

You will see the curds and whey develop.
Line colander with dampened muslin
and stand it in shallow dish.
Spoon curd into colander with
perforated ladle.

Knot corners of cloth, hang over bowl
and leave for 30 minutes to allow whey
to drain. Scrape cheese from sides
of muslin and put in new muslin cloth.
Hang it over bowl for another half hour.

Remove cheese from muslin.
Add salt to taste and wrap in greaseproof paper.
Refrigerate and eat how you like
within the next few days!

People who find that they cannot easily digest cheese should try making it with cultured buttermilk

Additives According to the English Cheese Bureau, there is absolutely no reason why chemical additives should be put in cheese. They recommend harmless vegetable dyes, such as *annatto,* which gives many red cheeses colour. Various firms do put powerful agents like sodium nitrite in their cheese. The best way to avoid this is to use a reputable wholefood supplier of cheeses.

Can cheese be frozen? Yes, if you do not mind the crumbly texture that develops. In the case of certain blue cheeses this does not matter. Freeze hard varieties in packs not more than 3 cm (1 in) thick, wrapped tightly in freezer paper or foil. Keep for a maximum of six months, and thaw gradually in the refrigerator.

To store cheese Soft cheeses are highly perishable and will only keep in the refrigerator for a few days. All cheese should be kept tightly wrapped in foil or an airtight container in the least cool part of the refrigerator. An ideal temperature range is from 8-12°C (45-55°F). Bring the cheese out at least one hour before serving or the flavour will suffer.

If cheese goes hard and dry, grate it and store in an airtight jar in the refrigerator. This way, it will keep for several weeks.

Comfrey

Comfrey was valued by the Ancients for its medicinal value. Pliny the Elder described its healing properties and both the Greeks and Turks used it for healing wounds. Early English herbalists called it knit-bone or boneset and put it very high on the list of healing plants. They used it to soothe and heal internal organs as well as external wounds. Modern analysis has revealed many reasons why comfrey is so effective.

Comfrey is not a legume, but a member of the borage family. Its long roots can reach 3 m (10 ft) down into the subsoil and draw up plant foods usually only tapped by tree roots.

In 1870 a Quaker farmer called Henry Doubleday began to import a particularly fine strain of comfrey from Russia. The plants were carefully dug up from the garden of Catherine the Great in St Petersburg and sent to Henry Doubleday's small farm in Essex, England. From these he grew the hybrid *Symphytum peregrinum* which is used today. The popular name Russian comfrey stuck and it is widely called that in the U.K. today. In the U.S.A. and Canada it is usually called Quaker comfrey. Both names are used in Australia.

It is ironic to note that Catherine the Great's garden is now a Park of Rest and Culture and the comfrey plants were long ago pulled up as weeds. No Russian comfrey had been grown as a crop in Russia for many decades. Then, in 1976, a symposium of scientists in Leningrad urged the Soviet Government to grow comfrey as 'an outstanding crop'.

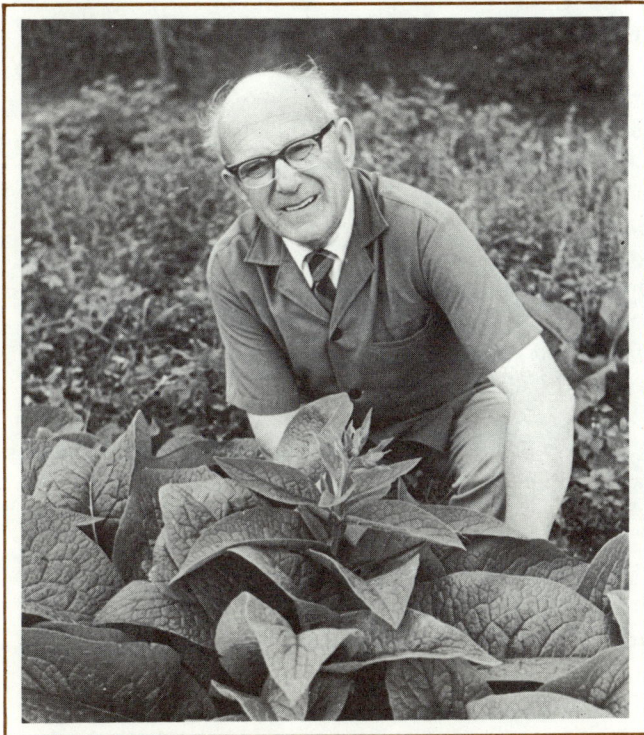

Nutritional content

Comfrey is a good source of the B complex group with the important addition of B12. It is rich in vitamins C and E. The Henry Doubleday Research Association has published this analysis of dried Bocking mixture comfrey leaves: every 100 g (4 oz) contain: 0.5 mg B1 (thiamine), 1 mg B2 (riboflavin), 5 mg nicotinic acid, 4.2 mg pantothenic acid, 0.7 mg B12, 100 mg vitamin C, 30 mg vitamin E, and 0.18 mg allantoin. It is 22% protein and has traces of iron, calcium, vitamin A, manganese, and phosphorus.

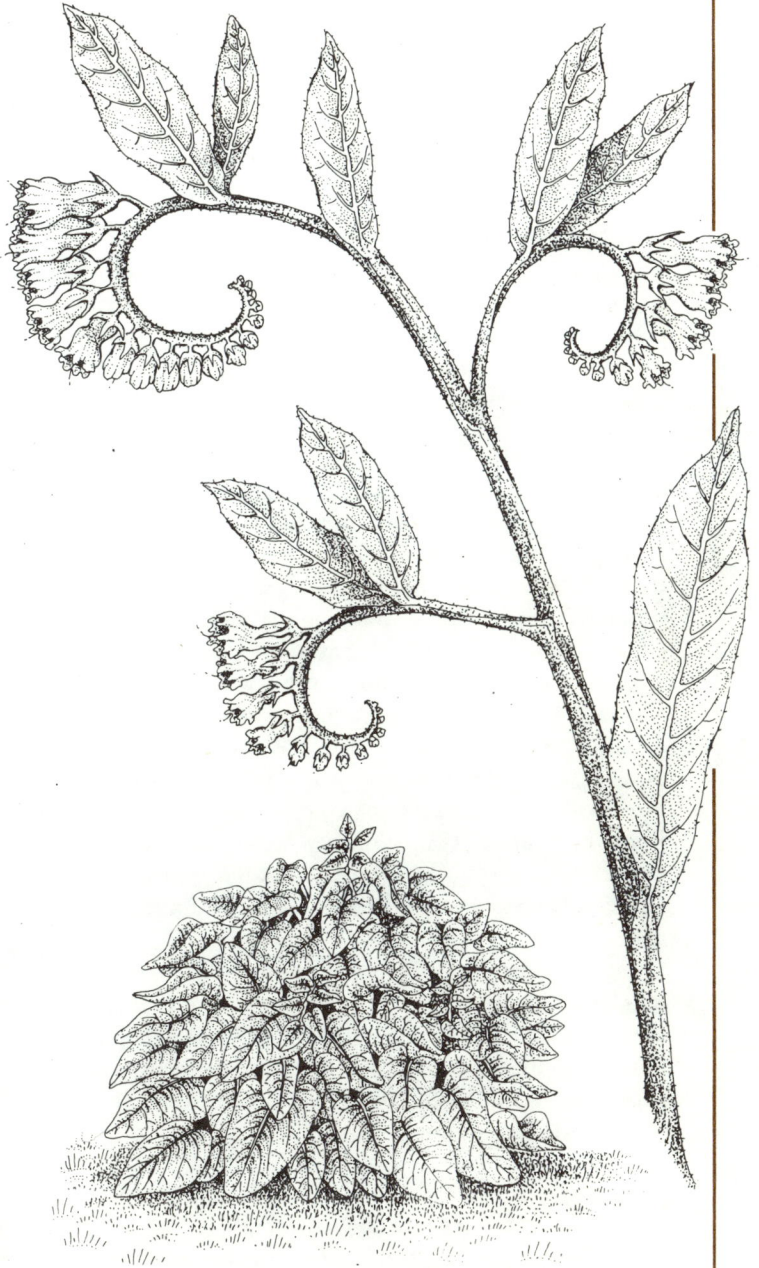

Lawrence D. Hills, Director of the Henry Doubleday Research Association with comfrey plants

Comfrey and B12

Comfrey has been widely written about as the only land plant containing B12. This is a source of controversy. Some authorities believe that comfrey only contains B12 if it has been grown in certain organic matter already possessing the vitamin.

Particular value

The healing power of comfrey is thought to be due to the agent allantoin occurring in a plant with natural antiseptic and mucilage and a wide range of well-balanced vitamins. Allantoin is a substance which promotes the healing of damaged tissue and is used in orthodox medicine in the treatment of suppurating wounds and ulcers. The ancient healers had no powers of analysis but their observations were remarkably accurate. Registered herbalists prescribe comfrey tablets or liquid for bronchial complaints, asthma, and internal ulcers.

Comfrey ointment is recommended by herbalists for bruises, eczema, haemorrhoids, and dermatitis.

Comfrey leaves may be dried and used as a beneficial tea.

Comfrey flour can be bought in health food stores, or may be made as follows: Spread the leaves to wilt in the sun and when wilted but still bright green, place in an airing cupboard to dry until crisp. Break up the leaves and grind to a green flour in a coffee mill. Store in an airtight container.

How to store

All comfrey products are hygroscopic, that is they have the ability to draw moisture from the air. So it is essential to keep them in airtight containers. This is important in the case of comfrey leaves which are often sold in ill-sealed cellophane bags.

How to cook

Comfrey can be cooked as a green vegetable rather like spinach. Wash the leaves and chop the larger ones into small pieces. Heat a knob of butter in a pan. Add the leaves gradually. Keep the lid on for about two minutes shaking the pan to prevent burning. The leaves then give out their own moisture. Turn gently and cook for eight minutes. Serve with a sprinkling of nutmeg and butter.

Types of comfrey

Most modern comfrey is descended from the hybrid that Henry Doubleday made in 1870. The Henry Doubleday Research Association of Bocking, U.K., is perhaps the leading research centre testing comfrey today and has bred 20 variations on the original hybrid. Each variety is carefully graded and aimed at a special use. For example, Bocking no. 14 has thin stems and can be cooked as a vegetable. It is ready earlier in the season, rich in potash and is also a good poultry feed. Testers in the selection trials preferred the taste of Bocking no. 4 which has thicker stems. Rabbits and chinchillas agreed with the humans. They devoured Bocking no. 4 and merely picked at Bocking no. 14.

Growing comfrey

It is not worth buying comfrey seeds which take such a long time to develop. The plants can be obtained direct from the Henry Doubleday Research Association which has a licence to export worldwide. *See page* 154.

Dried fruit

Many fruits such as grapes, apricots, dates, and plums, have been dried since the time of the Pharaohs and are clearly shown in the wall paintings of the Egyptian temples. Hippocrates, the Father of Medicine, recommended raisins as a preventative against jaundice and fever. In the Bible, King David accepted raisins in lieu of taxes. His subjects dried their grapes by spreading them out in the sun. Today fruit dehydration is a highly scientific business.

Dried fruits are a rich source of protein and minerals such as iron and calcium, vitamins A, C, and several of the B vitamins.

How fruit is dried

Apricots, pears, peaches, nectarines, and apples are usually put in sulphur houses to retain their colour, then subjected to dehydration. In Australia and California the fruit is dried out in the sun. The sulphur houses fumigate the fruit by sulphur dioxide, a highly poisonous gas.

Raisins and sultanas are dipped into a potassium carbonate solution and then dried. Finally, the majority of commercially dried fruit is sprayed with food grade mineral oil to prevent sticking and to present a luscious and moist appearance. Mineral oil, also called liquid paraffin, prevents the body absorbing the fat soluble vitamins, A, D, E, and K. It can be removed from dried fruit by careful washing in hot water. Specialist shops sell dried fruit guaranteed unsprayed with mineral oil.

Storing dried fruit

Stored correctly in airtight containers, dried fruit can keep for up to one year. All dried fruit freezes well.

Apricots

Apricot trees were first cultivated in China. Traders took apricot stones over the great caravan routes to Armenia and across the Middle East and thence to Europe. Spanish settlers took their favourite apricot stock and grape vines with them to California where methods of drying the fruit were developed. The Chaffey brothers·went from their superbly irrigated fruit farm in California in the 1880s and took vines, apricots and plums to Australia to start the now thriving dried fruit industry.

Nutritional content

75 g (2½ oz) dried apricots contain: 4 g protein, 222 calories, 4.1 mg iron, 50 mg calcium, 75 mg phosphorus, 780 mg potassium, 8000 I.U. vitamin A, 9 mg vitamin C, 3 mg niacin, plus traces of B1 (thiamine) and B2 (riboflavin).

Sweet and sour apricot sauce

2 tablespoons salad oil
225 ml (8 fl oz) or 1 U.S. cup puréed apricots
1 tablespoon honey
pinch salt
1 teaspoon Worcestershire or soy sauce
2 tablespoons vinegar
100 ml (4 fl oz) or ½ U.S. cup tomato sauce
2 tablespoons grated onion
¼ teaspoon dried oregano

Combine all the ingredients together in a saucepan and bring to the boil. Cover and simmer gently for about 12 minutes.
This sauce is delicious with any meat, especially barbecued.

Particular value

Tests in the U.S.A. have shown that the iron in apricots is particularly well assimilated by the body. Liver produces the most haemoglobin, followed by kidneys, apricots and eggs in decreasing amounts.

Currants

Currants are dried from the tiny purple Corinth grape which originally came from Greece. They dry so easily that the preserving saline solution is not needed. They are the smallest of all dried fruit and have a hard, crisp texture. They are traditionally popular in buns and rock cakes.

Nutritional content

80 g (3 oz) dried currants contain: $1\frac{1}{2}$ g of protein, 240 calories, 1.9 mg iron, 41 mg calcium, 83 mg phosphorus, 400 mg potassium, 80 I.U. vitamin A, and traces of vitamin B1 (thiamine) and niacin.

Colonial potato cake

(From the *Australian Dried Fruit Cookbook*)

225 g (8 oz) or 2 U.S. cups wholemeal self raising flour
100 g (4 oz) or $\frac{1}{2}$ U.S. cup mashed potato
150 g (5 oz) or 1 U.S. cup currants
100 ml (4 fl oz) or $\frac{1}{2}$ U.S. cup milk

Sift the flour into a bowl and mix in the potato and currants. Mix to a soft dough with the milk, knead lightly on a floured surface, and form into a round shape. Glaze with milk and then place on a floured tray to bake in a moderately hot oven 200°C (400°F, Gas Mark 5) for about 15 minutes or until cooked and golden brown.

Dates

The date is one of the oldest known cultivated fruits, and was first grown in the fertile crescent between the Tigris and the Euphrates about seven thousand years ago. The date palm which bears these amber fruits is a fascinating tree and will grow in desert conditions where no other fruit-bearing tree could flourish. It is renowned for its longevity. A circle of date palms was planted by one of Alexander the Great's generals over two thousand years ago in the Himalayas and it is said still bears fruit today.

Dates, fresh and dried, form an important part of the Bedouin diet. They sap the palm tree to provide a sweetening agent and pierce the bark which oozes a liquid for drinks.

Stuffed date salad

12 dates, stoned
2 tablespoons of peanut butter
1 avocado pear
450 g (1 lb) or 2 U.S. cups cottage cheese
1 Lettuce
Make a nest of cottage cheese on crisp lettuce leaves and put a circle of diced avocado pear around it. Take the stone out of each date and fill it with peanut butter.
Put the dates on top of the cottage cheese.
(Serves 4)

Nutritional content

The date has the highest natural sugar content of all dried fruits. 178 g ($6\frac{1}{4}$ oz) of dried dates contain: 4 g protein, 505 calories, 5.7 mg iron, 105 mg calcium, 110 mg phosphorus, 1300 mg potassium, 100 I.U. units vitamin A, 3.9 mg niacin, with traces of B1 (thiamine) and B2 (riboflavin).

Prunes

Prunes come from special varieties of plums. These are shaken from the tree by mechanical shakers and fall into catching sheets. The plums are then washed and dehydrated by blasts of hot air for 20 hours and as the moisture dries out the fruit assumes its characteristic wrinkled skin.

Nutritional content

270 g ($9\frac{1}{2}$ oz) prunes contain: 3 g protein, 300 calories, 4.5 mg iron, 60 mg calcium, 100 mg phosphorus, 810 mg potassium, 1500 I.U. vitamin A, 1.8 mg

Prune whip

200 g (7 oz) or 2 U.S. cups dried prunes
700 ml (24 fl. oz) or 3 U.S. cups yoghurt
$\frac{1}{2}$ teaspoon lemon juice
1 tablespoon unflavoured gelatine
Dissolve the gelatine in 50 ml (2 fl oz) or $\frac{1}{4}$ U.S. cup of cold water and stir well. Cook the dried prunes until quite soft, take out the stones and purée them. Beat in the yoghurt and lemon juice. Add the gelatine and leave it to set. Garnish with chopped walnuts.

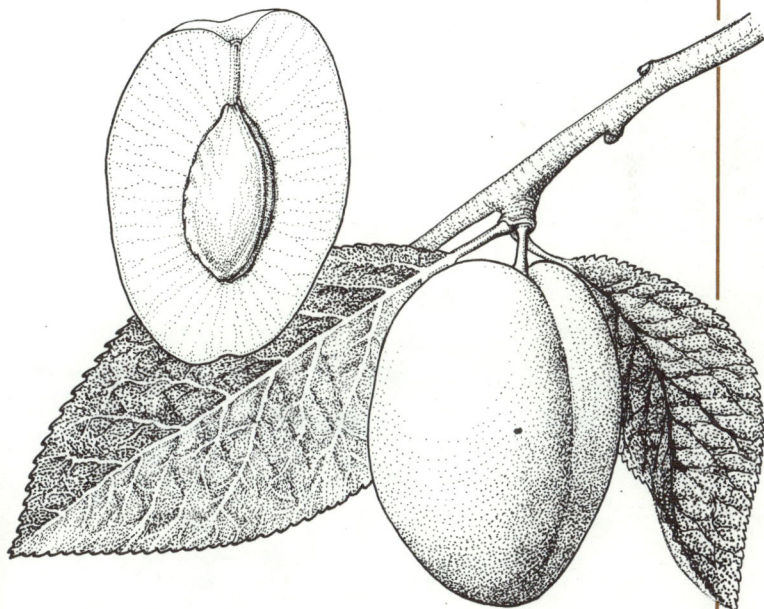

niacin, 3 mg vitamin C, with traces of B1 (thiamine) and B2 (riboflavin).

Particular value

The particular value of prunes lies in their natural laxative properties and the high vitamin A content.

Raisins

Raisins are dried grapes of the Muscat variety, medium in size and perhaps the most widely used of the three main dried grape varieties. They are hardier than sultanas, chewier than currants, and make an excellent addition to muesli, meat stuffings, sweet and sour rice dishes, and an infinite variety of puddings. Children can easily be encouraged to eat raisins instead of sweets.

Nutritional content

80 g (3 oz) dried raisins contain: 2 g protein, 230 calories, 2.8 mg iron, 50 mg calcium, 112 mg phosphorus, 575 mg potassium, 15 I.U. vitamin A, with traces of B1 (thiamine) and niacin.

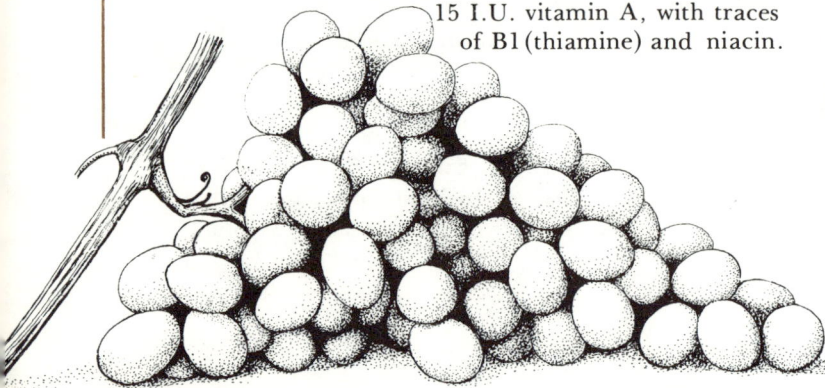

Frozen rum and raisin cream

(From the *Australian Dried Fruit Cookbook*)
150 g (5 oz) or 1 U.S. cup finely chopped
seeded raisins
225 ml (8 fl oz) or 1 U.S. cup dark rum
225 ml (8 fl oz) or 1 U.S. cup double cream
125 g (4 oz) or 1 U.S. cup macaroon crumbs
125 g (4 oz) or 1 U.S. cup chopped walnuts
850 ml (1½ pints) or 3½ U.S. cups softened
vanilla ice-cream
Soak the raisins in the rum for at least one hour. Whip the cream and fold into the mixture. Add the macaroon crumbs and walnuts. Gradually stir the mixture into the ice-cream and spoon into six dessert dishes. Place in the freezer until firm. Serve garnished with chopped walnuts.

Sultanas

Sultanas come from the seedless sultana grape. These are dipped or sprayed with a solution of emulsified oils and potash to help dehydration and preserve the golden colour. In Australia sultanas and raisins are treated with a cold dip based on olive oil.

Sultanas are softer and sweeter than either currants or raisins.

Nutritional content

80 g (3 oz) dried sultanas contain: 2 g protein, 230 calories, 2.2 mg iron, 60 mg calcium, 90 mg phosphorus, 450 mg potassium, 15 I.U. vitamin A, and traces of B1 (thiamine) and niacin.

Sultana, banana and grapefruit bake

1 large grapefruit
1 large banana
1 tablespoon brown sugar
2 tablespoons sultanas
lemon juice
Peel grapefruit and cut between the sections to remove the flesh. Put in buttered fireproof dish. Peel the bananas and cut them in half first across and then downwards. Roll them in lemon juice to prevent discolouration. Sprinkle with sugar and sultanas. Tightly cover and bake at 190°C (375°F, Gas Mark 5) for about 15 minutes.
Serve hot with yoghurt.

Eggs

Eggs have always had a unique place in the search for food as it was realized that the fragile oval shell contained not only good nourishment but also the developing embryo of a bird. So the egg became the symbol of fertility and life itself.

Many ancient cultures viewed the egg with a mixture of superstition and fear. Even today in Papua and New Guinea some tribes will not allow pregnant women to eat eggs on the assumption that the live embryo within the shell might affect the life within the womb.

The Chinese have always had a sensible attitude to the egg as a useful food. Centuries ago, they perfected the craft of preserving eggs. A leading restaurant in Peking specializes in rare delicacies and puts one-hundred-year-old egg soup at the top of the menu.

The Romans brought egg cookery to a fine art for their sumptuous banquets and when the conquering legions landed in Britain in 55 B.C., they were surprised to find that the primitive natives were already expert at raising chickens.

A Church edict in the fourth century A.D. forbade the eating of eggs during Lent. This started the tradition of hard boiling the eggs and decorating them to celebrate Easter. Modern observance of this old tradition places less emphasis on beautifully painted eggs and more on large chocolate shells.

Nutritional content

Eggs are excellent sources of vitamins and minerals. Two standard eggs each weighing 56 g (2 oz) contain: 12 g protein, 150 calories, 56 mg calcium, 2.54 mg iron, 205 mg phosphorus, 129 mg potassium, 1000 I.U. of vitamin A, 0.10 mg B1 (thiamine), 0.35 mg B2 (riboflavin), and traces of niacin. The yolk also contains vitamins E and K.

Particular value

Eggs are rated very highly by nutritionists because their essential amino acids are balanced in such a way that 95% of the protein is available for use by the body.

Eggs and cholesterol

The controversy about cholesterol and heart attacks has led to a major reduction in the consumption of dairy foods and animals fats. The cholesterol content of a fertile egg is between 194 mg and 200 mg. The lecithin content of the egg is 1700 mg, or a ratio of 1:8, and breaks fat up into tiny globules that disperse easily, so helping the body to utilize cholesterol normally. Egg-marketing nutritionists believe that the lecithin content of egg offers good protection against high cholesterol levels in the blood.

Studies have shown that eggs fried in animal fats or hydrogenated cooking fats brought about a higher elevation in the blood cholesterol level than did boiled, poached eggs, or eggs cooked in vegetable oils.

Raw eggs It is not advisable to eat raw eggs regularly since they contain a substance called avidin which combines with the B vitamin biotin and prevents it from reaching the blood. Also the albumen protein of raw egg white may pass into the blood undigested and cause many allergies. Many recipes, such as ice-cream, use raw egg and should be treated with discretion.

Fertile eggs If an egg is fertile it simply means that the hen has mated with the cockerel. The embryo chick appears as a small brownish-red speck in the egg. The majority of battery eggs are not fertile. Eggs which have been fertilized contain many natural hormones.

How do you boil an egg?

The greatest insult to any cookery novice is to be told he 'can't even boil an egg'. It *is* simple, but some fundamental knowledge is required.

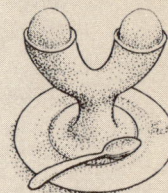

Protein albumen in the white coagulates at a lower temperature than the yolk. So always boil eggs gently at 96°C (205°F) just under boiling point. Too high a temperature will overcook the white and spoil its texture before the yolk is ready. It is safest to start the egg in cold water and bring it slowly to the boil; then start timing. A soft-boiled standard egg will take 2¾ minutes, a medium-boiled standard 4 minutes, and a hard-boiled standard, 9 minutes. Overcooking a hard-boiled egg causes sulphur to release from the white and combine with iron from the yolk to form a dark ring. To help prevent this, plunge the cooked eggs into cool water.

Take your choice: battery or free-range?

Battery or free range?

This is another area of raging controversy. The average shopper would not pay the additional cost for free range eggs but there are a growing number of people, however, who gladly pay extra for non-battery eggs. Research by the Ministry of Agriculture in Britain has shown that battery eggs can be 70% lower in vitamin B12 and 50% lower in folic acid than free range eggs.

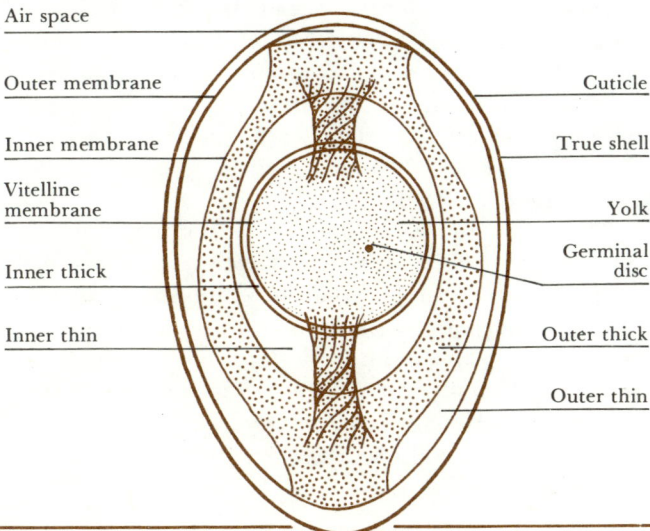

Air space

Outer membrane — Cuticle

Inner membrane — True shell

Vitelline membrane — Yolk

Inner thick — Germinal disc

Inner thin — Outer thick

— Outer thin

On the other hand, factory farmed can contain more calcium and iron depending on the food supplements given to the hens. Research in Oslo has shown that battery eggs are much more likely to have antibiotics and the residues of hormone injections and other drugs.

The influential Farm and Food Society, U.K., believes that the mental health of animals has a great effect on the food they produce. Their argument is that a hen kept in a small cage is bound to produce a less wholesome egg than a hen who scratches and pecks in the farmyard.

Storing eggs

The U.S. Department of Agriculture recommends buying eggs from shops that keep them under refrigeration in packed cases. They should be kept in the refrigerator, wide-end up, at an ideal temperature of 6°C (40°F). Bring them out to room temperature (13°C, 55°F) before plunging into boiling water.

Never store eggs next to strong-flavoured food as the shells are porous and will absorb smells.

43

Ginseng

The ancient Chinese called ginseng the 'root of heaven' and valued it more highly than any other plant, so much so that one Emperor paid the equivalent of £5000 ($9000) for one well-developed root.

Ginseng has never been cheap. Today, throughout the East poorer people would rather work many hours overtime than go without ginseng. It is used as a tonic and restorative, to increase sexual vitality, and to treat serious diseases. The plant's botanical name, *Panax ginseng,* means 'all healing' and illustrates its use as a panacea or universal remedy.

The plant likes to grow in deep, shady regions away from stagnant water. At least five years are needed for the roots to develop properly. Seven-year-old roots are considered more beneficial and this is obviously one reason for the high price of good ginseng.

The strange man-like shape of the root and the way the plant chooses secret locations to grow have given rise to many legends. One legend describes how the villagers of Shantan, in the Shensi province of China, were awakened each night by a terrible wailing. They took torches and staves and tracked the sound to a wood. There, they dug up a huge root shaped exactly like a man with arms and legs, which shrieked as they pulled it out of the ground. The mandrake, also shaped like a man, has had similar legends woven around it in Western mythology. Even now, special ceremonies are performed in certain areas when the ginseng roots are pulled up.

In China today, where old legends are not encouraged, ginseng still holds a special place on the list of curative herbs. It is used both by bare foot doctors and by modern hospitals.

It makes a very interesting study to see how the ancient uses of ginseng, and the powers attributed to it, are borne out by modern technology. In the *Vegas,* the old Indian scriptures, there is a hymn to ginseng calling it 'the root which is dug from the earth and strengthens the nerves'. The hymn continues: 'The strength of the horse, the mule, the ram, even the strength of the bull it bestows on him. This herb will make thee so full of lusty strength that thou shalt, when excited, exhale heat as a thing on fire.' This graphic passage picturesquely describes the belief held by the Chinese, Koreans, and Indians, that ginseng was a powerful sexual stimulant and aphrodisiac.

More seriously, it has been used as a disease preventative and general tonic. Illnesses ranging from gastritis to malaria and fever have been treated with a decoction of the root for many centuries.

The Russians began to become interested in ginseng when they occupied North Korea at the end of the Second World War. They took thousands of samples and cuttings and sent them back to the U.S.S.R. for propagation. Ginseng does grow wild in Siberia, but it is rare and hard to find. The first analysis of the plant at the Institute of Biologically Active Substances in Vladivostock described the root as having 'rare properties'.

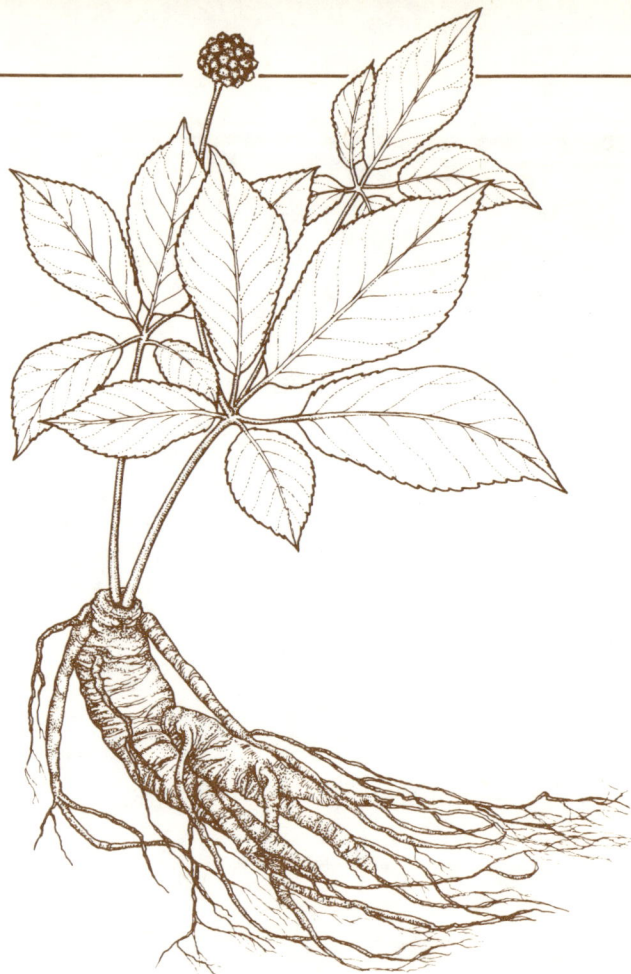

There is a variety of ginseng growing wild in North America. This had been used for centuries by Indian tribes in their medicine and folk lore. American ginseng is now exported in large quantities to China and Korea to meet demand.

Ginseng is sold commercially in several main categories. Chinese and Korean ginseng is the true *Panax ginseng* and is now cultivated in Japan. Wild Chinese ginseng is sometimes called Manchurian ginseng. Cultivated roots from both China and Korea are sometimes sold as Asiatic ginseng. These can be red or white depending on the curing process. Siberian ginseng is botanically related, but correctly called *Eleutherococcus senticosus;* American ginseng is called *Panax quinquefolium.*

The Chinese *Materia Medica,* the standard pharmacological handbook, lists the ginsengs in order of quality: first, the Manchurian white roots, rarely seen outside China; second, the Chinese and Korean red and white roots; third, the Japanese cultivated plants, and finally, the American white roots. However, all these varieties are closely related, so it is not unreasonable to suppose that the same qualities are common to each sort.

Other Russian tests have shown that ginseng acts as a stimulant on the central nervous system. Professor Petkov of the Institute of Advanced Medical Training in Sofia has found that ginseng actually increased the efficiency of cerebral activity. He found that brain-wave patterns in both animal and human subjects increased in speed. Professor Petkov has conducted 15 years of experiments on ginseng and in a paper published in 1976 he concluded: 'Ginseng stimulates the basic neural processes which constitute the functioning of the cerebral cortex, namely the excitation . . . and inhibition . . . which form the physiological basis of man's mental functioning as a whole.' Both professors stress the difference of ginseng's stimulation compared to other common stimulants such as drugs or alcohol. Professor Petkov writes:

Ginseng, in contrast to other stimulants, causes no disturbance in the equilibrium of the cerebral processes. This explains the absence of any pronounced sense of subjective excitement as is characteristic of all other stimulants . . . and also why this stimulant does not interfere with the normal bodily functions.

Scientific evidence for ginseng's value

The medicinal properties of ginseng are attributed to substances contained in the root. The active principles have been identified as six individual glycosides, called panaxosides. Ginseng also contains amino acids, organic acids, sterols, flavonoids, and vitamins including pantothenic acid, biotin, vitamin B12, B1 (thiamine), and B2 (riboflavin).

Extensive tests have been done on Chinese, Korean and Siberian ginseng by the Institute of Biologically Active Substances in Vladivostok. The earliest experiments were conducted by Professor Brekhaman, head of the Institute.

Ginseng as a stimulant

Professor Brekhaman devised a swimming test for mice to see if ginseng could increase stamina. The results proved that mice given ginseng were able to swim twice as long as the others. In another controlled experiment, scientists at the Institute gave ginseng to half a newspaper's proof readers to test their speed and accuracy. Those who had taken ginseng increased the numbers of letters they read by 12%, and decreased the number of mistakes by 51%.

Other qualities of ginseng

The Russians, who lead the world-wide research into ginseng, have also found that the root has powers as an adaptogen which can protect the body from stress. Professor Brekhaman observed that ginseng had the power to normalize the chemical changes that the human system undergoes whilst under stress. Only powerful modern drugs also have this effect.

A group of doctors in West Berlin found that patients with high blood pressure made a small but significant improvement after taking ginseng. In traditional Chinese medicine, ginseng is always given to heart patients. Further Russian research has led to the belief that ginseng can also increase resistance to infection. There are also well documented details of ginseng used as a sedative. It may seem odd that such a strong stimulant is also used as a sedative. It is exactly because of the action on the central nervous system that ginseng has this power. This same quality would appear to be linked with the legendary quality of ginseng to improve sexual virility. Russian clinical tests indicate that impotent patients became more tranquil after taking ginseng, as a result improving in sexual performance.

Dr Karzel of the University of Bonn conducted tests in sexual activity and reported: 'The occurrence of constituents with sex-like hormone-like activity in ginseng preparations thus seems to be proven . . . but questions concerning the ratios between male and female hormones remain to be solved.'

The Russians use extracts of ginseng in many of their medicines and gave tablets to the first of their astronauts. The ancient power of this man-shaped plant is well vindicated.

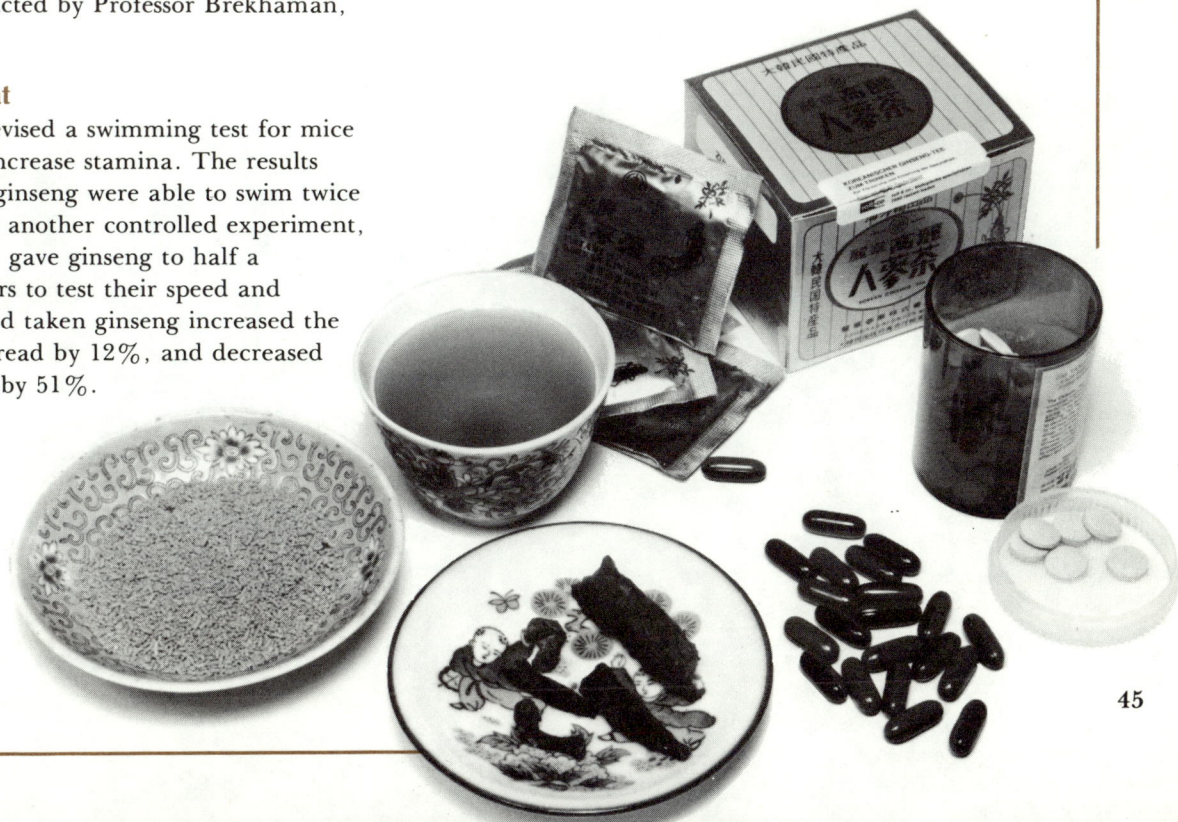

Grains

Grains or cereals are possibly the most important staple food in the world. This family of botanic grasses has had a profound effect on the history of mankind.

Stone Age Man's ability to farm cereal crops led him to live in groups rather than nomadic tribes and small villages were formed to till the earth, scatter seed, and tend the growing plants. The early communities sprang up in the fertile crescent surrounding the Mediterranean, and the river Nile in Egypt, where grain would grow easily.

As time went on, cereal grains became increasingly important. Wheat was baked into bread which was the 'staff of Life'. Millet was the basic food of the Vhina long before rice was introduced 12,000 years ago.

The Romans worshipped the Goddess Ceres as the provider of all the bountiful gifts of the earth. Grains, a vital food, were 'from Ceres' — hence the name cereals.

The staple grain varied with the geographical location. Wheat and rye were most important in the West, followed by oats, barley and millet. Rice and millet were the staples of the East, and sorghum and maize of prime importance to Africa and Central and South America.

Today, these divisions have blended until they no longer exist. Many grains have specific values which are described in each entry. The entire range of fascinating cereal grains from bulgur, through triticale to wheat might well be included in the repertoire of an enterprising wholefood cook.

Storage

All whole or hulled grains (sometimes called berries) will last longer than when they are ground into a flour. This is particularly true of 100% or 80% wholemeal flour. The recommended time for storage is two months because it still contains the oil-rich germ.

This is possibly the reason for the popularity of hand-grinding mills. Cooks can simply grind the flour as needed, or a week in advance for real freshness.

As a principle, all untreated, organic flours should be consumed within a few months of purchase. Keep all flours and grains in a cool, dark, dry place in air tight containers. The grains or berries will keep for about a year in such conditions. Millet is especially long lasting, and is good for at least two years.

Barley

Barley was the most important bread grain of the ancient Greeks, Romans and Hebrews. In the Sumerian civilization from about 4000 B.C. onwards, it was used as the monetary currency; Hammurabi's Code of 1700 B.C. gives clear instructions as to exactly how many sacks of barley were to be paid for each day's work.

In Europe, barley was gradually replaced by WHEAT and RYE until by the Middle Ages it had become comparatively insignificant except in certain fiercely individualistic areas. For example, Scotland where to this day there are many recipes for stews and soups incorporating barley, such as the classic Scotch broth. (*See* RECIPE).

Although barley lost cultural favour as a food grain, it remains of supreme importance in brewing beer. The grains are sprouted as part of the malting process. This increases the vitamin and enzyme content, making beer a good nutritional aid.

Types of barley

Pearl barley This is when the barley grain has been hulled to remove the two hard outer layers. Unfortunately, the aleurone part of the endosperm which contains the protein is often milled away in the process. Most whitish barley sold today has been pearled.

Whole grain brown barley (also known as Pot Barley) has had only the hard top layer removed, leaving the second casing and the aleurone cells intact. Whole grain brown barley is chewier and takes longer to cook. Nutritionally it is far superior. It is available from specialist stores. (*See* WHERE TO BUY *page* 152).

Nutritional content

100 g (3½ oz) pearl barley contain: 8.2% protein, 349 calories, 16 mg calcium, 189 mg phosphorus. 2 mg iron, 160 mg potassium, 3.1 mg niacin and traces of other B vitamins. In comparison, whole grain barley contains 10 or 12% protein, 30 mg calcium, 6 mg iron, 240 mg phosphorus, and 200 mg potassium.

Scotch broth

1 kg (2¼ lb) lean stewing cuts of beef or lamb
2.3 litres (4 pints) water
50 g (2 oz) or ¼ U.S. cup pearl barley soaked for 1-2 hours
50 g (2 oz) or ¼ U.S. cup dried peas, soaked overnight
2 onions   1 large leek
1 large carrot   1 large turnip
½ green cabbage
1 tablespoon chopped parsley
salt   freshly ground pepper
grating of nutmeg

Trim the meat, put it into a large saucepan with the soaked peas and pearl barley and cover with cold water. Bring it slowly to the boil and skim carefully as the scum rises. Let it simmer while you pare and slice the vegetables, then throw them all except the cabbage into the broth. Cover the pan and allow to simmer very slowly for 2½ hours. Add the shredded cabbage and seasoning of salt, pepper and nutmeg and simmer on, uncovered, for a further 20 minutes. (Serves 6)

Barley flour Most commercial barley flour appears to have been made from pearl barley. Whole grain barley flour is darker in colour and coarser grained. Most wholefood suppliers concentrate on barley flakes rather than flour. Barley flour and flakes have a light, nutty flavour.

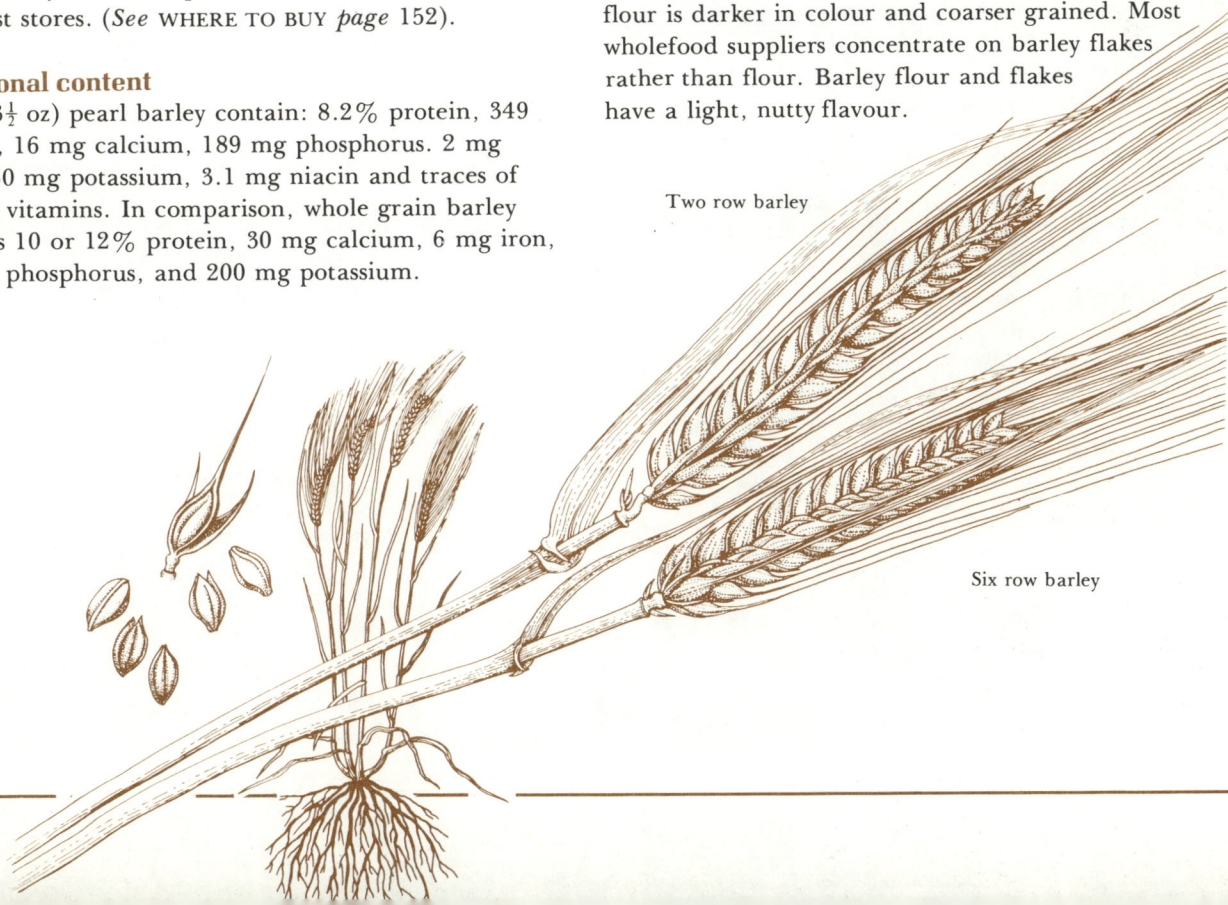

Two row barley

Six row barley

Bulgur

Bulgur is an ancient wheat product that has survived in eastern Europe. It is usually sold as cooked, parboiled wheat. When Genghis Khan celebrated his mighty victories the tables were loaded with bulgur delicacies to eat or fermented into a potent drink. The Biblical name for the grain is 'Arusah' and was the 'alien corn' that Ruth stood amongst when she left her homeland.

Bulgur has such an excellent taste and nutritional content that it is now being eaten in many parts of the world, sometimes in places where it has not been used for thousands of years.

Parboiled (parched) bulgur
Most manufacturers partially boil the bulgur grain before pearling. It will be marked precooked or parched on the label. These grains will be much quicker to cook.

Nutritional content
100 g ($3\frac{1}{2}$ oz) of bulgur contain: 11.2 g protein, 366 calories, 2.8 mg calcium, 338 mg phosphorus, 3.7 mg iron, 229 mg potassium, 4.5 mg niacin, 0.28 mg B1 (thiamine), 0.14 mg B2 (riboflavin).

How to cook bulgur
Use one cup of bulgur to two cups of water. Bring to the boil, and simmer very gently for 15 or 20 minutes.

Bulgur (Chinese style)
225 g (8 oz) or 1 U.S. cup bulgur (if not pre-cooked, put between kitchen paper and crack with rolling pin)
1 large chopped onion
700 ml (24 fl. oz) or 3 U.S. cups stock (vegetable or meat)
half a green pepper cut in strips
3 tomatoes, sliced
2 tablespoons vegetable oil
1 clove garlic, crushed   pinch salt
freshly ground black pepper

Heat the vegetable oil in a heavy pan or wok and add half the onion. After two or three minutes add the pepper, garlic and the tomatoes. Stir well. Gradually add the bulgur. stirring all the time to make sure that each grain is coated with the mixture. Add the stock, bring to the boil. Immediately lower heat and cover. It should take about 35 minutes to cook. Just before serving, sprinkle on the freshly ground black pepper and salt. (Serves 2)

Persian wheat

Einkorn

Particular value
The particular value of bulgur lies in the fact that the grain always remains whole. This is because the seed structure allows the wheat germ and bran to be retained even in modern steel-milling processes.

Bulgur flour is heavy in consistency and needs refrigerating since it contains the germ of the wheat. It is surprisingly hard to find in the shops. Perhaps this is because bulgur is only now growing again in importance in the West, and wholefood cooks are one step ahead of the flour manufacturers.

Bulgur grain respond well to home-grinding on steel blades (the oil from the wheat germ smears most stone buhrs). Bear in mind that pre-cooking has an effect on the gluten content within the grains, and the flour will require more kneading.

Maize (Corn)

A semantic sort out

The English-speaking countries have each developed their own names for grains to the utter confusion of travellers.

The world 'corne' was the old English name for the staple grain of a country. So when an Englishman says corn he means WHEAT, and when a Scotsman says corn he means OATS. To an American, the Zea Mays or maize plant is known as corn. This is because the first English settlers saw maize growing abundantly in the new colony and christened it 'Indian Corne'.

Maize (corn) was first used on a domestic scale 10,000 years ago in South America and became the staple food of the entire American continent. Both the North and South American Indians worshipped the Zea Mays plant, and called it variously, 'Daughter of Life' or 'Seed of Seeds'. The first boatloads of settlers to land in Plymouth Colony were probably saved from starvation by the 'Indian Corne' growing there.

Early European explorers took the maize seed from the Americas and planted it elsewhere in the known world but it was not often taken back to the European homelands as the sailors considered it to be inferior to wheat or RYE. Magellan took maize to the East Indies and the Philippines. During the sixteenth century explorers introduced it to Africa, India, Japan and China.

Types of maize (corn)

Sweetcorn (corn on the cob) When grown as a vegetable the maize plant is known as sweetcorn in the United Kingdom and Australia, and as corn on the cob in the United States. This plant is indeed much too sweet to be dried and ground as a flour or meal. It is essential to choose one of the field varieties for this purpose.

Flint corn is the natural successor to the 'Indian Corne' of the early settlers. It has a very hard endosperm which makes it difficult to grind. For this reason, flint corn is now mainly fed to animals.

Dent corn is the most widely available commercial corn in the United States. When the hard endosperm dries, it 'dents' the top of the grain. Corn meal and flour are ground from this grain, although some experts consider it to be nutritionally inferior.

Flour corn is the top quality field corn, but the seeds are quite difficult to buy. (*See* WHERE TO BUY *page* 152). Flour corn has a very thin endosperm and kernels of soft starch.

Popcorn The especially hard endosperms of popcorn make a good 'bang' when heated and are much loved by the sweet manufacturers. In fact, popcorn is nutritionally the poorest of all maize grains.

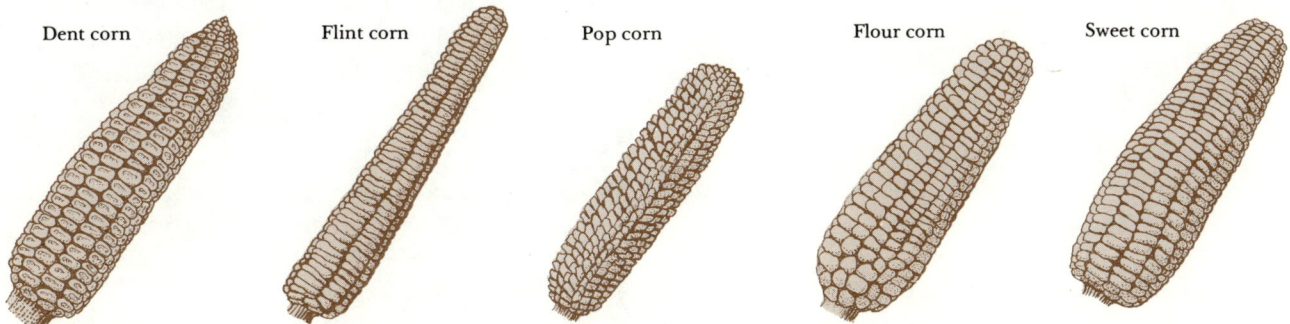

Dent corn · Flint corn · Pop corn · Flour corn · Sweet corn

Corn flour is generally made from the hard and soft starch layers which lie directly under the hard seed casing. It does not include the germ which contains all the nutrients needed for the life of the grain. Cornflour is often processed to make it very white and is a good thickening agent, but adds little nutritional value to food.

Corn meal Most wholefood recipes specify corn meal and when buying it, it is important to obtain stoneground whole corn meal. This is because the grain has sometimes been degerminated which literally means that the valuable germ has been taken out. Sifted or bolted corn meal simply means that the hulled, ground grain has been put through a mesh to a get a finer texture.

Nutritional content

Whole grain unsifted (unbolted) corn meal is rich in phosphorus, potassium, and vitamin A. 100 g ($3\frac{1}{2}$ oz) unsifted corn meal contain: 9% protein, 324 calories, 20 mg calcium, 256 mg phosphorus, 2.4 mg iron, 284 mg potassium, 510 I.U. vitamin A, 2 mg niacin, and traces of B1 (thiamine) and B2 (riboflavin). Sifting (bolting) the meal takes out about 40 mg each of phosphorus and potassium and 30 I.U. of vitamin A. Field corn dried has about 10% more of every vitamin and trace mineral. This is assuming that the grain is

This American Indians' fertility dance, known as Green Corn, was performed in honour of corn

ground and used immediately. Sweetcorn (corn on the cob) contains: 3.3% protein, 3 mg calcium, 89 mg phosphorus, 0.6 mg iron, 196 mg potassium, 400 I.U. vitamin A, 1.4 mg niacin, and 9 mg vitamin C.

Millet

Millet was possible the first cereal grain to be used for domestic purposes and was the staple food in China before rice was introduced about 12,000 years ago. It is still an important staple food in parts of Africa such as Ethiopia, in India, and in Asia.

In Western countries millet has been relegated to the budgerigar's cage. This lowly rating is all the more surprising since the grain has long aroused the interest of food experts, such as in the case of the Hunza tribe where millet is an essential item in the diet. The Hunzas are a remarkable tribe living in the Himalayan foothills and famed for their longevity and fitness. Every basic Hunza food such as YOGHURT and millet is now coming under scrutiny from modern nutritionists.

Types of millet

All whole grain millet has been hulled since the outer casing is so hard that not even budgerigars can crack it. The most common types of millet generally available are:

Foxtail millet — also known as Italian or yellow millet.

Pearl millet — also known as bulrush, cat tail or candle millet.

Prosso — also known as broomcorn or hog millet.

225 g (8 oz) or 1 U.S. cup whole millet
1 litre ($1\frac{3}{4}$ pints) or $4\frac{1}{2}$ U.S. cups
vegetable broth or stock
1 teaspoon salt
$\frac{1}{4}$ teaspoon fresh ground pepper
2 tablespoons vegetable oil
1 diced carrot   2 chopped onions
75 g (3 oz) or 1 U.S. cup sliced
mushrooms
(Serves 4)
225 g (8 oz) or 1 U.S. cup thick yoghurt
Preheat the oven to 180°C (350°F, Gas Mark 4).
Use a dry heavy casserole and first
carefully brown the millet on the top of the stove.
Remove millet and add oil to casserole.
Sauté the onions until lightly browned.
Return millet to dish and add carrot, salt
and pepper. Pour on the broth
and bake, tightly covered
for about $1\frac{1}{2}$ hours until
the millet is tender.
Stir in the yoghurt
and serve at once.

Common millet

Foxtail millet

Bulrush millet

Nutritional content

An average 100 g ($3\frac{1}{2}$ oz) millet contain: 9% protein, 312 calories, 20 mg calcium, 311 mg phosphorus, 6.8 mg iron, 430 mg potassium, 2.3 mg niacin, with traces of B1 (thiamine) and B2 (riboflavin).

How to cook millet

This tiny grain swells enormously when heated and always requires four or more parts of water. It has a rich flavour and a fluffy texture and provides more servings per 450 g (1 lb) than any other cereal.

Bring four or five cups of water to the boil. Stir in one cup of whole millet with a pinch of salt. Lower the heat and put a tight-fitting lid on the pan. It will need about 15 or 25 minutes for the grain to absorb the water.

Millet stew
225 g (8 oz) or 1 U.S. cup whole millet
100 g (4 oz) or $\frac{1}{2}$ U.S. cup chick peas
1 chopped onion
1.2 litres (2 pints) or 5 U.S. cups
vegetable stock
1 tablespoon soy sauce
a pinch of thyme
225 g (8 oz) or 1 U.S. cup diced vegetables
in season
Heat the oil in a saucepan and sauté the onion. Add diced vegetables and stir well. Add the millet, stock, soy sauce, herbs, and chick peas, bring to the boil, cover and Simmer for about 25 minutes. (Serves 4-6)

Let the fluffy cooked millet cool and add chopped strawberries or any juicy fruit. Stir in chopped walnuts. Mix well. Pour over thick yoghurt and serve.

Particular value

Among the grains, millet is well balanced in essential amino acids. It has more iron than any other cereal. The protein utilization value of millet is greatly increased by the addition of legumes.

Millet flour As millet is such a small grain, the flour is only marginally more nutritious than the whole grain. The flour is a particularly tasty thickening agent, and adds colour and flavour to soups and casseroles. Millet lacks gluten, so bread made with it does not rise very high. The national loaf of Ethiopia, *Injera*, is made from millet flour.

51

Rye

Rye does not have the neolithic antecedents of WHEAT or BARLEY. To the ancient Greeks rye was merely a vigorous weed and it was the Romans who tamed the 'weed' and began to plant rye as a crop. By the Middle Ages rye had become the staple grain throughout Europe; the basic loaf in England was made from roughly ground rye and barley. In eastern Europe, especially Germany, rye has retained its popularity and both the Russians and the Scandinavians prefer the distinctive flavour of dark rye bread. Early settlers from Holland took rye seeds with them to America where, by the middle of the nineteenth century, thousands of acres were under rye cultivation. Rye whisky was distilled and is now a major export from the U.S.A.

The growing rye grain is subject to attack from a virulent fungus called ergot. The affected grain can then cause the disease ergotism which has an important place in European history. Modern historians now believe that several of the plagues so virulent in the Middle Ages were in fact ergotism. The weird 'dancing sickness' in which whole villages literally danced themselves to death was caused by eating diseased rye. The virus affects the central nervous system and produces hallucinations and trances, which played such an important part in the history of witchcraft.

Selling wholemeal bread at Cranks Health Foods in London

St. Anthony caring for a sufferer of ergotism

Nutritional content

100 g (3½ oz) whole rye grains contain: 12% protein, 360 calories, 38 mg calcium, 376 mg phosphorus, 3.7 mg iron, 467 mg potassium, 1.6 mg niacin, and traces of B1 (thiamine) and B2 (riboflavin). Dark (unsifted or unbolted) rye flour contains in each 100 g (3½ oz): 16% protein, 54 mg calcium, 540 mg phosphorus, 4.5 mg iron, 860 mg potassium, 2.7 mg niacin, 0.61 mg B1 (thiamine), 0.22 mg B2 (riboflavin).

Types of rye

Rye flour is low in gluten, so bread made from all rye will rise less and be flatter than high gluten grains like wheat. On the other hand, rye bread is more filling and scores highly for taste. Rye flour packets are often labelled 'dark' or 'light'. The light flour has been sifted (or bolted) and contains less bran.

Rye groats are the whole grains of rye. They may be soaked and cooked like rice, or cracked with a rolling pin for shorter cooking.

Rye bread
375 g (13 oz) or 3 U.S. cups rye flour
15 g (½ oz) or 2 U.S. teaspoons dried yeast
pinch of salt
275 ml (½ pint) or 1¼ U.S. cups warm water
Rye bread is very tasty but it is low in gluten and will be heavier than other breads.
Mix the yeast and warm water in a bowl and add the salt. Allow the yeast to rise for five or ten minutes, then gradually add the flour, stirring all the time with a wooden spoon.
Turn out the mixture on a floured surface and knead well. Put the dough in a large oiled bowl and cover with a clean cloth. Leave it in a warm place for 18 hours. During this time the dough will rise slightly. Knead again briefly and place in a well oiled dough tin — let it rise again for several hours.
Cook for about 1 hour at 190°C (375°F, Gas Mark 5).

Sorghum

According to archaeologists, sorghum was used for domestic purposes long before recorded history. A carving has been found showing sorghum under cultivation in Egypt in 2500 B.C. This extremely hardy, drought-withstanding grain gradually became the staple of hot, dry countries and is still the major cereal grain throughout Africa today. From the seventeenth century onwards, slave traders took sorghum seeds from Africa with them on their voyages to the West Indies and America.

Today, Western cookbooks rarely mention sorghum and many an average reader might have no idea what it is. Yet a recent United Nations survey on food consumption ranked sorghum the third most important cereal in the world after WHEAT and RICE. In Africa, sorghum grain is freshly ground and cooked as a sort of porridge. The Chinese and Japanese cook it in the same way as rice.

Types of sorghum

Kafir, a native of South Africa, is also called Kafir corn. It has smallish seeds varying in colour from white through pink to red.

Milo, from eastern Africa, has larger seeds of salmon or pink colour.

Feteritas, from the Sudan, has very large white seeds.

Shallu, from India, but known also as Egyptian wheat, has large white seed heads.

Nutritional content

This varies according to the variety, but an average variety of sorghum contains per 100 g (3½ oz): 11% protein, 370 calories, 28 mg calcium, 287 mg phosphorus, 4.4 mg iron, 350 mg potassium, 3.9 mg niacin, with traces of B1 (thiamine) and B2 (riboflavin).

Sorghum flour is gluten free and so produces flattish bread. The whole sorghum grain is always ground into flour or meal. This ensures a high nutritious content,

Quick sorghum stew

450 g (1 lb) or 2 U.S. cups cooked sorghum
1 large diced onion
150 g (5 oz) or 1 U.S. cup diced green peppers
3 large diced tomatoes
1 litre (1¾ pints) or 4½ U.S. cups vegetable stock
½ teaspoon salt
½ teaspoon freshly ground black pepper
1 clove of garlic finely chopped
1 tablespoon vegetable oil
Fry the onion gently in the vegetable oil until transparent. Add the green peppers, garlic and tomatoes and stir well. Cook gently until the tomatoes are soft and the peppers still a little crisp. Add the vegetable stock, bring to the boil and stir in the cooked sorghum. Simmer for a few minutes to allow the flavours to blend.
(Serves 4)

but it does mean keeping the flour under refrigeration as the oil in the embryo will quickly go rancid.

How to cook sorghum

The different varieties of this grain have slightly different moisture requirements, but never use less than four parts of water to one of sorghum. Put one cup of sorghum grains in a pan and add four cups of water. Bring to the boil, add a pinch of salt, cover tightly and simmer gently for about 1 hour. Check the absorption rate after 30 minutes and add more water if necessary. The sorghum is ready when the grains are separated and slightly chewy. Use it much as you would rice.

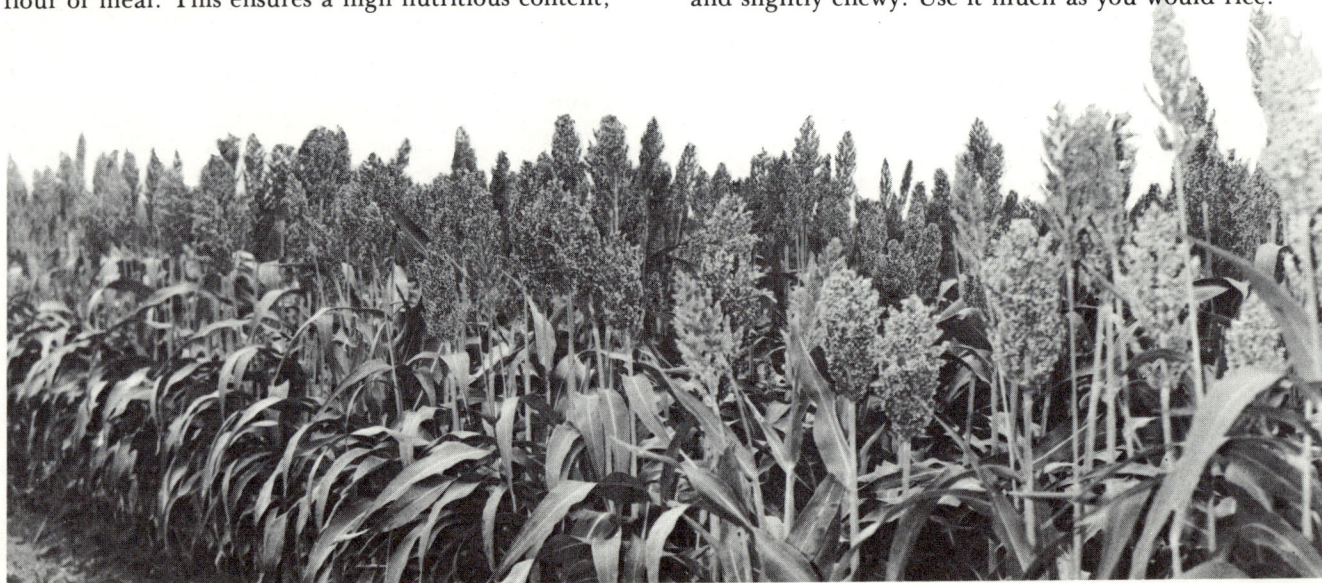

Triticale

This 'man-made' grain was formed by crossing WHEAT (*Triticum*) with RYE *(Secale),* hence the name, Triticale. Wheat and rye have been growing in fields alongside each other for centuries and hybrid plants have always occurred naturally. Yet somehow these illicit offspring were never able to reproduce. It took a hundred years of genetic research to create fertile triticale seeds.

The first fecund seed-producing wheat/rye plants were raised in Sweden in the 1930s. A genetic breakthrough came when the plants were injected with colchicine, an alkaloid from the crocus. The plant chromosomes doubled, and thus became capable of reproduction.

This genetic engineering feat captured the imaginations of scientists and space fiction writers. Dr Norman E. Borlaug, director of the International Center for Maize and Wheat Improvement in Mexico City said of triticale: 'This is the first time that man — scientific man — has been able to reproduce the great feats of neolithic women who domesticated wheat, oats, barley, rye, sorghum, and corn.'

The International Center in Mexico City and the University of Manitoba in Canada are the two major research centres for the new grain. They have bred strains of triticale which combine the high lysine content of rye with the protein content and hardiness of wheat.

Particular value

Dr Borlaug testified before a Senate Select Committee on Nutrition and Human Needs in the United States and said: 'Comparing triticale to wheat under similar conditions we have evidence that indicates it is likely to have 2% more protein and that the amino acid balance, the nutritive value, will be better than wheat.'

Triticale bread

550 g (1¼ lb) or 4 U.S. cups triticale flour
½ teaspoon salt
¼ teaspoon vitamin C powder (or 1 small tablet crushed)
1 tablespoon dry yeast
2 tablespoons vegetable oil
2 tablespoons honey
400 ml (14 fl. oz) or 1¾ U.S. cups (approx) water

Stir the vitamin C into a small amount of hand-hot water. Add the dry yeast. Measure the flour into a large, warm bowl. Mix together the oil, water, honey and salt and add gradually to the flour. Add the frothy yeast. Mix with your fingers until the moisture is absorbed. Turn out onto a floured board and knead very gently. Put into a greased loaf tin and allow to rise. (Triticale does not require double rising or proving.) Bake for about 1 hour at 190°C (375°F, Gas Mark 5).

Nutritional content

100 g (3½ oz) triticale grain contain: 19 g protein, 340 calories, 4.6 g fat, 38 mg calcium, 540 mg phosphorus, 5.7 mg iron, 7 mg sodium, and 508 mg potassium.

How to cook triticale

Triticale has a lighter, softer gluten than either wheat or rye and thus requires a different method of cooking. Triticale flour is readily available and excellent bread can be made from it. Handle the dough as little as possible, and use smooth, gentle kneading.

How triticale was created

Rye   Wheat

Wheat

Wheat is the universal grain. Half the population of the world relies on it to provide a staple food. It has become synonymous with our daily bread which has been the 'staff of Life' since recorded time. The first wheat began to grow at least 10,000 years ago in the fertile crescent surrounding the eastern Mediterranean. Man's skills in grinding and storing the grain eventually led to a more settled way of life. By about 4000 B.C. the early Egyptians had brought wheat cooking to a fine art. They isolated yeast as the mysterious ingredient which could cause the dough to rise. In their clay ovens, the Egyptians baked exotic high-rising domed, coiled and plaited bread and Egypt became the grain basket for the Roman Empire. The majority of Cleopatra's 'treacherous vessels' were used for carrying wheat to Rome. In turn the wheat seeds were taken to Britain and Gaul by the Roman Legions.

Over a thousand years later, in 1493, Columbus carried wheat grains with him to the West Indies. Cortes took wheat with him to Mexico in 1519. During the whole period of English colonization wheat grains were shipped to Australia, North America, and South Africa.

It is a tribute to this truly versatile grass plant that it has grown and flourished in every climate.

Types of wheat

The many varieties can be divided basically into hard or soft wheat. British wheat is generally soft and American wheat is generally hard, the difference being caused by climate. Hard wheat contains more gluten and is generally better for baking bread. Soft wheat is good for cake and biscuits. Flour manufacturers often combine wheat from several countries to get a good mixture. Hard grain flour is often marketed under the name 'Strong Flour'.

Durum wheat has amber coloured grains. It is used exclusively in pasta products.

White wheat is low in protein and very starchy. It is used mainly in pastries and breakfast cereals.

Hard red winter wheat has been developed in Canada and takes only 90 days between sowing and harvesting. It is excellent for making bread.

Maris dove is the most common British wheat. It is a soft, winter wheat, high in protein.

Kibbled wheat. The whole wheat grains are cracked in a small machine called a kibbler so that they are broken into little pieces rather than milled. It is used in bread-making and in cereals.

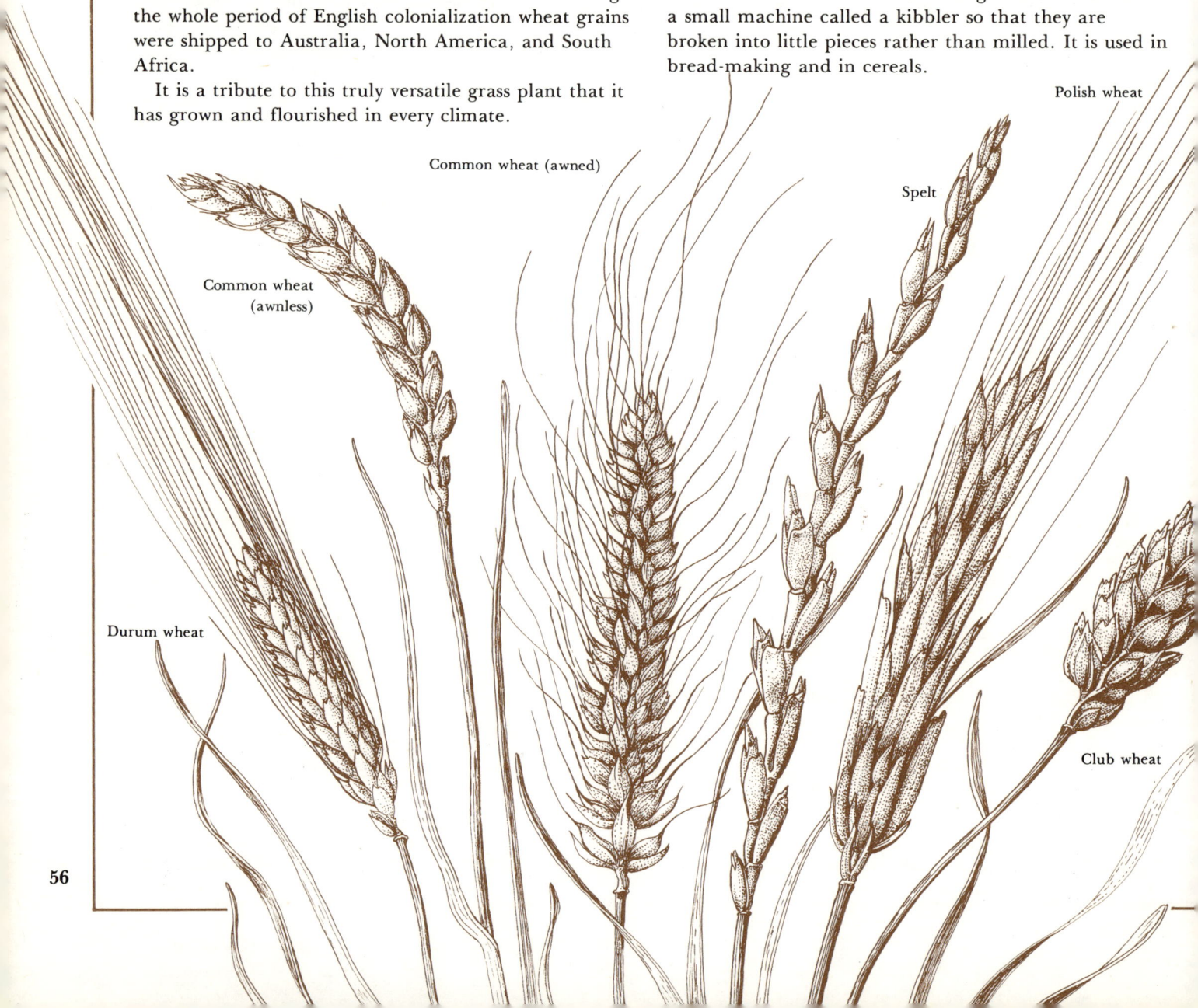

Common wheat (awned)

Common wheat (awnless)

Polish wheat

Spelt

Durum wheat

Club wheat

Cracked wheat The whole wheat grain is cracked by pressure machinery. Splitting the hard outer casing retains the nutritional value while ensuring that the grain cooks much faster.

Wholemeal flour contains all the wheat grain including the bran and the wheat germ. It is much coarser in texture than other flours, and higher in nutritional value. Wholemeal flour is sometimes sold as '100% extraction' and, by law, is only permitted to contain one additive — caramel, whereas wholemeal (or wholewheat) *bread* may contain, with the exception of bleach, all the additives permitted in white bread.
Stoneground wholemeal flour is worth buying since the steel or roller plate mills distribute the wheat germ oil unevenly throughout the flour. The steel plates reach such a high speed that the generated heat affects the quality of the flour and might cause the wheat germ to become rancid. Stone buhrs distribute the embryo oil much more smoothly at slower speeds and maintain cooler temperatures. (*See* WHEAT GERM *page* 117 and BRAN *page 26*)
White flour Wheat flour has actually been whitened for centuries. The popular demand has traditionally been for whiter bread since white has always been associated with purity. In the Middle Ages, all the richer burghers bought 'white' bread and so it became linked with quality. In fact, the bakers whitened the grain with chalk, alum, and in some cases, arsenic powder, or ground-up bones from the graveyard.

White flour is made from the starchy endosperm of the grain. In the milling process, 35% of the grain, bran and surface endosperm is removed, leaving creamy granules. These are then bleached by chlorine dioxide, the same bleach used by housewives to clean drains.

Modern flour does get enriched with certain vitamins and minerals, which put some of the goodness back. For several decades, it was thought that this enriching made white flour the equal of wholemeal. Recent research has reversed this attitude. (*See* NUTRITION AND MEDICINE)
Brown bread Many manufacturers put bread labelled 'brown' on the market which is in fact made from bleached white flour with added brown colourants, usually caramel. Why should they bother to do this? The wheel of public opinion has come full circle. Darker bread is now thought to be better than white, but the flour millers realize that people have become accustomed to a lighter textured, more nondescript taste. It is easier to achieve this by simply adding colour to white. If in doubt, buy bread labelled 100% wholemeal.
81% or 85% extraction flour is usually sold as wheatmeal. The miller is aiming at a finer flour by extracting the coarser parts. Sieving 19% of the ground grain removes the bran and some of the aleurone layer.

Wheat into flour: **1** the flour-milling process begins with removing dirt and impurities, the cleaned wheat **2** is then separated and sieved several times **3, 4, 5**, to give the varying grades of flour **6**

Depending on the variety of grain the coarse extraction will take out between 15% and 19% of the grain. Extraction wheatmeal flour does not contain bran.

Nutritional content
100 g (3½ oz) of:

	Protein	Calories	Calcium mg	Iron	Phosphorus	Potassium	Thiamine	Riboflavin	Niacin
whole grain (hard wheat)	14	312	36	3.1	383	370	0.57	0.12	4.3
whole wheat flour	13.3	320		3.3	372	370	0.55	0.12	4.3
enriched white flour	10.5	342	16	2.9	87	95	0.44	0.26	3.5

Quick method wholemeal bread

450 g (1 lb) 100% wholemeal flour
25 g (1 oz) vegetable fat or oil
25 g (1 oz) fresh yeast or
15 g ($\frac{1}{2}$ oz) dried yeast
50 mg vitamin C tablet
275 ml ($\frac{1}{2}$ pint) (approx) warm water
$\frac{1}{4}$ teaspoon salt

Dissolve the yeast in hand-hot warm water. Crush the vitamin C tablet and stir it into the liquid. This causes the yeast to act much faster. While the yeast is becoming frothy (between 5 and 15 minutes), sieve the flour into a warm mixing bowl, add the salt and vegetable oil. When the yeast is ready, stir it into the flour. Expert cooks often use their fingers, held closely together for this part. When the mixture firms up, turn it out onto a floured board and knead until nicely elastic. Put the dough in a greased bread tin, cover with a clean cloth and let it rise in a warm place to almost double its size. You can knead once more for a really fine textured bread, but if time is short bake at 200°C (400°F, Gas Mark 6) for 10 minutes, reduce heat to 180°C (350°F, Gas Mark 4) for another 40 minutes. A well cooked loaf should sound hollow when tapped on the base.

Wheatfields in Alberta (*above*) and in Saskatchewan (*below*)

Common causes of failure

• Having the water either too hot or too cold for the yeast. It must be lukewarm, 32-43°C (90-110°F)
• Letting the rising dough stand in a draught or get cold
• Allowing the dough to rise too high before baking. It will go on rising in the oven.

It is possible to make a wholemeal loaf without kneading at all. The bread will be denser and coarser in texture.

Honey

Honey has a special place in the history of food and has become intertwined with man's emotions in a most evocative way. The Israelites were promised a land 'flowing with milk and honey' and in the Song of Solomon is the advice, 'my son use thou honey for it is good'. Honey has assumed an almost mystic quality over the centuries, due to this value lent to it by many religions. The Prophet Mohammed said: 'Honey is a remedy for every illness, and the Koran is a remedy for all illnesses of the mind. Therefore I recommend you to both remedies, the Koran and honey.' In the Hindu marriage ceremony the bridegroom says: 'The speech of thy tongue is honey; in my mouth lives the honey of the bee, in my teeth lives peace.' The ancient Egyptians were practical in their approach. They dressed wounds and burns with honey poultices and used it in many potent medicines. Ancient Britain in the time of the Druids was known as the Isle of Honey. Pliny the Elder noted wryly that the inhabitants consumed great quantities of honey, especially in the form of intoxicating mead.

How honey is produced

Honey bees collect nectar from the flowers of plants and trees. This nectar first consists of a weak solution of sugars in water and is carried to the hive in the honey stomach of the bee. Sucrose is converted into the predigested sugars levulose and dextrose by the enzymes present in the bee's stomach.

The bee deposits the nectar into the honeycombs of the hive where the process of conversion continues. A large amount of water gradually evaporates in the warmth of the hive. The bees then cap the honey with wax when it is ripe.

The actual composition of honey will depend on the flowers, the weather, the season and other infinitesimal variations of nature. The nectar flow from one plant species at a given location might dominate in the bees collecting and the honey will take on the characteristics of that species. In this way, with the help of a skilled beekeeper we get honey from an identified source, such as clover honey, heather honey, and gum tree honey.

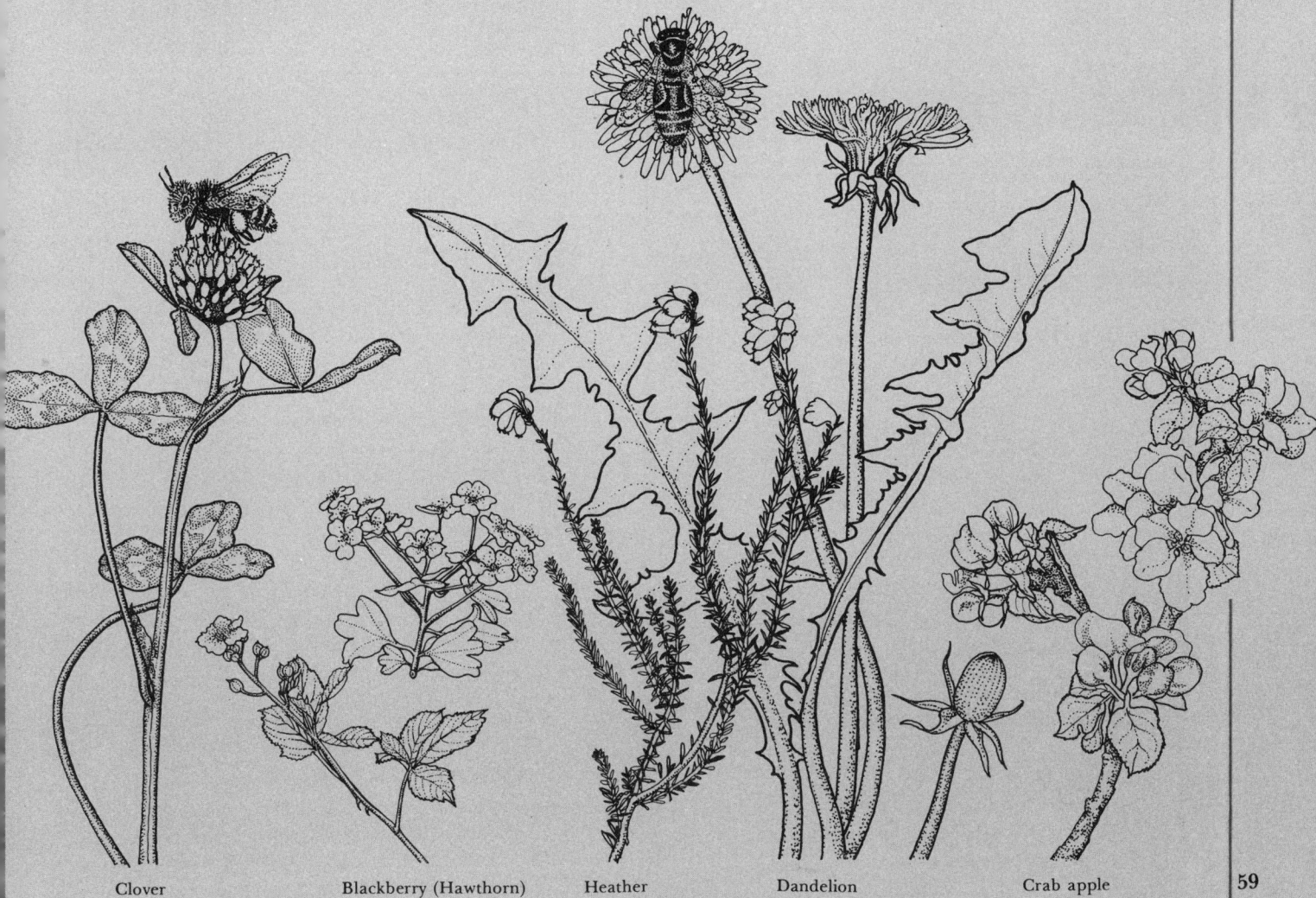

Clover   Blackberry (Hawthorn)   Heather   Dandelion   Crab apple

Nutritional content

Honey contains vitamins B1 (thiamine), B2 (riboflavin), B3, pantothenic acid, B6, biotin, and folic acid. It can contain large amounts of vitamin C. Naturally, this varies with the type of nectar. Very efficient filtering processes may remove some of the vitamins. In fact, honey is an excellent medium for vitamin stability.

The minerals in honey are important: iron, copper, sodium, potassium, manganese, calcium, magnesium and phosphorus are present. The sugars dextrose, levulose, sucrose, and maltose represent a major constituent as do the acids cluconic, citric, malic, succinic, formic, butyric, lactic, pyroglutamic and amino. Honey also contains several enzymes. Generally speaking, the darker the honey, the more minerals and vitamins present.

Particular value

As the bee has predigested the nectar, the sugars are already converted into a form readily available to the human body. Other sugars require a complicated digestive process in the human stomach, but honey can go straight into the blood stream. This makes it a powerful boost to energy and much appreciated by athletes.

An outstanding property of honey is its hygroscopicity, which means that it attracts moisture. This makes it a great natural healer because disease germs need water to multiply. Honey is also a natural

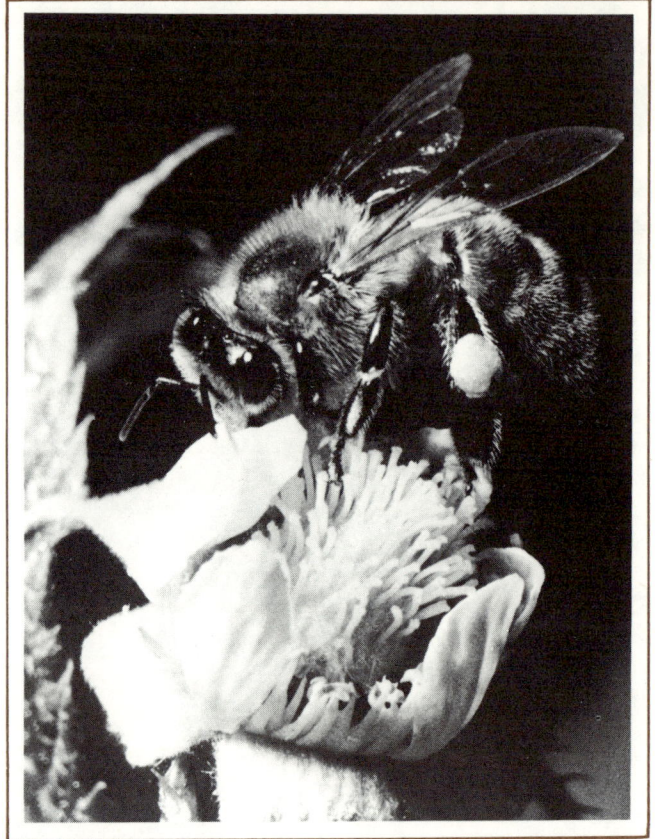

Honey bee foraging on raspberry flower

antiseptic and antibiotic. Research by Professor Remy Chauvin of the Paris Institute of Bee Research proved that bees manufacture several kinds of antibiotics. These they inject into the honey, honeycomb and the beeswax in varying strengths. This explains the specific medicinal qualities of these honey products.

Although honey has been used for about 15,000 years and subjected to close laboratory tests for the past 40 years, there are several ingredients which still defy analysis.

Dr Jarvis, the authority on folk medicine (*see page 62*), gives seven reasons for using honey and not sugar: Honey is non-irritating to the lining of the digestive tract. It is easily and rapidly assimilated and quickly furnishes the demand for energy, and enables athletes and others who expend energy heavily to recuperate rapidly from exertion. It has also a natural and gentle laxative effect, and a sedative value. It is easier for the kidneys to process honey than it is all the other sugars.

The medicinal value of honey

Several hospitals in Britain, including the Reading General and the Norwich General, use honey for dressing burns. Honey's hygroscopic quality draws the moisture from the burn and promotes healing. The natural antibiotics and antiseptic helps too.

Honey is also an important ingredient in many proprietary cough medicines. Dr Jarvis describes how to

Alice Springs honey lamb

(From the *Australian Honey Board*)

1 kg (2¼ lb) lean shoulder lamb

1 clove garlic

salt and pepper

3 tablespoons malt vinegar

4 tablespoons white wine

50 g (2 oz) butter

2 medium onions

450 g (1 lb) or 2 U.S. cups cooked puréed dried apricots

2 level tablespoons curry powder

10 level tablespoons honey

Cut meat into small cubes. Melt butter in a heavy pan, add chopped onions and crushed garlic and cook until soft and golden. Add apricot purée, salt and pepper, curry powder, vinegar and honey, and simmer for 10 minutes. Add wine, then pour mixture over meat in bowl and leave overnight. Remove meat from the sauce and thread on skewers kebab-style. Grill for 15 minutes at medium heat until browned. Serve on a bed of fluffy rice. Reheat sauce and pour over the meat. (Serves 6)

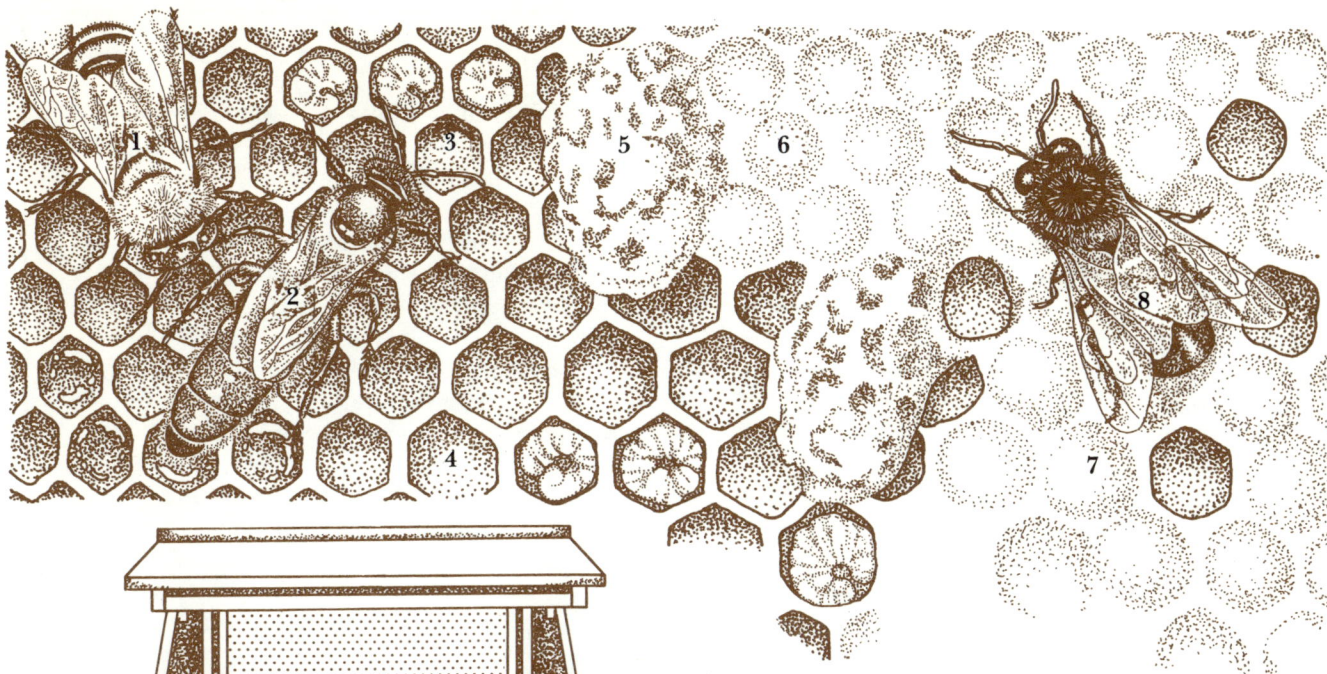

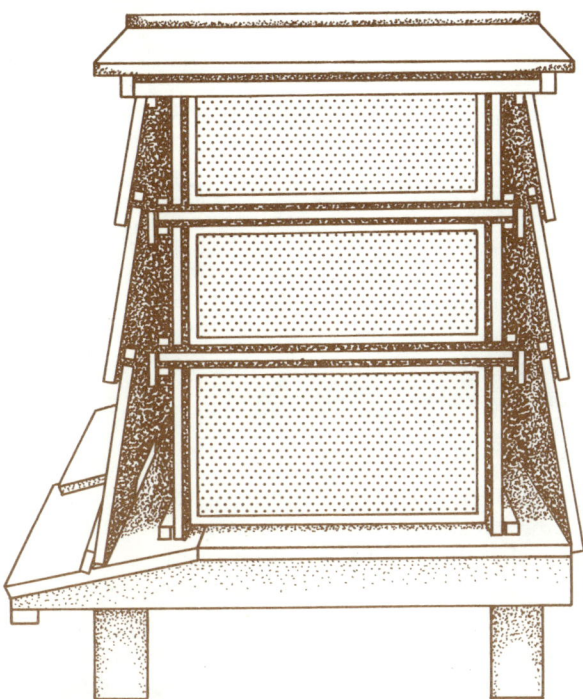

Cross-section of modern hive.

make a quick and easy cough relievant at home: boil a lemon for 10 minutes to soften it, extract the juice and add two tablespoons of glycerine. Mix in a glass and top up with honey. Stir well and take one teaspoon of this medicine several times a day.

Honey and infant feeding

Research by Dr Schultz and Dr Knott at the University of Chicago showed that babies tolerate and assimilate honey better than other sugars. *'Honey has the advantage over sugars . . . since it does not cause the blood sugar to rise to higher levels than can be easily cared for by the body.'* The doctors noted also that infants fed on honey rarely have colic since the rapid absorption prevents fermentation from taking place, and conclude: *'It is strange that honey has not enjoyed a wider use, especially in the feeding of infants and children.'*

Honey products

Propolis is the substance used by the bees to glue the hive together. They inject it with enzymes and antibiotics and many claims have been made for its medicinal value. It is available in liquid and tablet form, and also pleasant tasting sweets.

Pollen tablets An extraction and elimination process has produced an extract of pollen without the factors to which many people are allergic. Some nations use these tablets when training Olympic athletes.

61

FOLK MEDICINE by Dr D. C. Jarvis

Folk Medicine subtitled 'The honey and cider-vinegar way to health' is an outstanding book as Dr D. C. Jarvis has probably done more than any other person to bring the natural way to health to a wider public. The book was published nearly 20 years ago and millions of copies have since been sold. Many books have been published since on cider-vinegar and honey, but Dr Jarvis remains the great authority. As a doctor specializing in ear, nose and throat, he began to practise in his native State of Vermont in the United States. He found that his patients gargled with apple-cider vinegar to cure sore throats, used honeycomb for hayfever, and rubbed corn oil on brown age spots.

Instead of scoffing at these country people, Dr Jarvis watched for results. Then he threw the weight of his training into finding out why cider-vinegar and honey and other natural agents were so effective. The whole approach of *Folk Medicine* is analytic and readable. Not content with human beings, Dr Jarvis thought nothing of pursuing a herd of cows into a field and analysing the leaves and grass eaten by the ruminants. His litmus paper was applied to the very cow pats to see if they were acid or alkaline.

Dr Jarvis gives analyses and sources to satisfy the scientific, such as monitoring a patient's urine and blood pressure for months before coming to a conclusion.

The book deals with the treatment and prevention of many illnesses. Dr Jarvis cites case histories and treatments for the common cold, hayfever, arthritis, kidney trouble, digestive disorders, overweight, high blood pressure, chronic fatigue, and many others.

Honeycombs are the hexagonal cells of wax that the bees have made to support the honey. Many people chew it to relieve hay-fever and sinus complaints.

Bee brood (or baby bees) In some places bees do not survive the winter and the colony is killed off and the hive re-stocked in spring. The colony contains bee larvae and pupae rich in vitamins A and D, and protein. The larvae are marketed as a delicacy and can be fried, smoked or grilled.

Royal jelly is a jelly-like honey which the bees make to feed the young Queen. It is rich in enzymes and natural hormones. Royal jelly is widely used and marketed as health tablets, cosmetics, and food. Many claims are made for it. A worker bee can be turned into a Queen simply by eating this substance.

Honey cappings When the honey is ripe, the bee caps it with a layer of wax. This has its own particular qualities, somewhat similar to honeycomb.

Mead Diluted honey is fermented to make this alcoholic drink which was the traditional old English banqueting drink until the Middle Ages when it was superseded by wine. Mead is reputed to have health-giving properties. The malic acid in mead is alleged to counteract gout and rheumatism.

Does it matter what sort of honey you buy?

In some cheaper brands of honey the bees are fed on a sugar solution placed just outside the hive. This means that the complicated enzyme reaction and the minerals and vitamins are missing. The motto: buy from a good supplier. Do not be put off by cloudy honey as the cloudiness is caused by pollens which are valuable nutrients.

Storing honey

Honey should always be kept covered in a dry place at room temperature. Tight-fitting lids are best. The hygroscopic qualities that are so valuable in honey make it draw moisture from the air so it must always be very well covered.

Honey tends to go darker and taste stronger with age. It may crystallize with very old age, or if the temperature is too cool. To make it liquid again, place the honey pot in a pan of warm water.

Honey in cooking

Honey can replace sugar in most recipes but when doing so, use only three-quarters the amount of honey instead of sugar. Any liquid must be reduced by a fifth for each half tea-cup of honey used.

Kelp

Seaweed is possibly the oldest crop known to man. The Romans, Greeks and Chinese used it as a food, medicine and fertilizer. Pliny the Elder praised its virtues in his book *Natural History* in the first century A.D.

Kelp is a member of the seaweed family of flora. It grows deep in the rocky bottoms of the ocean, taking hold on the rocks with tentacles called 'holdfasts'. There are nearly a thousand species of kelp. The one most often used in the preparation of kelp tablets and granules has the botanical name *Macrocystis pyrifera*. Other members of the group include laver, agar agar, carrageen, Irish moss and Icelandic moss.

Nutritional content

Seaweed and kelp vary with the region and the time of year. The Norwegian Institute of Seaweed Research has provided this analysis of average kelp: It contains 13 vitamins, 20 essential amino acids, and 60 trace elements. Kelp is an excellent source of iodine, B1 (thiamine), B2 (riboflavin), niacin, pantothenic acid and vitamins A, B12, C, and D.

The B12 content is important to non-meat eaters as there are so few sources of this vitamin.

Particular value

The vitamins and trace elements in kelp, as in most sea plants, occur in a natural state of biological balance. Sea water and human blood have almost an identical chemical constituency. The iodine content of kelp makes it prized as a natural medication. The Greeks used it to treat goitre. They knew it worked, but they did not know it was because of the iodine content. A regular intake of iodine is vital for the thyroid gland to function properly and a prolonged lack of it can cause goitre. Even a small lack can cause nervous irritations and the inability to sleep.

Another factor is that under halogen displacement, chlorine displaces iodine from the body. Many local authorities add chlorine to the drinking water and this is one of the reasons why many people use the water filter described in KITCHEN UTENSILS. (*See page* 144) Some regions, particularly those inland, are very deficient in iodine in the soil. This is generally known to local authorities and doctors are able to pinpoint the areas most at risk. Including iodine-rich sea plants such as kelp and seaweed in the diet makes sense for the inhabitants of such areas.

Kelp was introduced into Japan in the seventeenth century and the Japanese today make extensive use of it in many national dishes. Many of the dried seaweed and kelp products now available in easy-to-use packages are of Japanese origin. The Irish and Welsh also make daily use of seaweed — the Irish with carrageen, or Irish moss, and the Welsh with their laver bread. Perhaps it is no coincidence that these people are also renowned for their energy.

Seaweed is a very important organic fertilizer and foliar feed.

A marine biologist collecting kelp (*Macrocystis pyrifera*) on the east coast of Tasmania

How to use kelp or seaweed

These are available in tablet and powder form. The powder may be added in very small quantities to stews and casseroles. A good way to include these rich sea plants in the diet is to use the products listed below.

Agar agar has strong jelling properties and is widely available as a powder under various proprietary names. This may be used instead of commercial gelatine which contains additives and colour.

Hiziki is packaged in long, thin, black strands. This may be boiled and used in much the same way as spaghetti. (*See* PASTA *page* 102)

Kombu may be sold in thick green strands, or cut more finely like hiziki.

Wakame can be sold in sprouts or bunches in which case it must be carefully picked over for tough stems.

Nori is similar to wakame, but sold in thin sheets.

Carrageen moss and dulse are also available in dried, packaged form, which can be slowly simmered until of a similar consistency to jelly.

Laver or sea lettuce looks like spinach, and may be gathered around the coast at low tides. Obviously it is not a good idea to gather any sea plants where there is a source of effluent discharge. Laver is widely available partly cooked in Wales where it is fried and served with eggs and bacon.

Carrageen surprise

1 packet of Carrageen moss or Irish moss, or else gather the moss and carefully dry it. First soak for 10 minutes and rinse carefully. Then slowly boil until it is the consistency of jelly. To this mixture add yoghurt and honey or fruit juice and honey.

Wakame and rice plums

Wash the wakame carefully and soak it for 15 minutes. This is to allow any bits of sea sediment to sink to the bottom. Strain the water into a pan and bring to the boil. Break the wakame into convenient pieces and add to the boiling water. Add half an onion and boil for 10 or 15 minutes until tender. Take one umeboshi plum per person. Serve with freshly cooked organic rice. With both hands mould each portion of rice into a bird's nest shape. Drop an umeboshi plum into the middle. Serve with wakame slotted across the top.

The brown holdfasts which attach the seaweed to rocks

Lecithin

Lecithin is a substance which is manufactured by the body and occurs naturally in all cells. It is also present in foods such as SOYA beans and EGGS. Research over the past few years has proved that lecithin is very effective in reducing blood cholesterol levels. Leading medical authorities throughout the world agree that high cholesterol levels are definitely linked with coronary heart disease. So not unnaturally, there has been a surge of interest in lecithin as a food supplement.

What is lecithin?

Lecithin is a complex mixture of substances called phospholipids and consists of essential fatty acids, the B vitamins choline and inositol, and phosphorus. The vital property of lecithin is that it can break down large particles of fat into smaller ones and disperse them throughout the body. In other words, it is an emulsifier. Think of how eggs with their lecithin content blend oil and water into a smooth liquid. Inside the body, lecithin works with the amino acid methionine to keep cholesterol in an emulsified state. Lecithin can keep the cholesterol flowing and prevent large fatty deposits building up on the artery walls. If these deposits build up, they lead to conditions such are arteriosclerosis and heart disease.

Wholemeal bread

Milk

Oil

Eggs

Liver

Nuts

Black-eyed peas

Kidney beans

Do we need a lecithin supplement?

Lecithin is present in cold-pressed vegetable OILS, such as sunflower, safflower and soya; eggs, soya beans, the seeds of LEGUMES, NUTS, wholewheat cereals, offal such as liver, heart and brain, and WHEAT GERM.

Since lecithin occurs naturally in foods it is quite reasonable to ask if it is necessary to take an extra amount as a dietary supplement. The fact is that the lecithin content of foods is easily destroyed, such as by frying an egg in saturated fat, or heating cold vegetable oils. Food processing removes the lecithin from the fats and oils used to make cakes and biscuits and many other products. So, unless the diet is carefully planned, it would be fairly easy to be short on lecithin from daily food.

In the body, lecithin is manufactured by the liver. It goes into the intestines and is absorbed by the blood. The body's production of lecithin can be affected by stress and over-exertion, as well as prolonged dietary insufficiencies. For these reasons, a growing number of people supplement their diet with one of the many lecithin products now available.

For complete good health, the lecithin-cholesterol relations of the body must be finely balanced. If an imbalance occurs it can lead to diseases such as gallstones and diabetes, or through faulty absorption, to a variety of skin complaints. (*See* NUTRITION AND MEDICINE *page* 16)

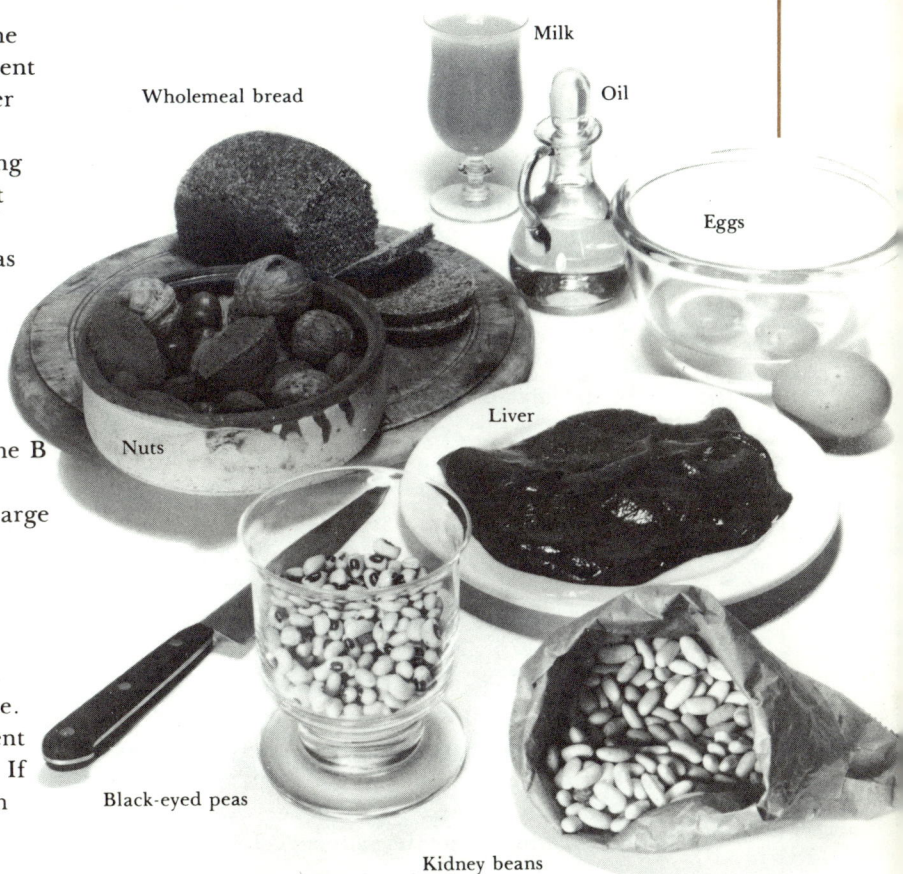

Lecithin supplements

Lecithin supplements are available as granules, powders, flakes, oils or tablets. The majority of commercial lecithin aids are extracted from soya beans. This is cheaper than the richest lecithin food source of egg yolks. Also, there is some controversy about whether egg lecithin is 'saturated' and therefore less effective. Soya beans provide a high choline phospholipid content and have been used in the major lecithin researches.

Lecithin supplements can be stirred into drinks and juices, shaken with milk, scattered on cereals, or added to any cold food. Or they can be liquidized with wheat germ and milk to make a high protein drink.

Nutritional content

Two tablespoons of granular lecithin contain: 105 calories, 1.2 g linoleic acid, traces of iron and calcium, 500 mg phosphorus, trace potassium, and good amounts of choline and inositol.

Legumes

Legumes (beans and peas) provide a good, cheap source of protein. They can be grown in every climate and have a high protein content ranging from 17-25%, which is roughly double that of cereals, and higher than that of meat, fish and EGGS. SOYA BEANS rate exceptionally high with 38% protein. PEANUTS or ground nuts have an average of 26% protein in the total nutritional content.

Most of the common legumes contain little fat. They are good sources of calcium, iron, and vitamins B1 (thiamine) and niacin. Although dried legumes do not contain vitamin C, the germination or sprouting process actually manufactures this vitamin. (*See* SPROUTING SEEDS *page* 113)

The World Health Organization (WHO) and the United Nations, in their joint studies on malnutrition during the past 25 years, have acknowledged the importance of legumes in the fight against protein-deficiency diseases.

In English speaking countries the bean and pea species are still referred to as pulses. The Latin word *puls,* meaning pottage, was absorbed into the language after the Norman French invasion of England in 1066. The word pulses is not understood in the U.S.A. and leads to some confusion in international cookbooks.

Cooking legumes

At first glance, it seems against all the tenets of wholefood cookery to advise long soaking of any food. With legumes this is absolutely essential. All raw beans and peas contain glycosides, alkaloids, saponins and other substances which are deterimental to the digestion.

Long soaking, changing the water before cooking, and boiling inhibits the action of these adverse properties. The long soaking process does not, as may be thought, spoil the nutritional value of the beans or peas. Experiments in the U.S.A. with LIMA and KIDNEY BEANS have shown that after soaking for 16 hours, then boiling for 1½-2 hours, 70% of the vitamin B1 (thiamine) and 85% of the niacin content were retained. Other tests have shown that ordinary boiling destroys 25% of the water soluble nutrients. Vitamin B1 (thiamine) appears to be the most vulnerable. The values given in the nutritional content descriptions are taken from cooked legumes.

Storage

Properly stored, dry legumes will keep well for several years. Good storage means keeping the beans and peas in airtight containers in a cool position away from moisture, high termperatures, and insects. Tests have shown that beans stored at 19-24°C (66-76°F) retain palatability but show reduced nutritional value, particularly in vitamin B1 (thiamine).

Cranks Wholegrain Shop in London

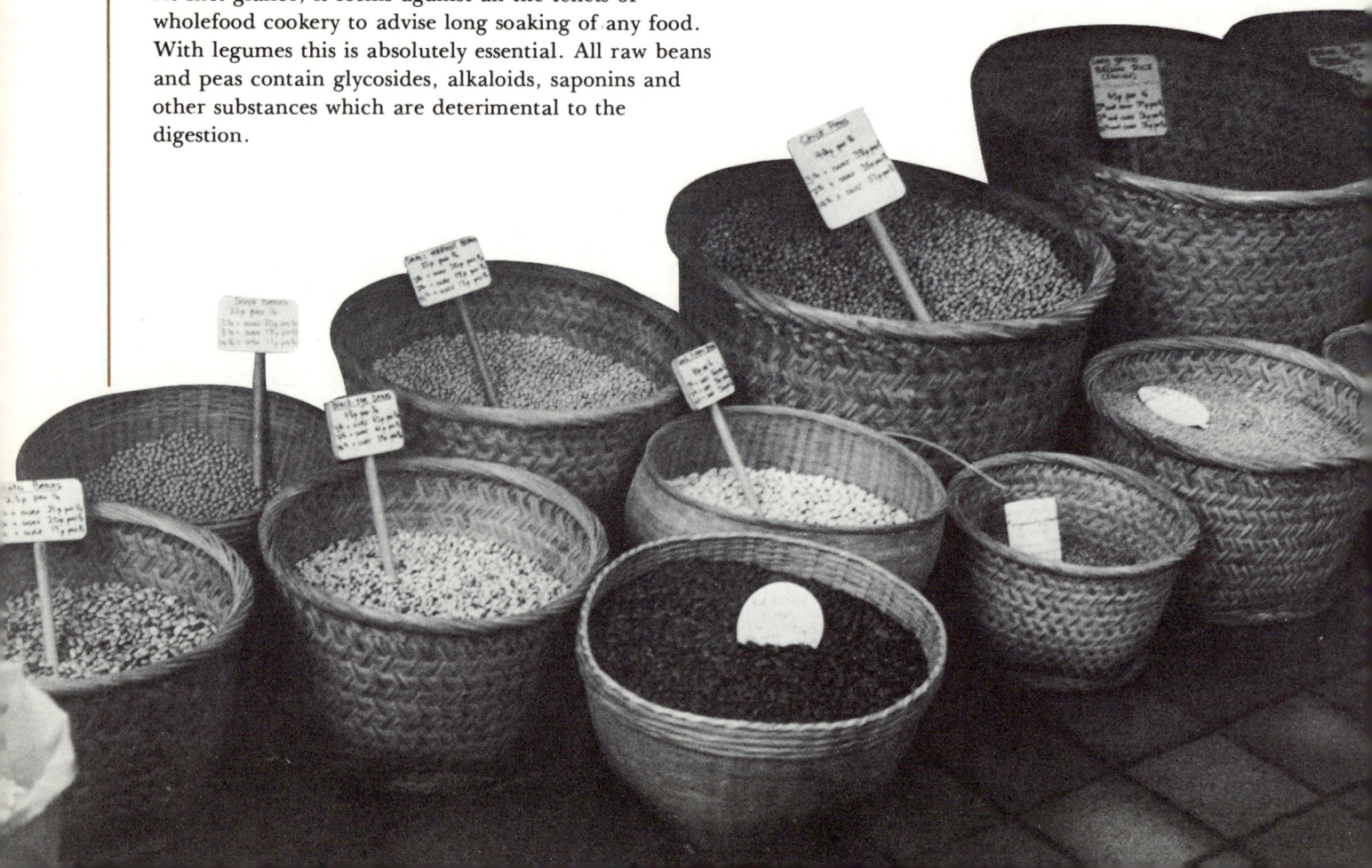

Aduki bean

Botanical name — *Phaseolus angularis*

Known also as adsuki, adzuki, feijao bean

The aduki bean is a native of Japan but it has been cultivated for centuries in China and Korea. In Japan it is known as 'The King of Beans' and was very little known or used in the West until the macrobiotic culture emerged. George Ohsawa, the founder of macrobiotics, specified the aduki bean as an important staple food. He felt that it could be eaten in larger quantities than most other legumes with no ill effects on the digestion.

The aduki bean is the seed of a bushy plant which grows to a height of 25-75 cm (10-30 in). There are several varieties within the main strain, but the seeds or beans are generally oblong-shaped and reddish or brown in colour.

In Japan and China the beans are usually left to ripen, and used dried. They are then soaked and boiled for use as part of a main meal, or pounded into a fine paste and made into cakes.

Aduki and medicine

For many centuries Chinese and Japanese herbalists and bare foot doctors have used aduki beans to help in kidney complaints. To make the juice they prescribed, soak two tablespoons of aduki beans overnight. Boil them in nearly 2 litres (4 pints) or 10 U.S. cups of water until they are soft and at least half the liquid has evaporated. Add a small pinch of salt substitute. Drain, and drink three times a day.

Nutritional content

100 g (3½ oz) cooked dry aduki beans contain: 25.3 g protein, 325 calories, 5.7 g fibre, 252 mg calcium, 7.6 mg iron, 15 I.U. vitamin A, 0.57 mg B1 (thiamine), 0.18 mg B2 (riboflavin), 3.2 mg niacin.

Aduki stew

200 g (7 oz) or 1¼ U.S. cups cooked aduki beans
175 g (6 oz) or 1½ U.S. cups chopped carrot
175 g (6 oz) or 1 U.S. cup chopped and diced onions
clove garlic crushed
1.2 litres (2 pints) or 5 U.S cups of water or stock
75 g (3 oz) or 1 U.S. cup mushrooms (tinned or fresh)
1 tablespoon miso
¼ teaspoon basil
pinch salt

Sauté the onions in vegetable oil and stir in the carrots, mushrooms and garlic. When they are well coated with oil, add the aduki beans, rice, basil, and salt. Pour on the water and bring to the boil. Cook slowly for about 40-45 minutes. Add the miso and cook for 3 minutes more.

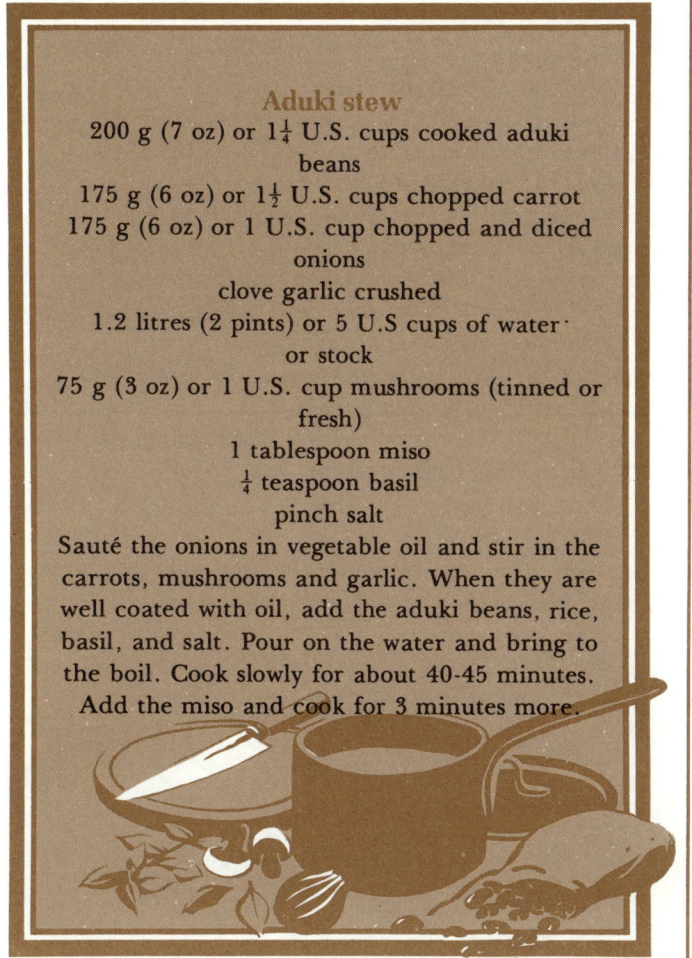

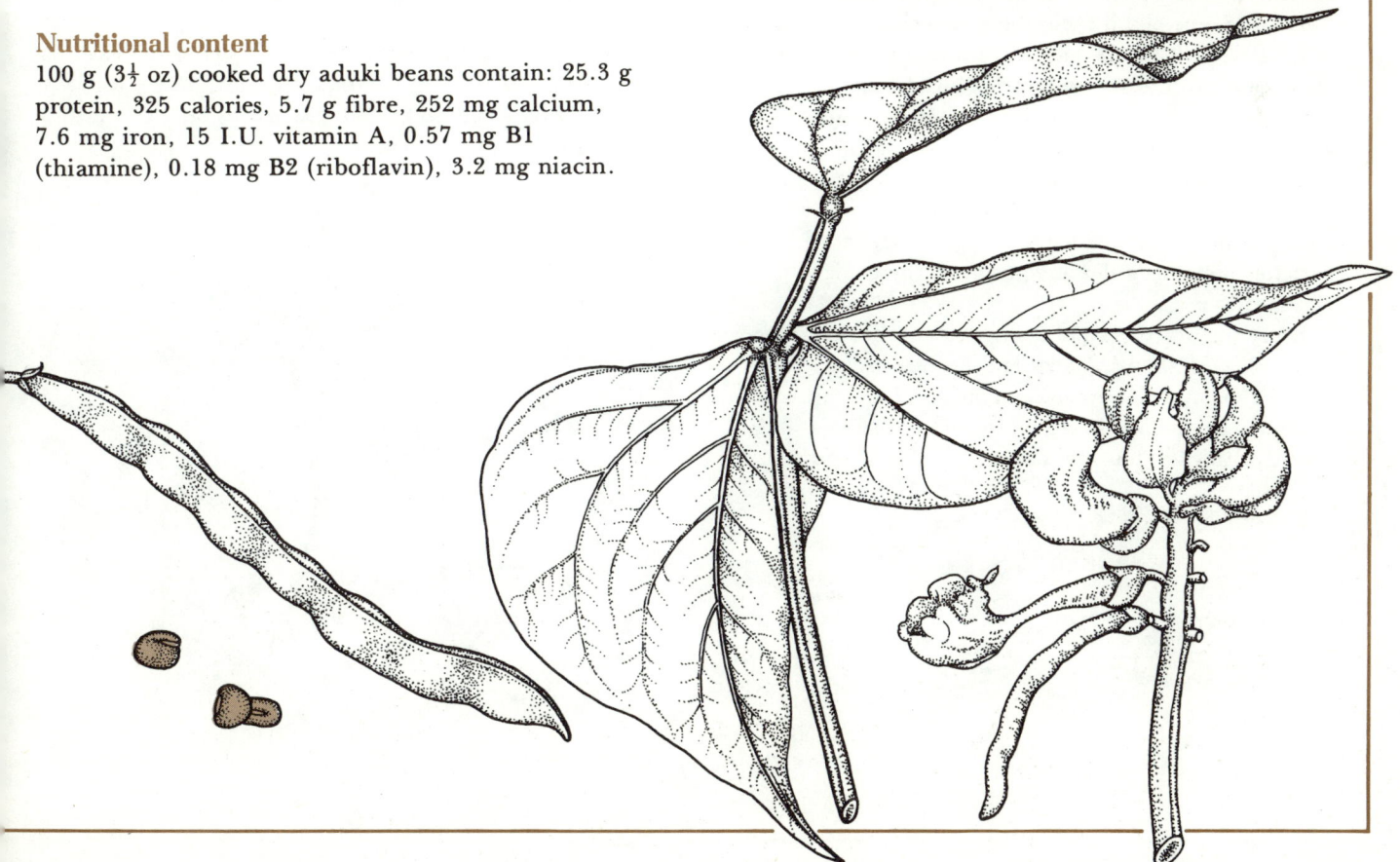

Asparagus bean

Botanical name — *Dolichos sesquipedalis*
Known also as yard-long bean.
This plant has a similar delicate flavour and is often
confused with the ASPARAGUS PEA (Goa bean). It
originated in Asia and is now cultivated on a large
scale in California by Chinese vegetable farmers. The
asparagus bean is eaten in the immature state before
the pod is ripe, and served as a vegetable.

Nutritional content

100 g (3½ oz) raw asparagus bean pods contain: 22 g
protein, 32 calories, 5.3 g fibre, 280 mg calcium, 8 mg
iron, 40 I.U. vitamin A, 0.4 mg B1 (thiamine), 0.15 mg
B2 (riboflavin), 1.6 mg niacin, 5 mg ascorbic acid.

Cooking

Both the asparagus bean and the asparagus pea pods
should be dropped in boiling water and cooked
quickly. Drain and serve with butter or a mild white
sauce.

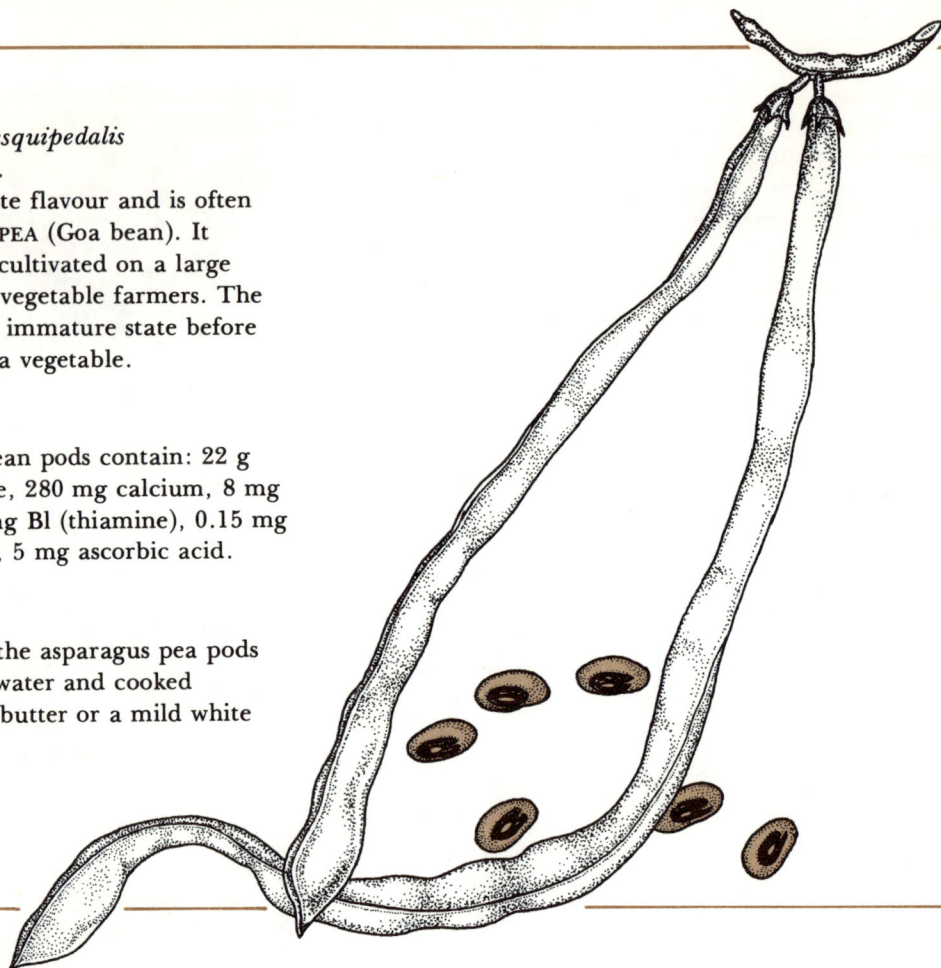

Asparagus pea

Botanical name — *Psophocarpus tetragonolobus*
Known also as Goa bean or winged pea.
The asparagus pea is a climbing perennial vine which
originated in tropical Asia and which has been an
important crop in the tropics for hundreds of years.
The plant is chiefly grown for the immature pods that
are cooked as a vegetable like French beans. The
delicate, aromatic flavour of the pod and seeds have
made this plant widely popular, and Australia and
America now cultivate it on a large scale. More hardy
varieties have been developed to suit the colder
climates.

Every part of the asparagus pea (Goa bean) can be
eaten. Young shoots, leaves and flowers are used as
vegetables, and the tuberous roots can be eaten raw or
boiled. The ripe seeds are often roasted in Asia and
served with rice, but are also sold as dried legumes.

Nutritional content

100 g (3½ oz) raw, immature pods of asparagus peas
contain: 1.9 g protein, 38 calories, 5.7 mg
carbohydrates, 0.2 mg fats. 100 g (3½ oz) of the ripe,
dry seeds contain: 37 g protein, 15 g fat, 28 g
carbohydrate. The plant contains traces only of vitamin
B1 (thiamine) and niacin.

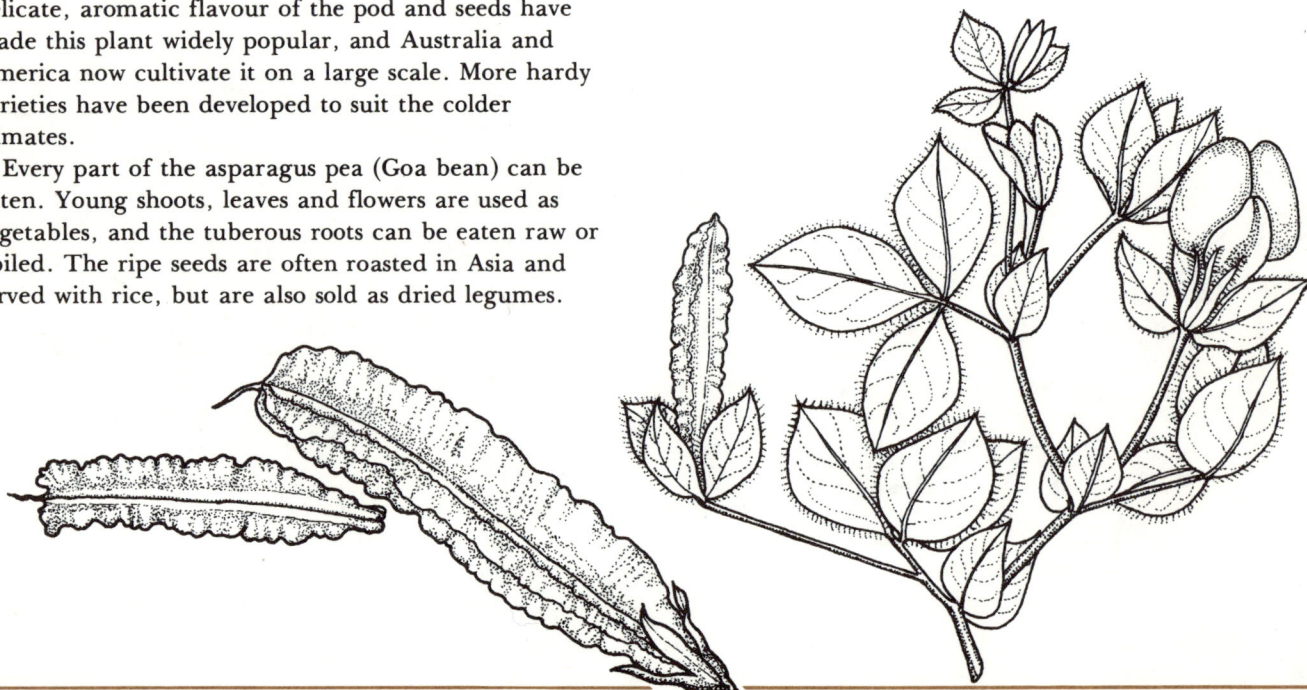

Black-eyed pea

Botanical name — *Vigna unguiculata*

Known also as black-eyed bean, cowpea, kaffir bean, Hindu cowpea, yard-long bean.

The black-eyed pea or bean came originally from Africa where it is still an important staple food. This is another legume native to the tropics that has been taken up in a big way by America, both North and South.

The black-eyed pea originally came to Europe via Egypt and Asia and explorers took it with them to the West Indies and America in the seventeenth century.

Today, the plant is cultivated all over the tropical world and America, plus many parts of southern

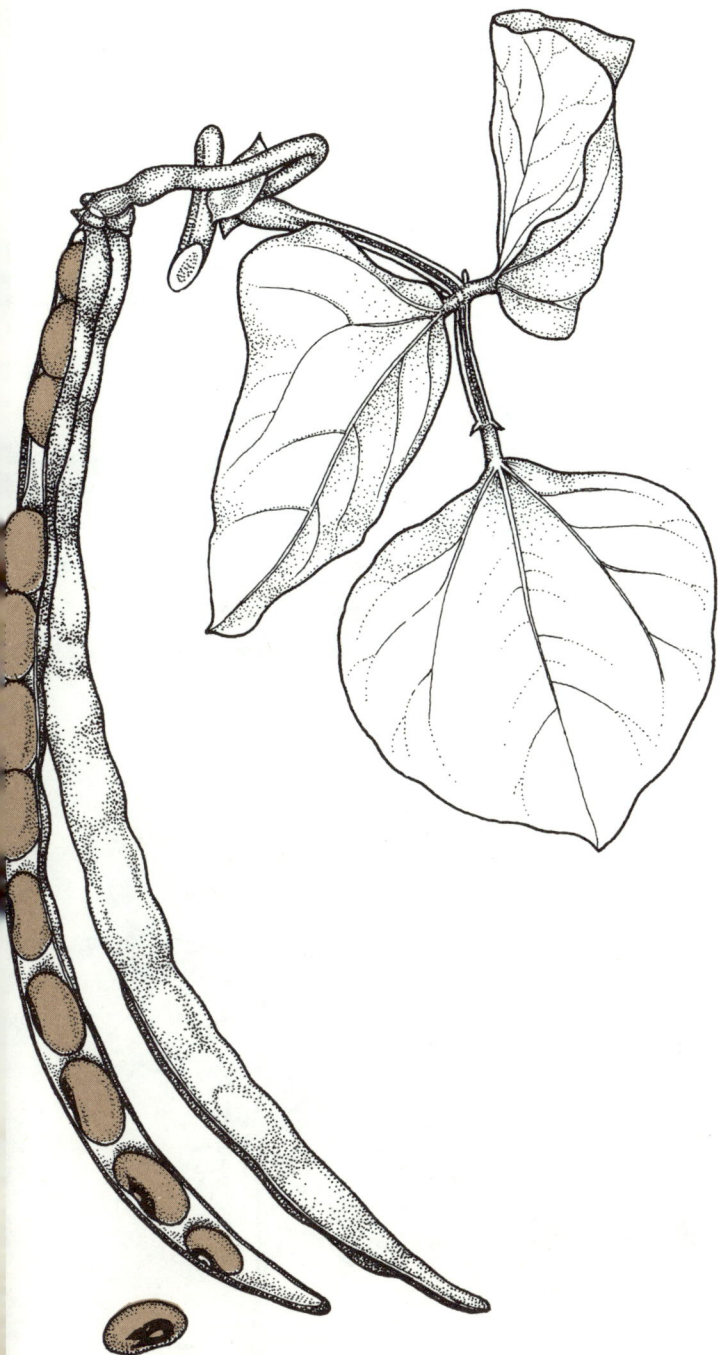

Hoppin' John

Black-eyed peas and rice are traditionally served in the southern parts of the U.S.A. on New Year's Eve.

200 g (7 oz) or 1 U.S. cup dried black-eyed peas
150 g (5 oz) or 1 U.S. cup brown rice
220 g (8 oz) or 2 U.S. cups bacon pieces
1 teaspoon fine herbs
salt and pepper to taste
1 large onion (well chopped)
1 clove garlic (crushed)
25 g (1 oz) or 1 loosely packed
U.S. cup chopped parsley
2 tablespoons vegetable oil
1.2 litres (2 pints) or 5 U.S. cups stock

Sauté the bacon pieces in the vegetable oil and add the onion, garlic and herbs. Lift out a spoonful of the bacon pieces and reserve. Drain the peas from their soaking water and add them to the cooking bacon, carefully mixing so that the vegetable oil clings. Add the washed rice, stir well. Pour on the stock and simmer for 45-60 minutes until the peas and rice are well cooked. Just before serving add the reserved bacon pieces and salt and pepper to taste.

Europe. The distinctive black-spotted legume has become popular throughout the world and colder climates import the dried pea.

There are several main varieties including the asparagus cowpea which is cultivated for the extremely long pods reaching up to 1 m (3 ft) in length. In parts of the U.S.A. where this is in demand it is known as the yard-long pea or bean.

In Africa, the dried seeds are ground into a coffee substitute. The young developing shoots are eaten like spinach, and the tender pod used as a green vegetable.

Nutritional content

100 g (3½ oz) cooked, dried black-eyed peas contain: 23.4 g protein, 342 calories, 4.3 g fibre, 76 mg calcium, 5.7 mg iron, 40 I.U. vitamin A, 0.92 mg B1 (thiamine), 0.18 mg B2 (riboflavin), 1.9 mg niacin, and 2 mg vitamin C.

Broad bean

Botanical name — *Vicia faba*

Known also as Windsor bean, haba, horse bean.
The broad bean was the only bean known to Europeans before the discovery of America. Its long history, starting possibly in the Mediterranean region, can be traced back to the Swiss lake dwellings of the Bronze Age.

Although broad beans were very common in the Ancient world they were held in low esteem. Egyptian priests decreed that only the common people should eat this bean, and no high ranking person would touch it. For this reason, the species is a notable omission from the tomb paintings and frescos of the period. The Greeks and Romans, too, thought of the broad bean as food fit only for peasants.

This down-grading of the *vicia faba* is possibly connected with the fact that it can cause the weird disease called favism whose main symptoms, high temperature and jaundice, occur soon after eating broad beans or within minutes of inhaling the pollen of the flower.

Favism is almost entirely confined to people of Mediterranean origin, and is very common in southern Italy and Sardinia. Scientists are still baffled as to why the disease should only attack one ethnic group. There is some evidence to suppose that people originating in the Mediterranean basin are more likely to inherit a biochemical abnormality of the blood.

The Greek philosopher Pythagoras who lived in the sixth century B.C. forbade his followers to eat beans. This greatly puzzled his loyal adherents, who reasoned that Pythagoras was not capable of illogical thought and, therefore, beans were bad. With modern hindsight we can deduce that the great philosopher suffered from favism. In fact, Pythagoras met his death at the edge of a field of flowering broad beans where a group of enemies had pursued him from the town of Croton. Rather than run through the beans, Pythagoras allowed himself to be captured and killed.

The broad bean is the white, flat seed of the plant. In France, the beans are cooked within the young pods. Dried broad beans are widely used, particularly in South America. In Brazil they are roasted and ground into a flour. Many poor South Americans make up huge pots of broad beans which are reheated day after day. These are known as 'awakened beans'.

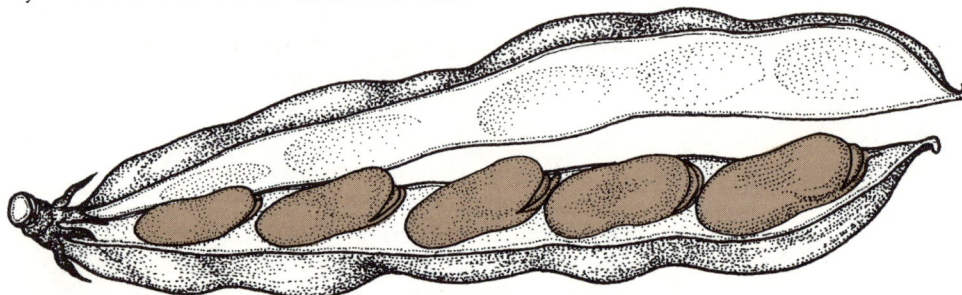

Broad bean salad

(Serves 4)

450 g (1 lb) or 2½ U.S. cups broad beans
225 g (8 oz) or 1 U.S. cup natural yoghurt
50 g (2 oz) or ⅓ U.S. cup cottage cheese
juice of half a lemon
1 teaspoon vegetable oil
fresh chopped herbs

If the beans are really young and tender cook them in the pod. If, not, pod them and cook until not quite soft. Mix the lemon juice with the oil and pour over the cooling beans. Blend the yoghurt with the cottage cheese and pour it over the beans. Finely chop fresh herbs (thyme, sage or chives) and sprinkle on top.

Nutritional content

100 g (3½ oz) cooked, dried broad beans contain: 23.4 g protein, 342 calories, 7.8 g fibre, 90 mg calcium, 3.6 mg iron, 100 I.U. vitamin A, 0.54 mg B1 (thiamine), 0.29 mg B2 (riboflavin), 2.3 mg niacin, and 4 mg vitamin C.

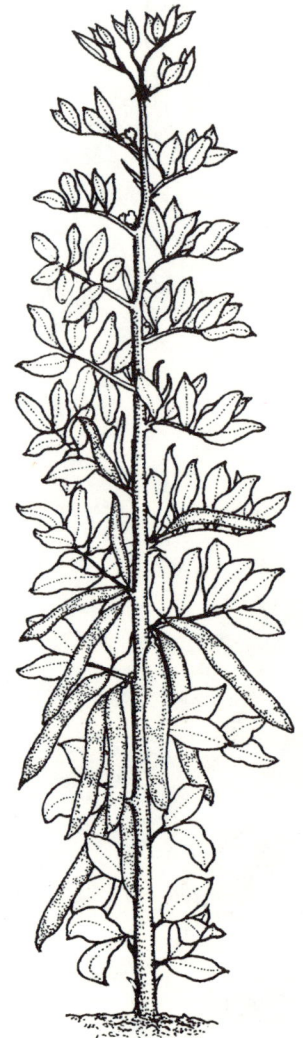

Chick pea

Botanical name — *Cicer arietinum*

Known also as *garbanzo* pea, Bengal gram, Egyptian pea, *Pois Chiche*, or *Ceci*.

The origins of the chick pea are rather mysterious. Archaeologists agree that the 'wild' chick pea grew in Egypt in the time of the Pharaohs. It is thought that it originated in western Asia. The pea spread from here through Palestine and Mesopotamia, then east to India. Merchants and explorers introduced the plant into Africa and South America and it is now grown commercially in Australia.

The chick pea has become of major importance in almost all Mediterranean countries where it is ground into a paste and mixed with garlic, oil and lemon to make *houmous*, or *hummous* as it is known in the West. In North Africa dried chick peas are ground into flour to form the essential part of *couscous*.

Seeds (or peas) develop inside the curious hooked pod. The peas can be white, yellow, brown, red, and sometimes almost black. They usually have a distinctive hook at each end. The dried, mature seeds can be boiled, baked or ground into a flour and in some countries such as South America and India entire unripe pods and the young shoots are used as a green vegetable.

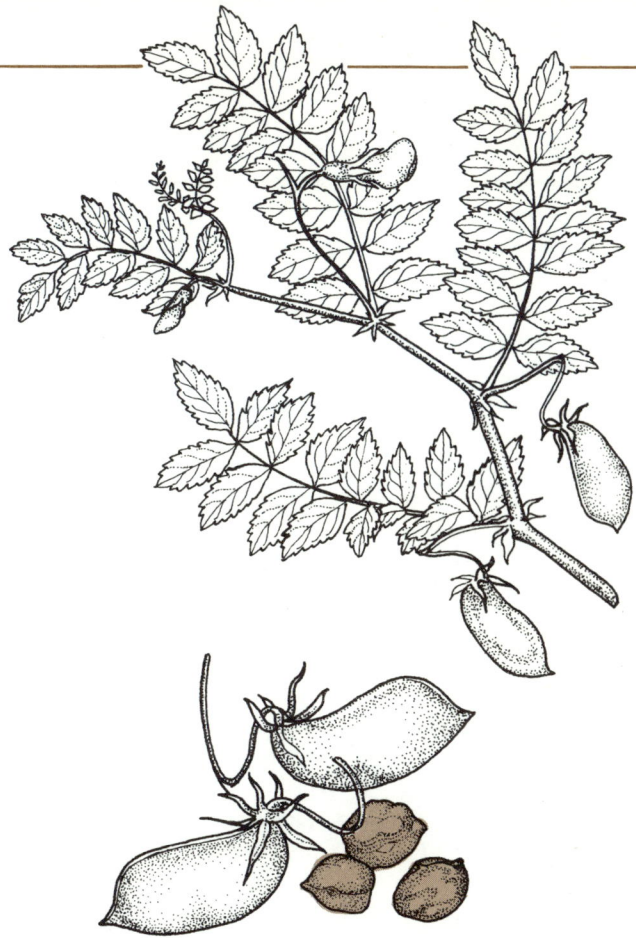

Chick peas and nutrition

Dr W.R. Ackroyd and Mrs Joyce Doughty in their well-researched book *Legumes in Human Nutrition* refer to tests with chick-pea supplements in India. Children suffering from the protein deficiency disease kwashiorkor were given a mixture of chick-pea flour made from germinated grains and banana mashed with unrefined sugar and water. Their report read:

Taken in amounts providing about 60 g of protein daily, this preparation produced a good clinical response, comparable to that seen in similar children receiving skim milk powder. Edema disappeared and weight gains were satisfactory. It was reported that the chick-pea supplement controlled diarrhoea more rapidly than the skim milk supplement.

In other tests in India, children given roasted chick peas and skim milk gained more weight and grew taller than other groups given only supplements based on skimmed milk.

Chick peas are known as *garbanzos* in Spanish-speaking countries and in many parts of the U.S.A., *ceci* in Italy and Bengal gram in India.

Nutritional content

100 g ($3\frac{1}{2}$ oz) cooked chick peas contain: 20 g protein, 358 calories, 4.9 g fibre, 149 mg calcium, 7.2 mg iron, 300 I.U. vitamin A, 0.40 mg B1 (thiamine), 0.18 mg B2 (riboflavin), 1.6 mg niacin, 5 mg vitamin C. The chick pea thus provides more vitamin C and nearly double the usual amount of iron than most legumes.

Hummous

450 g (1 lb) or 2 U.S. cups cooked chick peas
2 tablespoons olive or vegetable oil
1 or 2 cloves garlic
about $\frac{1}{2}$ teaspoon paprika (or to taste)
1 tablespoon sesame seeds (optional)
pinch salt
2 teaspoons lemon juice

Mash the beans well with a fork, add the oil and lemon juice and blend well. The consistency needs to be fluid enough for spreading. Add more or less oil if necessary to achieve this. Add the paprika, salt and sesame seeds and mix thoroughly. The whole operation can be done in a blender, but is easy enough to do by hand. Hummous is traditionally served as an hors d'oeuvre with raw vegetables. In the U.S.A. and Australia it is popular as a sandwich spread. The sesame seeds make the paste fairly crunchy, so leave them out if a smooth hummous is wanted.

Hyacinth bean

Botanical name — *Lablab niger*

Known aslo as lablab bean, Egyptian or Indian bean, *dolichos* bean, or field bean.

Hyacinth or lablab beans are native to India where they enjoy great popularity. The plant has been cultivated in the East for thousands of years and is produced on a large scale in Malaysia, Egypt and Ethiopia.

The *Lablab* family includes climbing and bush varieties, both of which are grown for the tender green pods as well as dried seeds. Hyacinth beans must not be eaten raw since they contain a poisonous glycoside which must be destroyed by soaking and boiling. The beans are considered highly palatable but they do require longer cooking than most legumes. This non-hardy climbing perennial can grow easily up to 6 m (20 ft). The seeds or beans vary in size and colour and have a characteristic white streak along the edge. The green pods are used in Asia and Europe as a green vegetable. In India, the ripe seeds are generally bought as a split dried legume.

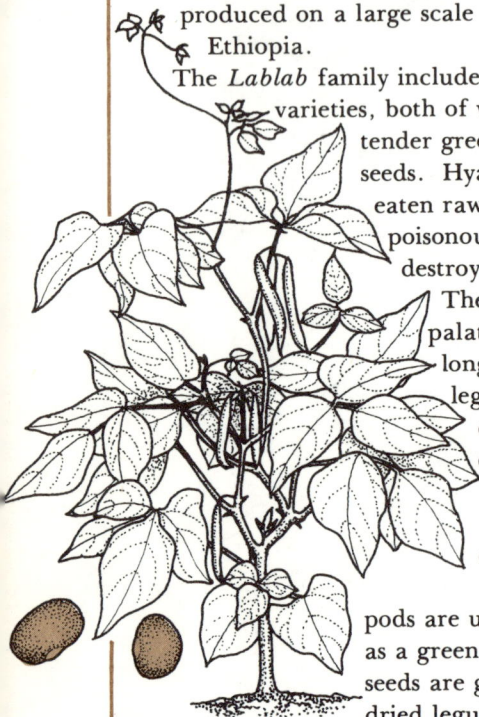

Bean loaf

200 g (7 oz) or 1 U.S. cup cooked beans
150 g (5 oz) or 1 U.S. cup chopped peanuts
50 g (2 oz) or 2 U.S. cups bran flakes
1 egg   1 tablespoon vegetable oil
200 ml (8 fl. oz) or 1 U.S. cup tomato juice
Mash the beans well, stir in the bran flakes, peanuts and vegetable oil. Whisk the egg up in the tomato juice and blend in with the bean mixture. Turn into an oiled loaf tin and cook at 190°C (375°F, Gas Mark 5) for 30-40 minutes. Dish up with a savoury sauce and a crisp green salad. (Serves 4)

Nutritional content

100 g (3½ oz) cooked dried hyacinth beans contain: 22.8 g protein, 340 calories, 4.6 g fibre, 92 mg calcium, 4.6 mg iron, 250 I.U. vitamin A, 0.63 mg B1 (thiamine), 0.16 mg B2 (riboflavin), 1.6 mg niacin, and 1 mg vitamin C.

Kidney bean

Botanical name — *Phaseolus vulgaris*

Also known as French bean, haricot bean, navy bean, pinto bean, snap bean, common bean, *frijoles,* or *opoca.*

This is the bean used in the great American invention 'baked beans with tomato sauce'. Cans of baked beans are on kitchen shelves from Woolloomoolloo in Australia to Wisconsin in the U.S.A. and have found a place as one of the most popular foods of our civilization.

The *Phaseolus vulgaris* species includes not only haricot, kidney and French beans but also the various coloured pinto beans, green and wax beans and great northern beans. In fact it is the most commonly used bean in the world today.

Kidney or French beans have been cultivated by American Indians since prehistoric times. Remains of *vulgaris* beans at the archaelogical sites in the Tehuacan valley in Mexico have been carbon dated as 7000 years old. The early explorers were surprised at the luxuriant growth of legumes in the New World. In

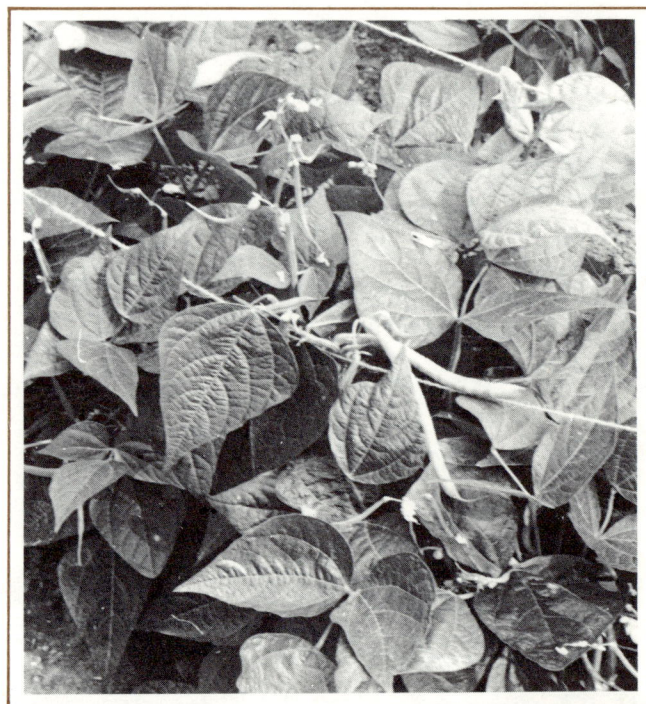

1492 Columbus described in detail a bean growing on the island of Cuba. It was quite different from anything to be found in Europe. Later in Honduras, he saw the same plant with red or white seeds. Cartier and Hudson and other explorers mentioned the excellent local beans. All these legumes were undoubtedly of the same *vulgaris* family of kidney and haricot beans. These legumes generously provided by the newly discovered lands also made further voyages possible as they became a rich source of non-perishable protein for the sailors.

The kidney bean was brought back to Europe in the sixteenth century. At first was a luxury, afforded only by the very rich, but soon its cultivation spread throughout Europe, reaching England from France in 1594; it was promptly christened the 'French bean'.

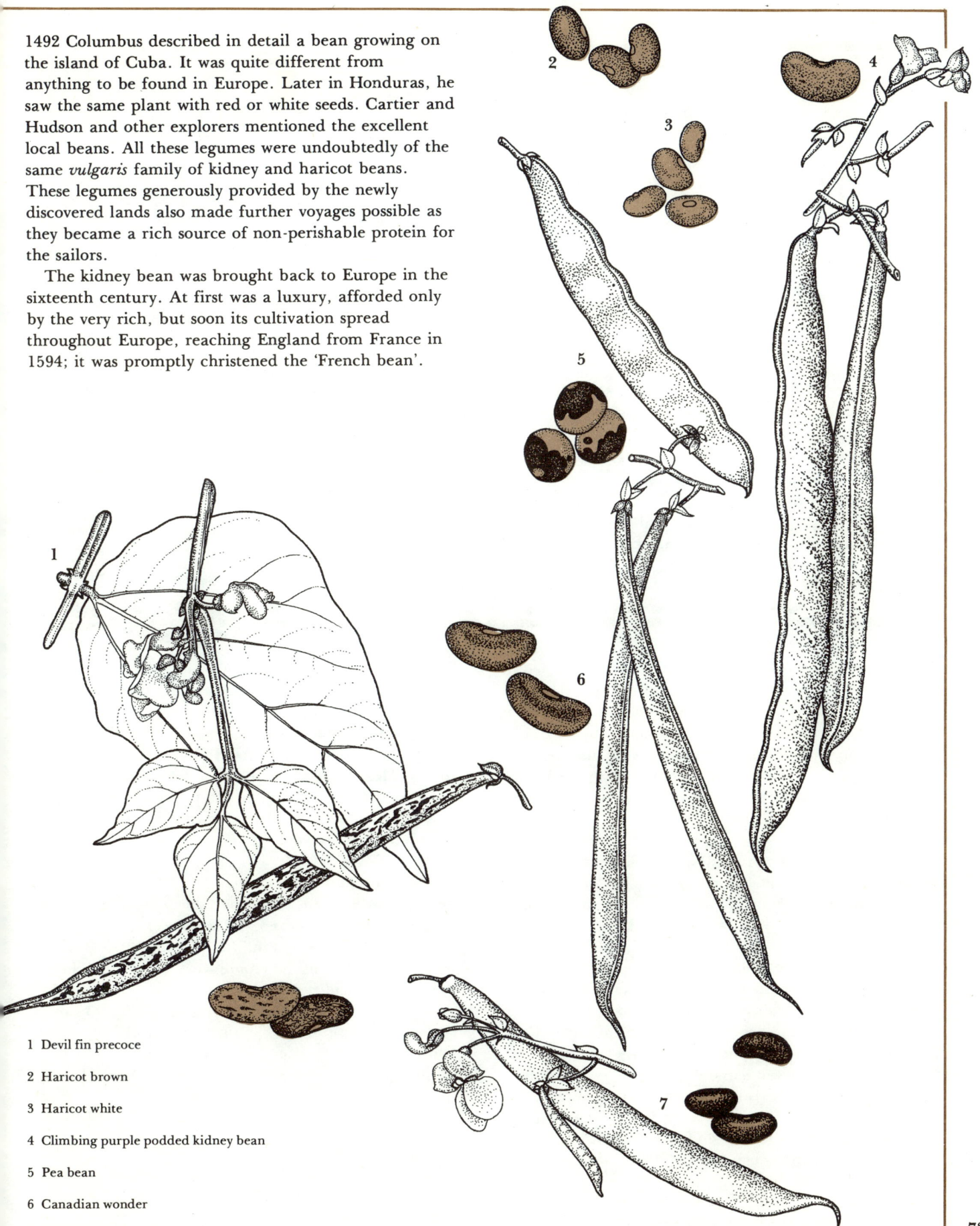

1 Devil fin precoce

2 Haricot brown

3 Haricot white

4 Climbing purple podded kidney bean

5 Pea bean

6 Canadian wonder

7 Mexican black

Boston baked beans

175 g (6 oz) or 1 U.S. cup haricot beans
75 g (3 oz) salt pork
1.2 litres (2 pints) or 4 U.S. cups stock
50 g (2 oz) molasses
1 teaspoon mustard
pinch salt

Soak the beans in water overnight. Next morning change the water and bake them for 45 minutes in the stock. Put the beans in a deep baking dish (preferably a bean pot) and reserve the stock. Score the pork deeply, put half of it in the bottom of the dish, the other half at the top with the rind uppermost. Mix the molasses and the mustard with the stock. Pour it over the beans in the baking dish. Cover the dish tightly, and bake in a slow oven, 150°C (290°F, Gas Mark 2) for 6-7 hours throughout the day. Check for dryness and add a little hot water if the beans seem dry. During the last hour, take the lid off, so that the pork and beans can brown.
(Serves 2-3)

Chili con carne

450 g (1 lb) ground beef
3 medium onions
1 tablespoon Mexican chili powder
1 teaspoon brewer's yeast
175 g (6 oz) cooked red kidney beans
1 large can tomatoes or 225 g (8 oz) fresh tomatoes skinned
600 ml (1 pint) or 2½ U.S. cups stock

Put the meat in a large, heavy pan. Turn it until the juices start to run, then add the well chopped onion and chili powder. Stir well. Add the tomatoes and brewer's yeast and the stock. Fit a tight lid and simmer for 30-45 minutes on a very low heat. Add the cooked kidney beans and a reasonable amount of their cooking liquid to top up. Mix well.
(Serves 4)

Many years passed before the Old World learned to cook the new beans with the skill of the American Indians. The Pilgrim Fathers endured bitter winters in New England before MAIZE and other crops were successful. During this time settlers were sustained by the beans given to them by friendly Indians. A recipe invented of necessity has come down to us as 'Boston baked beans'.

The *Phaseolus vulgaris* plant has hundreds of different cultivars or varieties, and the bean colours can range from white, to red, to black. Commercially, two basic types are developed: plants grown for their pods, and those grown for their dried seed.

French beans

It is generally accepted that French beans are the raw, young pods which are cooked as a green vegetable. The beans are widely cultivated for their pods in the U.S.A., where they are available fresh throughout the year, and in France. Stringless varieties are preferred, and are often cooked without slicing.

Snap beans are also the unripe pods from either the bush or climbing variety of *vulgaris*. The pods can either be green or yellow, and often have fibrous strings along pod sutures which must be taken off before cooking.

Navy beans are grown for their dry, mature seeds, and have been developed to be resistant to moasaic virus disease. They are usually sold as dried white beans.

Frijoles is a variety of medium field bean, very popular in South America. It is grown for the dried seed that has a pinky-beige colour.

Marrow red kidney beans are a variety bred especially for the dried red seeds. These red beans, sometimes sold as Mexican beans or red wonder beans, are the most commonly used legumes in Central and South America, and Mexico. They are the correct beans to use in *chili con carne*.

Nutritional content

100g (3½ oz) cooked, dried red kidney beans contain: 22 g protein, 341 calories, 4.2 g fibre, 137 mg calcium, 6.7 mg iron, 30 I.U. vitamin A, 0.54 mg B1 (thiamine), 0.18 mg B2 (riboflavin), 2.1 mg niacin, 3 mg ascorbic acid (vitamin C).

190 g (6½ oz) cooked common, white or navy beans contain: 14.8 g protein, 95 mg calcium, 281 mg phosphorus, 5.1 mg iron, 790 mg potassium, 0.21 mg B1 (thiamine), 0.13 mg B2 (riboflavin), 1.3 mg niacin.

Lima beans

Botanical name — *Phaseolus lunatas*

Known also as butter bean, sieva bean, curry bean, or pole bean.

Lima beans come, as their name suggests, from Lima in Peru. They belong to a later species than the *vulgaris* bean, although both the kidney and lima beans were discovered together in pre-Inca tombs in Peru dating from 5000 B.C.

Long before Columbus, the bean was growing throughout America, both North and South, with a firm stronghold in Florida where it is still cultivated. The Spanish *conquistadores* took lima beans with them to the Philippines.

The lima bean plant is one of the 'quick escapers' of the horticultural world. By the seventeenth century, it was growing in tropical areas all over the world. Today, the lima bean is less widely distributed than the kidney bean, but it remains the main legume crop of tropical Africa.

The species produces two distinct groups: the large, flat varieties known as butter or lima beans, and the smaller variety which are called sieva beans.

Although lima beans willingly flourish in tropical conditions, nobody has persuaded them to grow in colder climates. In the U.K. and Europe imported lima beans have long been popular as 'butter beans' in canned, dried, or frozen form.

The seeds (or beans) can vary in colour from white, brown, red, to mottled. Butter beans may come from either variety, but are usually preferred as white.

The raw seeds contain a poisonous cyanogenetic glycoside but long soaking and boiling will remove this. Some authorities consider the white varieties to be less toxic than the darker ones and this has influenced growers to concentrate on the 'butter bean' varieties.

The lima bean is an admirable subject for freezing. This means that northern regions can now enjoy the tender young green bean sold packaged as 'baby limas'.

Succotash

This is a traditional New England dish which is thought to have originated in Peru.

175 g (6 oz) or 1 U.S. cup maize (corn) tinned, frozen, or fresh
175 g (6 oz) or 1 U.S. cup cooked lima beans
1 clove garlic (optional)
⅓ red pepper diced (optional)
2 tablespoons vegetable oil
salt and freshly ground black pepper

If you are using sweetcorn (corn on the cob), cook it until the corn is tender enough to be rubbed off the husk. For frozen or tinned maize (corn), follow the instructions and cook quickly. Heat the vegetable oil in a thick pan. Put the cooked lima beans into it, with the crushed garlic and diced red pepper. Add the maize (corn), stir well, and season with salt and pepper. Keep the mixture on the heat for a minute or two to let the flavours blend. Serve with grated cheese and a white sauce, or simply sprinkle with ketchup (catsup) or soy sauce.   (Serves 4)

Nutritional content

100 g (3½ oz) cooked, dried lima beans contain: 19.7 g protein, 120 calories, 4.4 g fibre, 84 mg calcium, 5.2 mg iron, 30 I.U. vitamin A, 0.46 mg B1 (thiamine), 0.16 mg B2 (riboflavin), 1.8 mg niacin, 1 mg vitamin C.

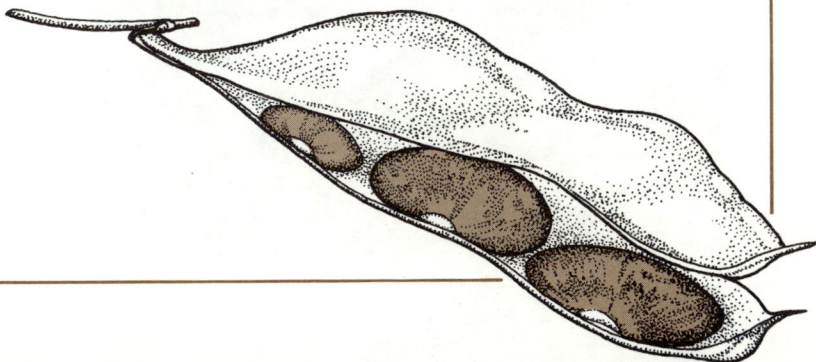

Mung bean

Botanical name — *Phaseolus mungo* or *Vigna mungo*
Known also as green gram, golden gram, black gram, or Oregon pea.

Most people think of the mung plant only in terms of a sprouting seed. In fact, this legume makes excellent dried bean dishes and is widely used as a flour in India. The mung bean is almost always used as a sprout in China where it plays an important part in the national cuisine. The Chinese usage has influenced America, and so the small, hard seed is commonly sprouted in the West. (*See* SPROUTING SEEDS *page* 115)

First cultivation of the bean took place in India before recorded history and, gradually, it became widespread and popular throughout Asia. In the East, the cooked, dried mung bean is often made into a porridge with a little glutinous rice. The only times the Malays eat mung beans or green grams is after the fasting month of Ramadan. The day after the sacred month has ended huge quantities of mung bean gruel are consumed. Indonesians use the mung bean therapeutically against protein deficiency and beri-beri.

The mung species has several main varieties, ranging in colours from green, yellow or golden to black. The

Idli

In India and Sri Lanka mung beans are traditionally decorticated (the seed coats are removed) and made into idli.
150 g (5 oz) or 1 U.S. cup cooked brown rice
50 g (2 oz) or ¼ U.S. cup mung beans
25 g (1 oz) cashew nuts (small pieces)
salt to taste
50 ml (2 fl oz) or ¼ U.S. cup water
Soak the mung beans overnight and try to rub most of the seed coats off. It might help to boil them for a few minutes and press through a sieve. Grind the beans until very fine. Grind or blend the rice with the water until it is a thick paste. Mix the rice and beans and cashew nuts together, salt, cover with a cloth and leave to stand overnight but not in the refrigerator. By the morning the mixture will have risen naturally. Grease some small cake tins and pour the batter in. Cook in a pre heated oven at 190°C (375°F, Gas Mark 5) for 25-35 minutes. Serve with curries, savoury meals or as a dessert.

green-seeded types are used generally for cooking or sprouting. The more rare black mung beans known as black gram in India are especially important amongst the high castes of Hindus. The golden coloured mung is increasing in importance in the U.S.A. and Europe.

Nutritional content

100 g (3½ oz) cooked, dried mung beans contain: 23.9 g protein, 340 calories, 4.2 g fibre, 145 mg calcium, 7.8 mg iron, 300 I.U. vitamin A, 0.56 mg B1 (thiamine), 0.17 mg B2 (riboflavin), 2 mg niacin, and 5 mg vitamin C.

Mung beans and chick peas have the highest amount of vitamin A among the dried legumes.

Pea

Botanical name — *Pisum sativum*

Known also as garden pea, *pois*, common pea.

The common or garden pea has one of the longest and most illustrious histories of the legumes. Some historians believe that it originated in the Garden of Eden, between the Euphrates and the Tigris rivers. Remains of peas have been found in the ruins of Troy and the pre-dynastic Egyptian tombs. Remains of cultivated peas at the site of a neolithic lake village in Switzerland have been carbon dated at 4500 B.C.

The word *pease* is of Sanskrit origin. It became *pisum* in Latin and pease in early English. The final '*e*' was dropped in the mistaken belief that it was a plural.

The ancient Romans cultivated the garden pea, but relegated it to the lowly position of other legumes. The Greeks prized it more highly. Theophrastus in his book *Enquiry in Plants* drew clear distinctions between the chick pea, the common pea and the vetch.

The pea escaped easily from cultivation and spread to Abyssinia and Africa. By the fourth century A.D. it had reached Asia, and from there it spread east to India and west to Europe. By the Middle Ages the dried pea had become an important legume all over Europe. At the court of Louis XIV in the seventeenth century, fresh green peas were all the fashion. 'This passion for peas is a madness', wrote Madame de Maintenon in her diary. She described how France's leading aristocrats would rush home from the theatre to consume large platefuls of young green peas. This French passion influenced the British, and young green peas became a rare and expensive delicacy. Nowadays, peas are most often eaten as a green vegetable, although the split pea has held its ancient popularity as a dried legume.

There are two main varieties of the common pea: the garden pea *(Pisum hortense)* or the field pea *(Pisum arvense)*. The seeds of the garden pea are yellowish or blue-green, wrinkled or smooth, and rich in natural

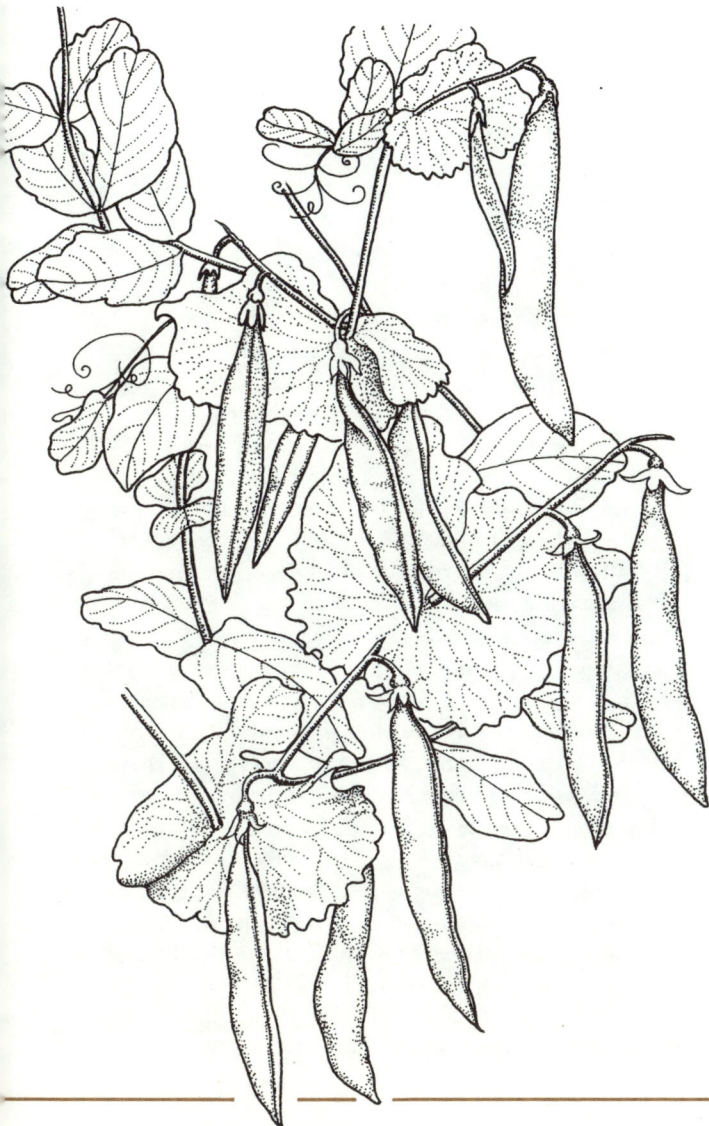

Pease pudding

Split peas are dried peas without the skins and they cook more quickly than most legumes.

200 g (7 oz) or 1 U.S. cup split peas
2 eggs
1 tablespoon vegetable oil
salt and black pepper

Soak the peas overnight and change the water. Simmer until well cooked and almost soft. Drain, and mash with a heavy fork, or grind in the blender. Add the beaten eggs, oil and salt and pepper to taste. The mixture should be quite stiff. Blend well. Oil a small pudding basin and scoop the mixture in. Press down, and cover with foil or waxed paper, securely fastened. Steam for about one hour. Serve hot or cold in slices. (Serves 6)

Green peas cordon bleu

900 g (2lb) fresh young peas (podded)
1 tablespoon oil
1 tablespoon butter
8 shallots diced small
6 large lettuce leaves
salt to taste

Put the vegetable oil in a pan and heat slightly. Arrange the clean lettuce leaves in the pan so that they cover the bottom and spread up the sides: Add the peas, shallots and butter. Cover with another lettuce leaf and tightly cover. If the peas are really young they will cook in 5 minutes. Older peas will need up to 20 minutes. Keep the lettuce leaves and juices to use in soups or stock. (Serves 4)

sugars. Field pea seeds are often spotted, greyish, with a high starch content.

The plant is an annual climber which prefers northern climates, but can be grown as a crop in Australia and tropical areas.

The great commercial emphasis today is on canned or frozen young green peas and each country has a preference of varieties. British manufacturers add green colour and sugar to canned peas, because, they say, national taste demands it. In most of Europe no colour is added to peas. *Petits pois* are used in freezing and canning. They are not a special variety but are picked when very young and small and have a lower sugar content.

The young, immature pod is usually topped and tailed and boiled whole. The common pea is marketed according to size and sugar and starch content as: sugar peas, snow peas, marrowfat peas or *petits pois*.

Nutritional content

200g (7 oz) cooked split peas contain: 16 g protein, 230 calories, 22 mg calcium, 178 mg phosphorus, 3.4 mg iron, 592 mg potassium, 80 I.U. vitamin A, 0.3 mg B1 (thiamine), 0.18 mg B2 (riboflavin), 1.8 mg niacin.

160 g (5½ oz) cooked frozen peas contain: 8.2 g protein, 109 calories, 30 mg calcium, 138 mg phosphorus, 3 mg iron, 216 mg potassium, 960 I.U. vitamin A, 0.43 mg B1 (thiamine), 0.14 mg B2 (riboflavin), 2.7 mg niacin, 21 mg vitamin C.

160 g (5½ oz) cooked fresh peas contain: 116 calories, 37 mg calcium, 158 mg phosphorus, 2.9 mg iron, 314 mg potassium, 860 I.U. vitamin A, 0.45 mg B1 (thiamine), 0.18 mg B2 (riboflavin), 3.7 mg niacin, and 32 mg vitamin C.

Pigeon pea

Botanical name — *Cajanus cajan*

Known also as red gram, Angola pea, Congo pea, or yellow dhal.

The pigeon pea is probably a native of Africa. It was under cultivation in ancient Egypt by at least 2000 B.C. as demonstrated by seeds which have been discovered in tombs of the Seventh Dynasty. The species also found its way to India where it flourished and diversified into many types.

The plant is a perennial which can be cut back and used as a crop for up to three years depending on the climate. It bears seeds in pods twisted like a helter skelter. The pigeon pea is an important crop in hot climates since it is resistant to drought and extreme temperatures. Australia, the Pacific Islands, and parts of America have successfully introduced this legume as a commercial crop.

It is known as yellow dhal in India where it is extremely popular. Like all dhals, the hard seed-casing is removed before cooking. In Africa, where the pigeon pea grows easily, it is only eaten in areas influenced by large Indian communities.

The tender young pods with their convoluted twists are sometimes easten as a green vegetable. However, the seeds, or peas, are generally used as a dried legume; they vary in colour, but are usually red, brown or yellow.

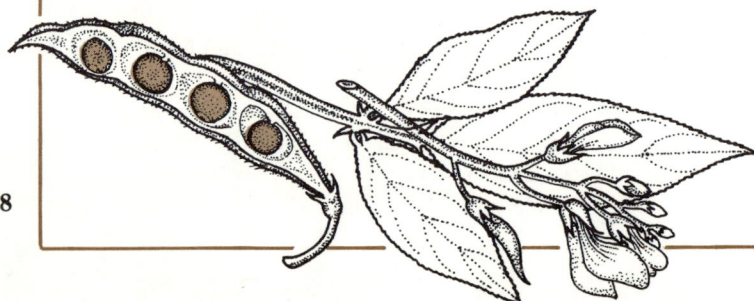

Nutritional content

100 g (3½ oz) cooked, dried pigeon peas contain: 20.9 g protein, 343 calories, 8 g fibre, 129 mg calcium, 5.8 mg iron, 130 I.U. vitamin A, 0.50 mg B1 (thiamine), 0.14 mg B2 (riboflavin), 2.3 mg niacin, and 4 mg vitamin C.

Stuffed cabbage rolls

200 g (7 oz) or 1 U.S. cup cooked pigeon peas
1 tablespoon grated coconut
1 medium onion, finely diced
½ teaspoon salt   freshly grated black pepper
1-2 tablespoons olive oil (or other vegetable oil)
1 medium-sized cabbage
150 ml (¼ pint) or ⅔ U.S. cup stock

Pound or blend the cooked peas with the vegetable oil, garlic, coconut and diced onion until a stiff paste is formed. Sprinkle on the salt and freshly ground black pepper. Carefully separate and clean the leaves of a medium-sized cabbage. Bring a pan of water to the boil, put in the cabbage leaves, cover tightly and boil for 8-10 minutes. Each leaf should be cooked but not so that it becomes floppy.

Drain the cabbage leaves and spread them out. Put one or two tablespoons of the bean paste in each leaf. Roll it up and fasten with a cocktail stick if necessary. Put the stuffed leaves in an earthenware dish and pour on the stock. Cover with foil or a tight-fitting lid and cook in a moderate oven, 190°C (375°F, Gas Mark 5), for 40 minutes. (Serves 4)

Runner bean

Botanical name — *Phaseolus coccineus* or *Phaseolus multiflorus*

Known also as scarlet runner bean or multiflora bean. The scarlet runner is a tall, climbing plant which produces spectacular flowers usually of a vivid scarlet. This bean is also a native of the New World. It was first introduced into England from America in 1683 by colonial merchants. For a long time the scarlet runner bean was cultivated only for ornamental value. The red flowers ran in profusion up cottage walls all around the country. When the long bean pods developed they were plucked off and thrown away as inedible. It was not until the eighteenth century that they were regularly cooked and eaten as a vegetable.

The runner bean is a good example of the ambivalent attitude towards legumes. In the U.S.A. the beans are still mainly grown for their flowers, whereas in the U.K. the scarlet runner bean has become one of the most popular vegetables. To cook, thinly slice the whole pod and boil quickly. Runner bean pods have a more distinct flavour than French beans, but a coarser texture. For tender, stringless runner beans, it is best to pick them at about 10-15 cm (4-6 in) long.

The twining shoots of this non-hardy perennial can grow up to 4 m (13-14 ft) in height. In practice, the growing points are pinched out at about 2 m (6-7 ft). Although the main varieties are scarlet, both the pods and flowers can vary in colour from red to white. In Central America the bean is important as a dried legume but western countries rarely use it as such. The bean can easily be dried within the pod and stored for later use.

Nutritional content

100 g (3½ oz) cooked green immature scarlet runner beans contain: 2 g protein, 25 calories, 0.6 mg fibre, 45 mg calcium, 0.9 mg iron, 204 mg potassium, 2 mg sodium, 830 I.U. vitamin A, 0.1 B2 (riboflavin), 0.6 niacin, and 16 mg vitamin C.

Cooking

Very tender young runner beans only need thin slicing and boiling for about 5 or 8 minutes. Toss about 1 tablespoon of butter in the pan and swirl around until the beans are coated. For a more elaborate method of serving (excellent for more elderly or frozen beans) make a garlic sauce. (*See* AIOLI *page* 125)

Runner beans with tomatoes

Longer, coarse beans can be turned into a tasty vegetable by this method.
Clean and slice 450 g (1 lb) of runner beans (or French beans past their best). Slice medium thick and boil in salted water for 8-10 minutes. Meanwhile, heat 2 tablespoons of vegetable oil in a frying pan. Add three large skinned tomatoes, or one large tin of tomatoes, two of cloves garlic, well chopped, and two teaspoons cider vinegar. Simmer slowly. Add the cooked beans, stirring well. Cook until the tomatoes have become nearly puréed. Serve with broccoli and garlic bread for lunch, or with rice as part of the main meal. (Serves 4)

Soya bean

Botanical name: *Clycine max*

Known also as soybean, haba soya or preta.

For thousands of years the soya bean has been known as 'The meat of the earth' in the Far East. Modern analysis has proved this ancient title to be very apt as it has outstanding nutritional value. It is one of the few sources of complete protein, i.e. it contains the eight essential amino acids the body cannot manufacture. As a result of research, the soya bean and its products have become a major growth industry, changing Western eating habits in certain ways.

The soya bean is a native of China, and was first recorded in 2800 B.C. by the Emperor Shen Nung, who described it as one of the most important crops in his country. The plant then spread to Japan and Korea and became equally important there.

The German botanist, Engelbert Kalmpfer, brought the soya bean back to Europe in 1712. It aroused great curiosity and samples were grown in the hothouses at Kew Gardens in England. Fifty years later, Commander Perry brought back two main varieties to the U.K. from his expedition to Japan. Even in the eighteenth century, the soya bean was recognized as having special, even unique nutritional qualities. However, it took another two hundred years before non-Asian countries began to produce soya beans on a large scale.

The explosion of interest in the West in the soya bean is due mainly to American influence. When research proved the unusual value of soya, the U.S. Government offered subsidies to farmers to turn their land over to the crop. By 1969, over forty-one million acres were under soya bean cultivation in the U.S.A., who are now one of the major exporters of the bean and its products; together with China they lead the world in its cultivation.

The boom in soya has become big business. Not only is the bean made into countless sorts of food, but new industrial uses are constantly being found. Soya extractions are used in paint manufacture, the plywood industry, brewing, pharmaceuticals and cosmetics. The natural emulsifying and binding properties of the plant continue to be investigated. Compounds of soya are added to foods as a natural preservative to prolong their shelf life.

The plant of the soya bean is an annual which grows to 60-90 cm (2-3 ft) tall. Seeds (or beans) of the plant can vary in colour from yellow through grey and brown to black. There are many varieties of this legume, but they may be classified into two main types: the edible vegetable bean, and the commercial field species used for soya bean oil, meal, and flour.

In the Far East, and more recently in the U.S.A., the tender young green pods are eaten as a vegetable and elsewhere in the world the seeds are used as a dried legume. Soya products include flour, oil, milk, textured vegetable protein, and the traditional fermented foods such as *miso* and *tofu*. These are dealt with in detail on *page 83*.

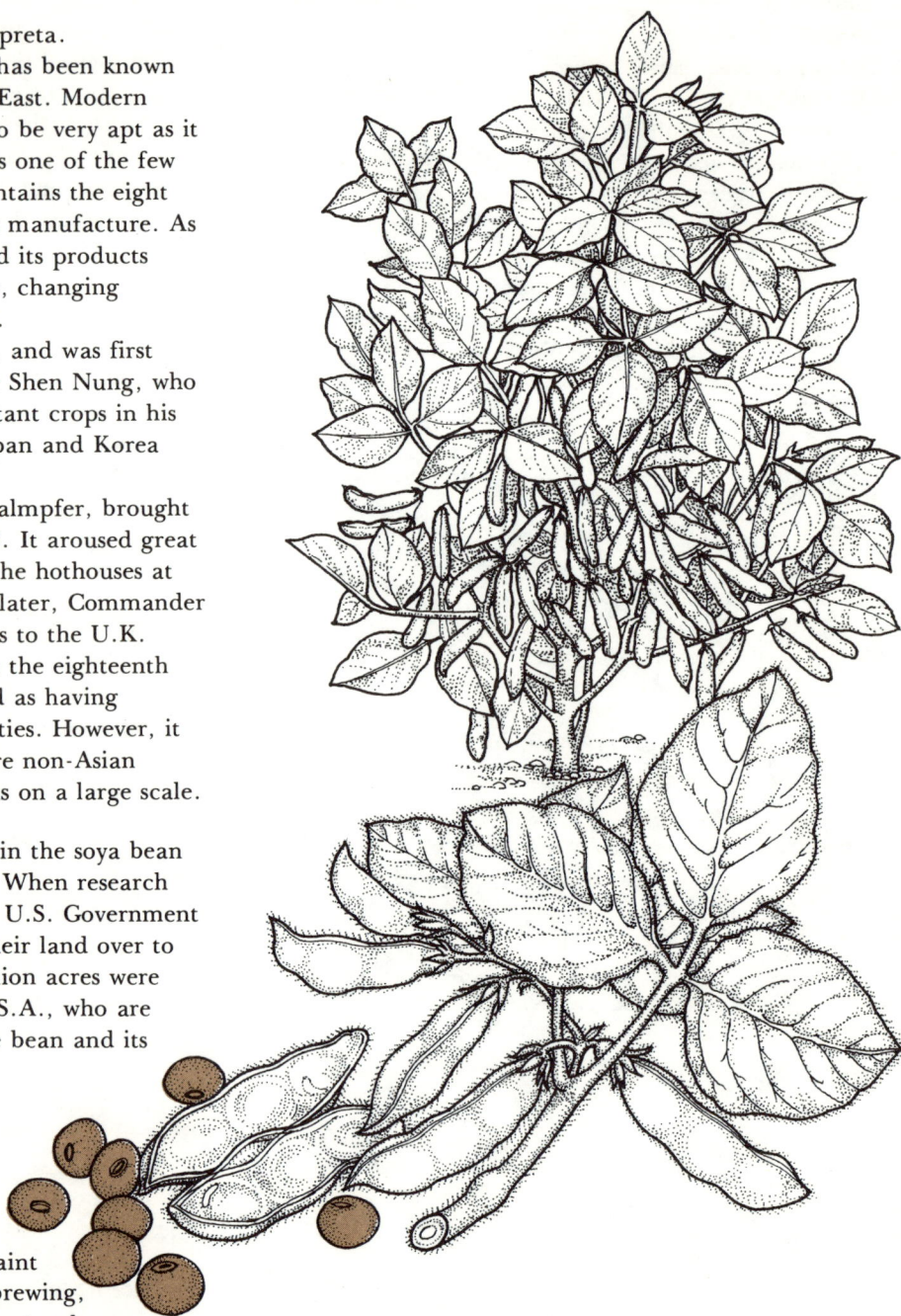

Nutritional content

200 g (7 oz) cooked, dried soya beans contain: 22 g of protein, 260 calories, 20 g carbohydrates, 3.2 g fibre, 7 g of linoleic acid, 5.4 mg iron, 150 mg calcium, 360 mg

phosphorus, 1080 mg potassium, 60 I.U. vitamin A, 0.4 mg B1 (thiamine), 0.1 mg B2 (riboflavin), and 1.2 mg niacin. The trace elements in soya beans include copper, magnesium, zinc, manganese, nitrogen, sulphur, calcium, potassium, phosphorus, and iron.

Particular value

Soya beans contain as much protein as top quality steak. 200 g (7 oz) or 1 U.S. cup provide 22 g of protein, and 85 g (3 oz) of lean steak also has 22 g of protein. The difference is that the beans contain unsaturated fats. Soya beans contain 54% of linoleic acid and a rich lecithin level, both of which have been proved to reduce the cholesterol levels in the blood.

The iron in soya products is in a much more assimilable form than in most other foods. Research at the University of Wisconsin, U.S.A., has shown that 80% of the iron in soya beans is actually assimilated by the body, as compared to 20% of the iron in spinach. Tests at the U.S. Bureau of Home Economics have illustrated that soya beans are one of the most alkaline of all foods, and can be used to correct over-acidity of the system. The Bureau has also stated that the soya bean provides the cheapest source of minerals and complete proteins on the market today. Although soya beans appear to contain only a moderate amount of vitamin A, they also have phosphatides which aid the absorption of carotene into the system. Other valuable ingredients include sterols which are used in the production of natural and synthetic hormones. The sterol stigmasterol is made commercially into progesterone which is used in the birth control pill, and sitosterol is turned into the male sex hormone testosterone.

A field of soya beans in North Carolina

Soya products

Soya grits The raw bean is broken into eight or ten pieces, which cook in minutes rather than hours. They can be used in any recipe which calls for cooked soya beans. The grits are particularly good in bean loaf or patties.

Soya bean sprouts The sprouted bean manufactures its own vitamin C. (*See* SPROUTING SEEDS *page* 115)

Soya as textured vegetable protein Spun and textured soya is now made to simulate beef, turkey, chicken, ham, and virtually every other sort of meat. Besides meat, textured vegetable protein (often called TVP) is being produced to simulate fruits, nuts, and cheese. All TVP comes in easy-to-use mixtures or tins. It is made from soya flour or soya protein concentrate which is extruded into small bits or granules. The dried chunks can be reconstituted into a main dish such as bolognese sauce, convenience dinners, and casseroles, or simply added to pies, cereals, and barbecue sauces.

Soya milk is useful not only to vegans but also to those who suffer from allergies to cow's milk. It is sold as canned, bottled, or as a spray dried powder. Soya milk is richer in iron than cow's milk but has less calcium, phosphorus and vitamin A. Most commercial soya milks compensate for this by being fortified with added vitamins and minerals.

It is easy to make your own soya milk with a grinder or blender machine. Soak 450 g (1 lb) of beans in 2.3 litres (4 pints) or 10 U.S. cups of water. Pour off the water and grind the beans to a fine paste. Gradually add fresh water and continue blending until you have about 2.3 litres (4 pints) or 10 U.S. cups of smooth white liquid. Strain out any bean remnants, and heat the milk to boiling point. Let it simmer for a few minutes. Cool, and skim off the skin then bring back to boiling point. Cool again and refrigerate.

Soya flour There are three types of soya flour generally available: full fat flour which contains 20% fat; medium fat flour, with 5% or 8% fat, and fat free soya flour. It is important to know what type of soya flour you are using because the amount of liquid in recipes may have to be adjusted to obtain good results; this applies especially to the low fat or fat free flours which require more liquid.

Soya flour is highly concentrated and even higher in nutritional values than the beans. It contains no gluten, but can safely be added to bread recipes at the rate of 2 tablespoons of soya flour per 225 g (8 oz) of wheat flour. The density of the flour makes it advisable to always use a sieve first. Add the flour to soups, gravies and casseroles as an easy way to achieve the best protein balance for a meal. There are a few uncooked soya flours on the market which are specifically intended for bread making. Refer to the word of caution below on uncooked soya.

Soya oil is obtained from the beans in two main ways: by the expeller process, in which a rotating shaft presses the cooked beans and by the solvent process where chemicals are used to extract the oil. Most reputable manufacturers preparing oil for the health food market would not use the chemical extraction. However, there is no indication on the bottle to state which method has been used.

Soya oil is rich in lecithin and linoleic acid. It is semi-drying, and used in cooking, margarines, cakes, pastries, dough, soups, and candies. The oil should be stored in a cool, dark place and after a few months may possibly change colour due to the presence of iron and copper which can be oxidized by the linoleic acid.

Growing your own soya beans

Soya beans are quite easy to grow, especially in hot climates. The English seed firm, Thompson and Morgan (*See* WHERE TO BUY *page* 154), has now promoted a variety of soya bean which is more suited to colder climates.

Fermented soya bean products

A good deal of ingenuity goes into the traditional processes which turn soya beans into pastes, sauces or cheese. Widely available products such as miso, natto, hamanatto, tempeh, tofu and soy sauce are described in detail below. The action of the micro-organisms such as *Bacillus subtilis* breaks down the proteins in the beans to readily assimilable forms of amino acids. This gives support to the ancient Chinese belief that fermented soya foods aid digestion. The fermentation process quite frequently produces natural antibiotics, particularly in the product tempeh.

Soy sauce (shoyu) Some Asian countries make exotic varieties of soy sauce with ginger and chicken and other ingredients. The basic method is the same in Japan and China and produces the soy sauce familiar in the West. The cooked beans are mixed with roasted wheat and treated with *Aspergillus oryzae*. Salt is added to quicken the growth of the fungus. The mixture is put in wooden vats or stoneware jars and allowed to ferment for times ranging from six months to five years. A long slow 'ripening' is considered essential for obtaining the best soy sauce and during the ripening time vats are stirred twice a day. When the beans are ready, the liquid should be a rich, dense brown. This is strained off and bottled, and the residues used as a fertilizer. Soy sauce is the eastern equivalent of tomato sauce and the bottle appears at every meal and is generously added to flavour foods from rice to hiziki. In traditional western cooking, soy sauce can be used much in the same way as Worcester sauce to impart a biting zest to foods and gravies.

Natto Buddhist monks devised the method of making

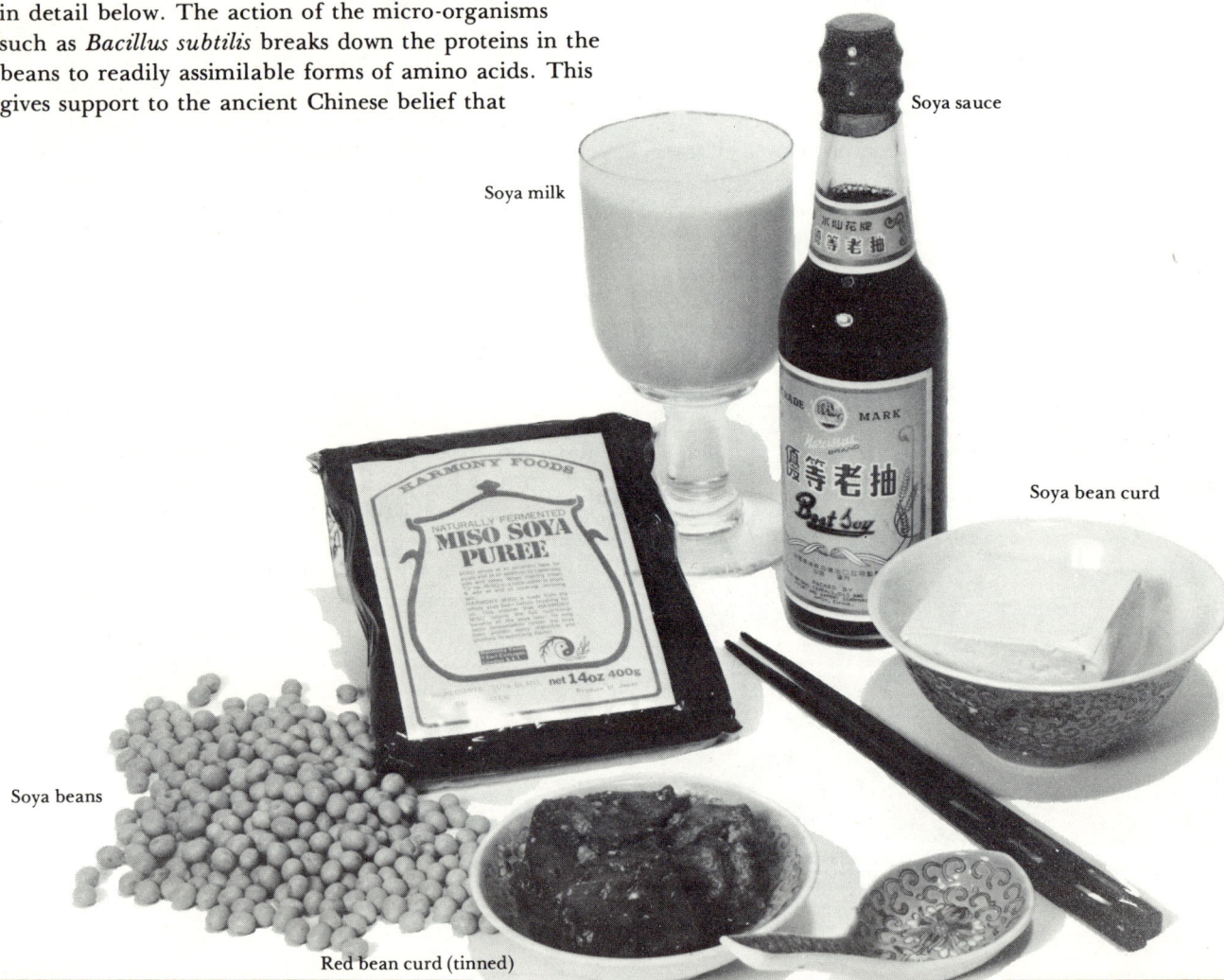

Soya sauce

Soya milk

Soya bean curd

Soya beans

Red bean curd (tinned)

natto thousands of years ago. It is another lengthy fermentation process during which the cooked soya beans are inoculated with the *Bacillus subtilis*. The beans are then wrapped in very thin sheets of pinewood and left to ferment for two days. Natto has a greyish colour and stiff texture.

Hamanatto originated in Korea where it remains very popular. The steamed soya beans are mixed with roasted wheat and fermented with a special mould. The mixture is dried in the sun and then put into wooden buckets with strips of ginger and salt. It is left to ferment for up to a year until it develops a reddish colour. The contents of the buckets are then poured onto wooden strips so that the hamanatto can dry in the sun until it is a black colour.

Tempeh is a sort of cheese made from fermented soya beans. It originated in Indonesia and is now popular throughout the East. The boiled and soaked beans are treated with the fungus *Rhizopus oryzae* and wrapped in banana leaves until a mould develops. Analysis of tempeh shows that it contains a powerful natural antibiotic, thus proving its traditional use as a disease preventative. It is best compared to gorgonzola cheese because of its strong smell and distinctive taste.

Miso is a soya bean paste produced by lactic fermentation. It has been an important product in Japan for over two thousand years. The miso or paste is made in a lengthy process during which cooked soya beans and cooked rice are impregnated with the organism *Aspergillus oryzae*. Salt is gradually added during long fermentation in wooden vats until a paste-like consistency is formed. Miso can vary in colour from black to white. Darker miso contains more soya beans (up to 90%) and a greater concentration of salt. White miso contains more rice and less salt. It can be made into soups, spreads, gravies, or use it like YEAST EXTRACT to enhance a simple casserole. Marinate vegetables in miso paste for an excellent home-made pickle.

Tofu is a soya bean curd, made by grinding the beans into an emulsion and curdling them with powdered gypsum, which has the same effect as rennin. It has a soft, delicate texture and pale colour and is sold in slabs or slices. The fresh curd should always be kept under refrigeration. The bean curd can be fermented to make cheeses, and the result is a highly flavoured cheese known in China as 'chou Tofu' — or stinking curd. Tofu and curd cheeses are widely used in China and Japan as the first solid foods for babies. It is slightly thicker than cottage cheese for which it can be substituted in every recipe.

A word of caution Soya beans and soya flour must not be eaten uncooked. The raw soya beans contain a substance known as a trypsin inhibitor, which appears to prevent the assimilation of the amino acid methionine by the body.

Basic cooked soya beans

Rinse the beans well and soak for 24 hours. This small, hard bean doubles in size during soaking, so allow at least three times the amount of water. Next day, change the water, bring the beans to a boil, and simmer for between two to four hours. The last hour of cooking is the time to add flavourings such as onions, celery, oil, spices, and soy sauce. Never add the salt until just before serving.

Freezer short-cut method The long cooking time can be considerably reduced by using this method. Soak the beans for a minimum of several hours. Change the water and put them in a flat dish in the freezer or freezing compartment overnight. Next day, cook the frozen beans by dropping them into boiling water. Reduce heat, and simmer for about one and a half hours, or until tender.

Soya casserole

200 g (7 oz) or 1 U.S. cup cooked soya beans
2 tablespoons vegetable oil
1 clove garlic
1 bayleaf
75 g (3 oz) or 1 U.S. cup mushrooms (optional)
50 g (2 oz) tomato purée or
3 tablespoons tomato sauce
1 large chopped onion
75 g (3 oz) or 1 U.S. cup cooked
wholemeal macaroni rings
1 tablespoon soy sauce
900 ml (1½ pint) or 4 U.S. cups stock
Sauté the onions in the vegetable oil until they are a clear colour. Add the garlic, cooked beans, mushrooms, bayleaf, tomato purée, and soy sauce. Mix well. Add the stock and the macaroni and bring to the boil. Simmer for about 15 or 20 minutes to allow the flavours to blend. Take the bayleaf out.
(Serves 4)

Lentils

The 'mess of pottage' that Jacob gave to Esau was made of lentils and was so tasty that Esau subsequently sold his birth right for it. Lentils were one of the first cultivated crops, particularly in the East. They were introduced into the U.S.A. in about 1914 by a travelling seventh-day adventist minister from Germany who gave the seeds to an enterprising farmer.

Nutritional content

Lentils are about 25% protein, 54% carbohydrate, and contain vitamin A, some of the B vitamins, plus good amounts of minerals including iron and calcium. 200 g (7 oz) cooked lentils contain: 15 g protein, 212 calories, 38 g carbohydrate, 4.1 mg iron, 50 mg calcium, 238 mg phosphorus, 505 mg potassium, 40 I.U. vitamin A, 1.2 mg niacin with traces of B1 (thiamine), and B2 (riboflavin).

Particular value

Lentils are not a complete protein since they lack some of the essential amino acids. Nevertheless, they are an important source of protein in Third World countries where they are called 'poor man's meat'. Lentils are richer in protein than any other of the pulse group with the exception of SOYA BEANS. The high calorific value satisfies hunger as they generally stay in the stomach longer. The farm worker's comment that lentils 'stick to the ribs' has thus more than an element of truth.

Types of lentils

The two main types are Chinese and Indian. The Chinese vary from whitish to green, the Indian lentils are various shades of pink and red. Generally speaking the red lentils have more protein than the others.

As lentils cook fairly quickly, they do not need soaking long. However, some experts believe that this makes them more digestible. They should not be cooked in the water used for soaking.

Lentil soup

200 g (7 oz) or 1 U.S. cup lentils
1 large chopped onion
1 bayleaf
2 cloves garlic (crushed)
½ teaspoon ground cumin or
½ teaspoon turmeric
1.2 litres (2 pints) or 5 U.S. cups water
Simmer the lentils gently with half the onion, the bayleaf and one clove of garlic. Slowly fry the rest of the onion with the remaining garlic in a small amount of mixed butter and vegetable oil. When the onion is golden brown remove from heat and gently stir in the ground cumin. When the lentils are cooked (about 30 or 40 minutes) scoop half out and put in the blender, add the onion and cumin or turmeric mixture and blend until smooth. Pour the mixture back into the pan, stir well and bring back to the boil. Garnish with parsley.

Molasses

Molasses, also known as blackstrap molasses, is a by-product of the sugar refining industry. The sugar cane is crushed and processed to obtain refined white sugar. The residue, after this process has been completed, is called molasses. On the way to becoming 'pure' pristine white, sugar loses almost all of its valuable minerals and vitamins. The residue, thick dark molasses, is a rich source of nutrients. Generally speaking, the darker the colour, the richer the nutritive value. The darkest molasses is blackstrap and is marketed under that name.

Nutritional content

Dark molasses is a good source of many B vitamins, especially inositol and B6. It is rich in iron, copper, calcium, phosphorus and potassium. It contains more iron than does the same amount of liver, and several times more calcium than milk.

One tablespoon (20 g or $\frac{3}{4}$ oz) of blackstrap molasses contains: 45 calories, 11 g carbohydrate, 2.3 mg iron, 116 mg calcium, 14 mg phosphorus, 585 mg potassium. It provides the following vitamins: 30 mg inositol, 0.5 mg B1 (thiamine), 0.5 mg B2 (riboflavin), 0.54 mg B6, 0.52 mg pantothenic acid, and 0.03 mg biotin.

Particular value

Molasses is extremely rich in the vitamin inositol (other sources are WHEAT, CORN and OATMEAL). The human body has a great need of inositol. A hundred times more of this vitamin is found in a healthy body than of any other vitamin. Lack of it is thought by some experts to cause loss of hair. Research at the University of Columbia, U.S.A., does seem to indicate that the male need for inositol is greater than the female.

After yeast, molasses is the richest source of vitamin B6. As the B vitamins are water soluble and cannot be stored, various deficiencies can occur quite readily. The State University of Iowa College of Medicine, U.S.A., has done extensive research into vitamin B deficiencies. This research indicates that B6 is needed for the proper assimilation of iron; even huge supplements of iron prescribed to anemia sufferers are not utilized if B6 is undersupplied by the diet. As rich amounts of both iron and B6 occur naturally in molasses, this makes it especially valuable.

A word of caution Molasses contains a good deal of natural sugar and so should not be left in contact with the teeth. It is not a good idea to take molasses directly from the spoon unless you are prepared to visit your dentist more frequently. It is perhaps best stirred into liquid or used in recipes.

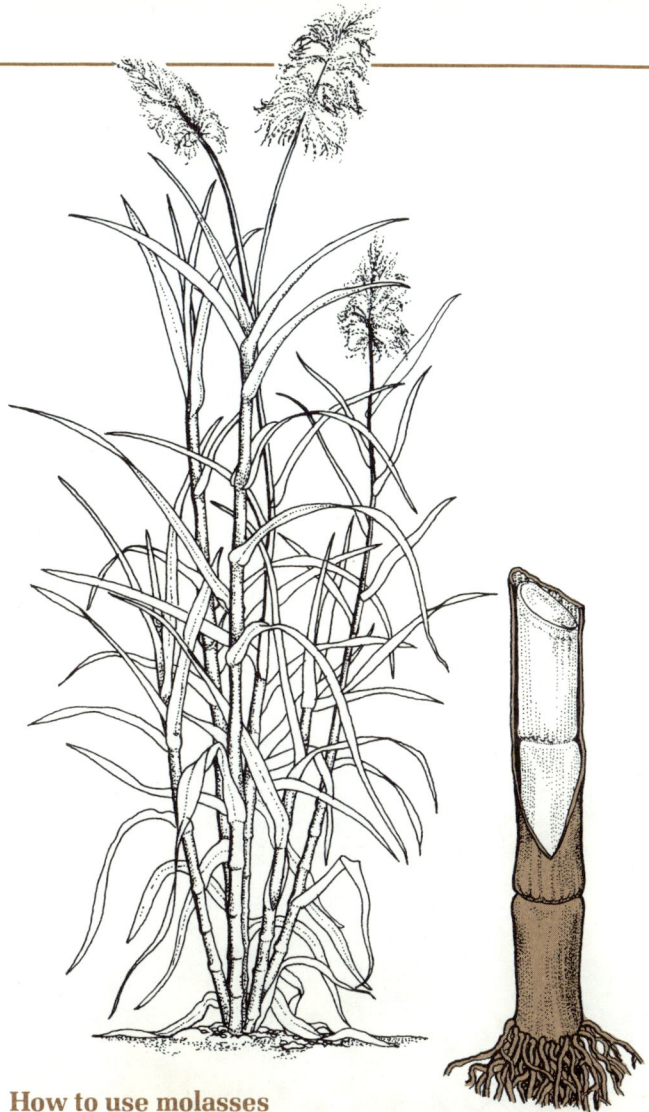

How to use molasses

Molasses is available in tins and jars. It can be diluted with a little warm water and stirred in a milk shake. It can also be substituted for honey in many recipes. Many forms of meat are delicious with molasses.

Sweet and sour spare ribs
Marinate 1 kg (2 lb) of spare ribs overnight in the following mixture:
2 or 3 tablespoons dark molasses
2 tablespoons apple-cider vinegar
575 ml (1 pint) or 2½ U.S. cups apple purée or diced apples
Pour off the marinating liquid and reserve. Put the meat in the oven to bake at 150°C (300°F, Gas Mark 2) It will take about 2 hours. During the last half hour of cooking, add a clove of garlic and dash of Worcester sauce to the reserved liquid and pour it over the meat. Baste once or twice. If there is no time to marinate, pour the liquid mixture over during the last 40 minutes and baste well.

Muesli

Muesli was first formulated by Dr Bircher-Benner in Zürich about 70 years ago. In Britain, America and Australia it has become regarded as a breakfast cereal, based on rolled OATS, fresh or DRIED FRUIT and served with milk or YOGHURT.

Dr Bircher-Benner was born in 1867 in Zürich and founded the Bircher-Benner Health Clinic in that city in 1897. At the Clinic he pursued his researches into food values and health. He became convinced of the curative powers of raw fruit and vegetables and juices. He was also a pioneer in the use of a machine to squeeze juice from fruit or vegetables.

Gradually, Dr Bircher-Benner evolved a carefully balanced formula for muesli to be a complete meal in itself. He felt that it was important for sick people to under rather than over eat. His formula was easy to

Dr Bircher-Benner

Dried fruit muesli
2 level tablespoons oats
1 level tablespoon wheat germ
1 teaspoon lemon juice
3 heaped tablespoons dried fruit
1 heaped tablespoon of nuts
2 level tablespoons yoghurt
brown sugar or honey to taste
milk to taste
The oats and milk can be mixed the night before for speed. Add fruit and nuts, sprinkle with lemon juice, mix well. Top with yoghurt, add honey to taste.

Muesli cake
150 g (5 oz) or 1 U.S. cup muesli base
(oats, wheat germ, and nuts)
125 g (4 oz) or 1 U.S. cup wholemeal flour
200 ml (8 fl. oz) or 1 U.S. cup vegetable oil
150 g (5 oz) or 1 U.S. cup brown sugar
2 eggs
25 g (1 oz) raisins
½ teaspoon baking powder
½ teaspoon ground nutmeg
Cream the oil and sugar together; add well beaten eggs; mix in raisins, flour, baking powder and muesli base. Bake in moderate oven for about 1 hour.

digest, while at the same time giving a feeling of fullness. Muesli was often served several times a day to his patients.

The muesli marketed today as based on the original Bircher-Benner formula contains 10 ingredients: WHEAT, oats, MILLET, unrefined sugar, dry apples, SULTANAS, roasted hazelnuts, roasted almonds, WHEAT GERM, and dry skimmed milk.

The classic Bircher-Benner formula has these proportions:
2 level tablespoons of oats (or a combination of oats/millet/wheat)
2 level tablespoons cream or yoghurt
1 level tablespoon chopped hazelnuts or almonds
1 fresh apple
1 teaspoon lemon juice
honey or brown sugar, milk to taste

Nutritionally this provides a complete protein, a rich source of calcium and the vitamin B complex group, together with a good range of the vitamins A, D, C, and E.

Dr Bircher-Benner felt that the fibre content combined with the lactic properties of milk or yoghurt were especially good in keeping the digestive tract healthy. Nutritional research during the 1960s and 1970s seems to have shown that Dr Bircher-Benner was thinking along the right lines fifty years ahead of general opinion.

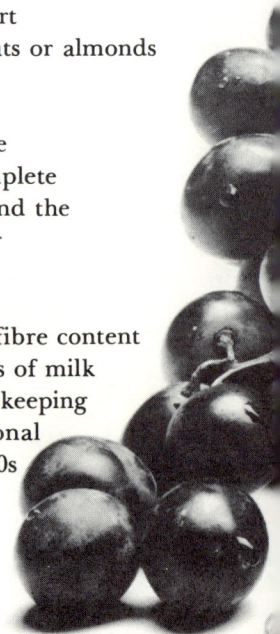

Some experts believe that optimum health can only be achieved by eating a complete protein at each meal. This is very difficult to do without overloading the system of a person who is not well. Another reason in favour of muesli is that oats and millet have been found to be more alkaline and less acid forming than the other grains. It is only in the last few years that orthodox doctors have written books urging the need for fibre in the diet. (*See* BRAN *page 26*)

Great emphasis was placed by Dr Bircher-Benner on the fruit additions to muesli. He used a great variety of fresh fruit in season and never allowed this to be peeled. Of course, nowadays our fruit is sprayed with a great variety of chemicals, and it is perhaps wiser to peel it if you are not certain of the source.

There is a strong body of expert opinion in favour of a good breakfast. Adelle Davis, the nutrition expert, advises: 'Eat breakfast like a king, lunch like a prince and supper like a pauper.'

Much research has been done into blood sugar levels from which we conclude that a person who eats little or no breakfast is in danger of poor functioning all day long. So, if you have neither the time nor energy to cook breakfast, muesli is the ideal way to get a nutritionally sound start to the day.

It is much cheaper to make your own muesli rather than buy packets. Experiment, and find the combination which your family likes best. There are endless variations on the basic theme — two of which are given below. Try to obtain sultanas and dried fruits unsprayed with mineral oil. This can cause fat soluble vitamins to be destroyed.

Nuts

Nuts are a high protein food that is rich in B vitamins, and minerals. They are worthy of being included in the diet more often than just as salted snacks. No vegetable can compare with nuts in the amount of protein they provide.

For example, black walnuts are 28% protein, and lean beef is 22% protein. Nuts do have a high fat content, but this is rich in linoleic acid which helps to control cholesterol. The high numbers of calories in this food puts would-be slimmers off. In fact, nuts take so long to chew that they are more satisfying than other 'empty calorie' foods.

Unshelled nuts are designed by nature to keep and store over long periods. Nowadays, nuts both shelled and unshelled are treated with preservatives, dyes, and inhibitors. Packaged commercial nuts are often fried in saturated or rancid fats or hydrogenated oils.

If you can get nuts from a reputable organic source, they deserve to be eaten regularly.

Nuts on sale in a Karachi market

Almonds

Almonds have been esteemed as a food since the days of the Old Testament. In one of the first recorded miracles, Aaron's rod was made to blossom and bear almonds. During the great famine Jacob sent almonds to his son Joseph in Egypt.

The almond tree itself is a native of the eastern Mediterranean. It produces a spectacular pink or white blossom in the spring, followed by a fruit which is eaten unripe as an aperitif. The almond seed or nut is found inside the fruit. There are two basic varieties:

Sweet almond

This is the type most usually used in both European and Eastern cooking. Sweet almonds can be used whole, ground, fried, or pounded into a sort of milky paste. They are a fine flavouring for soups, fish or meat dishes. Almond paste is mixed with sugar to make the marzipan which is so popular on cakes. Sweet almonds are very common in Arabic food and in Indian curry recipes. One delicious Middle Eastern dish combines almonds, rice and chicken.

Bitter almonds

Bitter almonds are quite a different variety to sweet almonds and can be distinguished by their broad shape. They have a powerful, pungent taste similar to that of peach or plum kernels. The powerful flavour of bitter almonds is due to an enzyme reaction which produces prussic acid. Fortunately, this poison is highly volatile and evaporates when heated. Raw bitter almonds should be avoided. Certain recipes specify bitter rather than sweet almonds. Indeed, the pungent flavour of bitter almonds can be an asset if used with discretion.

Almond oil can be pressed from either variety of almond. It is marketed as 'oil of bitter almonds' or 'sweet almond oil' and was one of the earliest cosmetic aids. Imperial Roman ladies used it as a favourite skin moisturizer. Medieval beauties used the oil to whiten their hands and keep their skins smooth and free from wrinkles. Almond oil is still a much used ingredient for face creams.

Nutritional content

70 g (2½ oz) sweet almonds contain: 13 g of protein, 425 calories, 8 g linoleic acid, 3.3 mg iron, 163 mg calcium, 353 mg phosphorus, 541 mg potassium, 0.2 mg B1 (thiamine), 0.2 mg B2 (riboflavin), and 2.4 mg niacin.

Almond yoghurt

425 ml (16 fl oz) or 2 U.S. cups natural yoghurt

100 g (4 oz) or 1 U.S. cup toasted blanched almonds

50 g (2 oz) or ⅓ U.S. cup curd cheese

juice of half a lemon

50 g (2 oz) honey

50 g (2 oz) orange juice

Blend the honey with the yoghurt and curd cheese. Add the lemon and orange juice and stir well. Crush half the toasted almonds and mix in the yoghurt. Use the other almonds to decorate the top. Chill and serve.   (Serves 4)

Brazil-nuts

These nuts have been a popular export to Europe since 1633. In Victorian England no dinner would have been complete without Brazil-nuts to hand around with the port. Their popularity has gradually grown in the U.S.A. until now half the entire crop of Brazil-nuts goes there. Surprisingly enough, very few Brazil-nuts are eaten in their country of origin.

The Brazil-nut is actually a large coconut-type shell weighing up to about 1.8 kg (4 lb). The seeds — what we call nuts — are neatly wedged inside, like chocolates in a box. The Brazil-nut tree grows to the vast height of 45 m (150 ft). The nuts drop to the ground when ripe, but even then, collecting them is a risky business as high winds hurl the shells down with the force of cannon balls, and the nut gatherers need protective head gear.

Nutritional content

70 g (2½ oz) unsalted Brazil nuts contain: 20 g protein, 914 calories, 4 g fibre, 24 g linoleic acid, 4.3 mg iron, 224 mg calcium, 880 mg phosphorus, 890 mg potassium, trace vitamin A, 1.2 mg B1 (thiamine), 0.2 mg B2 (riboflavin), and 2 mg niacin.

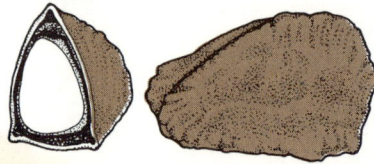

Cashew nuts

The cashew nut is the actual fruit of a tropical tree called *Anacardium occidentale* which is native to Brazil. The South American Indians called the fruit acajú which the Portuguese colonists heard as cajú, hence the name cashew. Portuguese sailors took cashew nuts with them to their Indian colonies in the sixteenth century, and India is now the largest exporter of cashews, which are used to enhance many an exotic curry or sauce.

The swollen pedicle on which the cashew is mounted is called an 'apple'. Many Brazilians simply detach the cashew and eat the 'apple' instead.

Most imported cashew nuts have already been roasted and had their outer layer removed since it contains an acrid fluid which produces blisters on contact with the skin. Cashew nuts are most popular as a salted snack.

Savoury nut loaf

50 g (2 oz) raw cashews 50 g (2 oz) raw peanuts
1 bunch spinach well washed and chopped
1 large onion finely chopped
25 g (1 oz) chopped parsley 1 egg
225 g (8 oz) or 1 U.S. cup wholemeal breadcrumbs
½ teaspoon thyme, ¼ teaspoon sage
Pound or coarsely grind the nuts. Steam or cook the spinach and parsley until tender. Purée the mixture until smooth and then beat in the egg. Add the ground nuts, puréed spinach and parsley, wholemeal breadcrumbs, finely chopped onion, and herbs. Shape into an oiled loaf tin. Brush lightly with olive oil. Bake in a moderate oven, 180°C (350°F, Gas Mark 4), for about 25 minutes. For additional protein, sprinkle with cheese during the last 10 minutes of cooking.

Nutritional content

70 g (2½ oz) unsalted cashew nuts contain: 12 g protein, 392 calories, 0.9 g fibre, 2 g linoleic acid, 2.9 mg iron, 29 mg calcium, 242 mg phosphorus, 325 mg potassium, 70 I.U. vitamin A, 0.3 mg B1 (thiamine), 0.1 mg B2 (riboflavin), and 1.2 mg niacin.

Coconut

Coconuts are the stones of the fruits borne by the coconut palm, *Cocos nucifera*, which originated in Malaya and now grows freely in all the tropical regions of the world. It is interesting to note that coconuts have actually spread themselves. The husky nut is very buoyant and can be carried on water currents across the oceans. Coconuts have even been taken by the Gulf Stream from Central America to Norway.

Coconuts have been an important food in the tropics for several thousand years. The Sanskrit name for the coconut palm was *kalpa vriksha* — 'The tree that sustains life'.

The coconut palm fruit provides shelter, food and drink. The fibrous outer skin is made into coir, or coconut matting, the embryo is the food, and the milk it contains makes a refreshing drink. Dried coconut 'meat' is known as copra and is used in margarines, soap, cosmetics and coconut oil.

Nutritional content

50 g (2 oz) shredded coconut contain: 1 g of protein, 274 calories, 2 g of fibre, a trace of linoleic acid, 1 mg iron, 8 mg calcium, 56 mg phosphorus, 176 mg potassium, 0.4 mg niacin, 1 mg vitamin C, plus traces of B1 (thiamine), and B2 (riboflavin).

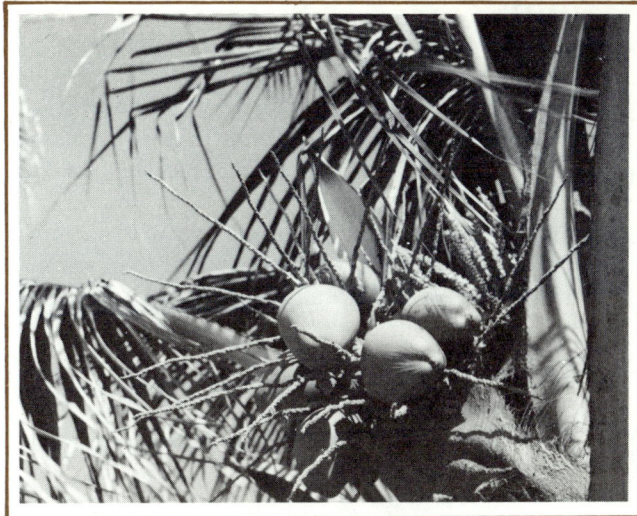

To crack a coconut

First pierce the eye of the coconut with an ice pick or an unused nail. Drain out the milk, then bake the coconut in the oven at a moderate heat — 180°C (350°F, Gas Mark 4) — for about 30 minutes. This will help the shell crack more easily. Tap lightly with a hammer all over the shell. Then use a sharp, pointed knife to prise out the flesh.

Hazelnuts, cob nuts, and filberts

These nuts are closely related members of the Corylus family of small trees which grow wild wherever the climate suits them in Europe, North America, Asia, and the Middle East. The Corylus tree obligingly adapts to many conditions and produces a slightly different nut depending on the climate. Thus, hazelnuts are more common in the U.K., and filberts and cobs more usual in the U.S.A. Spanish hazelnuts are commonly known as Barcelona nuts. Filberts have a longer, more slender shape than cobs or hazelnuts.

Haesil was the Anglo-Saxon word for head-dress, which is a neat description of the way the nut fits inside its cupule or covering.

Most countries today cultivate the species to provide good commercial specimens. Hazelnuts are widely used in chocolate manufacturing, and are an excellent addition to many puddings and sorbets. They are an essential ingredient of Romesco sauce.

Nutritional content

70 g (2½ oz) raw hazelnuts or filberts contain on average: 12 or 13 g protein, 364 calories, 10 g linoleic acid, 2 g fibre, 2 or 3 mg iron, 120 mg calcium, 460 mg phosphorus, 470 mg potassium, 0.46 mg B1 (thiamine), 19 mg niacin, and a trace of vitamin C.

To skin hazelnuts

Hazelnuts, cob nuts and filberts are skinned more easily if they are baked in a moderate oven for about 15 minutes. Let them cool and the outer cases should slip off between the fingers.

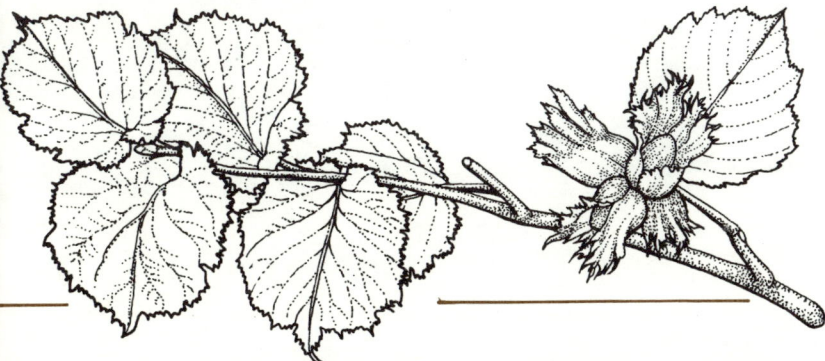

Peanuts

Peanuts are also known as ground nuts but, in spite of their name, they are a legume, the seeds of the annual plant *Arachis hypogae*. They originated in South America where recognizable peanuts have been discovered in Peruvian tombs dating from 950 B.C.

Portuguese explorers took peanuts from Brazil to East Africa in the sixteenth century and at the same time the Spaniards brought them to the Philippines. Peanuts quickly spread throughout the Old World and became an important food.

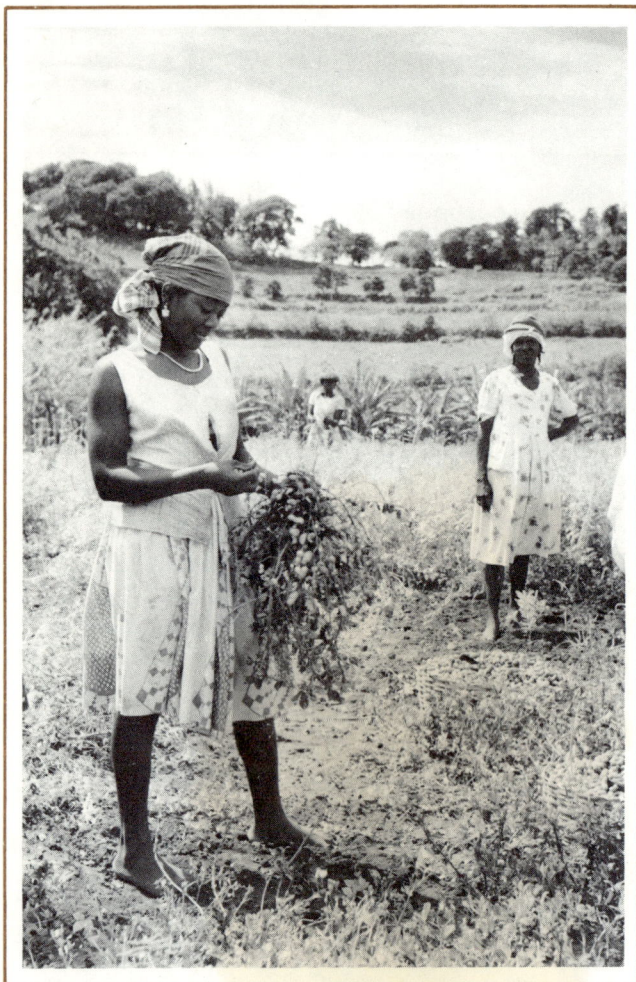

Picking the peanut crop in the Caribbean

Slave traders crammed the holds of their ships with enough peanuts to sustain the captured Africans on the voyage to the coast of America. Any nuts left over were planted out and cropped well enough to start a major industry in the U.S.A. The nuts grow on long tendrils below the ground, hence the name 'ground nuts'. Peanut butter can be a highly nutritious addition to the diet, but unfortunately most commercial nut butters are hydrogenated. Foods that are hydrogenated do not become rancid. However the additional hydrogen renders them useless as essential fatty acids.

Peanut oil also known as Arachis (*See* OILS)

Nutritional content

50 g (2 oz) roasted unsalted peanuts contain 13 g protein, 290 calories 7 g linoleic acid, 1 mg iron, 37 mg calcium, 200 mg phosphorus, 337 mg potassium, 8.6 mg niacin, 0.2 mg B1 (thiamine), and 0.1 B2 (riboflavin), plus 1.35 mg pantothenic acid, and 27 mg biotin.

Peanut butter 50 g (2 oz) peanut butter contain 13 g protein, 284 calories, 7 g linoleic acid, 1 mg iron, 30 mg calcium, 204 mg phosphorus, 337 mg potassium, 7.9 mg niacin, 0.5 mg B1 (thiamine), and 0.1 mg B2 (riboflavin).

Particular value

Peanuts do contain the eight essential amino acids, though some nutritionists consider them an incomplete protein because tryptophan and methionine are present in low amounts. They are rich in linoleic acid which has been shown to reduce the risks of cholesterol deposits. The high calorific value makes peanuts shunned by slimmers but sought by those who need quick protein foods. Peanuts provide a higher proportion of pantothenic acid than any food except liver.

A word of caution Substances in peanuts can under certain circumstances combine with iodine and prevent it from reaching the blood. Common sense is needed here, as in every aspect of food. If you happen to love peanuts, do not eat them every day, and use iodized salt in cooking.

Peanut butter

It is quick and easy to make your own peanut butter. Put one cupful of shelled peanuts, either raw or roasted, into a grinder. Add one or two teaspoons of vegetable oil and a pinch of salt. Grind until crunchy or smooth according to personal taste.

Pecan and hickory nuts

Hickory and pecan nuts are the stones of fruit borne by the Carya family of trees. Pecans are a species of the group and generally considered to be the superior nuts. They are indigenous to the southern states of the U.S.A. and are cultivated commercially in Texas and Oklahoma and transported from there to all over the U.S.A. Increasing amounts of pecans are being exported to Europe.

Hickory nuts grow wild in the northern states of the U.S.A. They are sometimes sold in markets, but more often enjoyed as 'food for free'.

The pecan and the hickory nuts were a vital staple in the North American Indian's diet.

Nut sauce

100 g (4 oz) or 1 U.S. cup ground nuts (any combination)

350 ml (12 fl oz) or 1¾ U.S. cups milk

½ chopped onion

75 g (3 oz) or 1 U.S. cup mushrooms (optional)

Grind or crush the nuts finely (choose hazelnuts, walnuts, brazils, or any combination you wish). Put in an electric blender with the milk and onion and buzz until smooth. Cook the mixture in a pan on top of the stove for about 30 minutes until it thickens. Serve hot with loaves, patties, rissoles, or rice dishes.

(Serves 4)

Nutritional content

56 g (2 oz) raw pecans contain: 5 g protein, 343 calories, 1.1 g fibre, 7 g linoleic acid, 1.2 mg iron, 36 mg calcium, 144 mg phosphorus, 300 mg potassium, 60 I.U. vitamin A, 0.4 mg B1 (thiamine), 0.1 mg B2 (riboflavin), and 0.4 mg niacin.

Pine nuts

Pine nut trees (pignolias) in many parts of the world bear edible seeds inside the hard mosaic casing of the cone. In the U.S.A. pine nuts are known as Indian nuts because the North American Indians used to raid the nests of pack rats which had gathered and stored the nuts for the winter.

The classic pine nut in Europe comes from the stone pine, *Pinus pinea*, which is a native of Italy. It is now cultivated all around the Mediterranean coast where pine nuts are especially popular in cooking. They are used in many Italian meat recipes and in *pesto Genovese*. Pine nuts are also chopped into stuffings, minced meat, aubergine dishes, sweet and sour sauces and rice bases.

The nuts can have a distinctive and pleasant taste, but they need long storing and cooking to dissipate the turpentine flavour. For this reason, pine nuts are always sold commercially as kernels. Northern hemisphere pine nuts in particular have a strong turpentine taste.

Nutritional content

56 g (2 oz) raw unsalted pine nuts contain: 17 g protein, 315 calories, 1 g of fibre, a trace of linoleic acid, 1 mg iron, 10 mg calcium, 56 mg phosphorus, 176 mg potassium, 0.6 mg niacin, with traces of B1 (thiamine) and B2 (riboflavin).

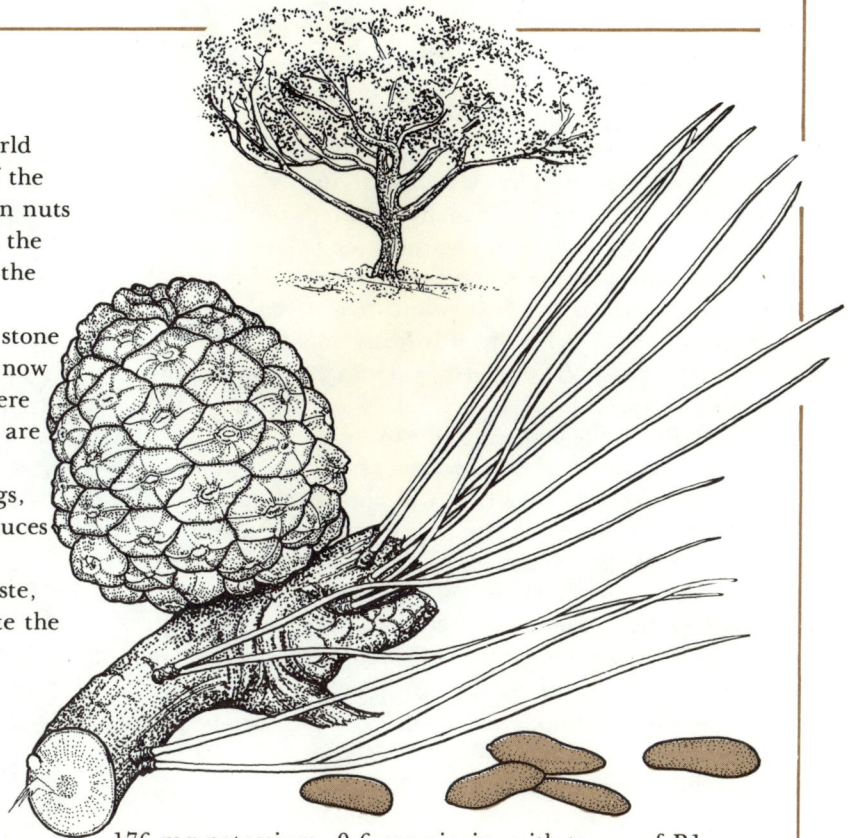

Pistachio nuts

The pistachio is one of the most popular nuts in the U.S.A. today, either eaten raw or mixed into ice-cream, puddings, or cookies. The pistachio is the seed inside the fruit of a small tree called *Pistacia vera* which is a native of Syria.

The famous Roman epicurean (some would call him glutton) Lucius Vitellius developed a passion for pistachio nuts when he was governor of Syria. He had vast amounts of the nuts exported to his native city and the Romans took them to the rest of the known world. Pistachio nuts have been cultivated for thousands of years in Turkey, Syria, Israel, Greece and Italy and huge plantations are now cropped in California and Texas.

These nuts are distinguished by their superb taste and delicate green colour, both of which enhance such

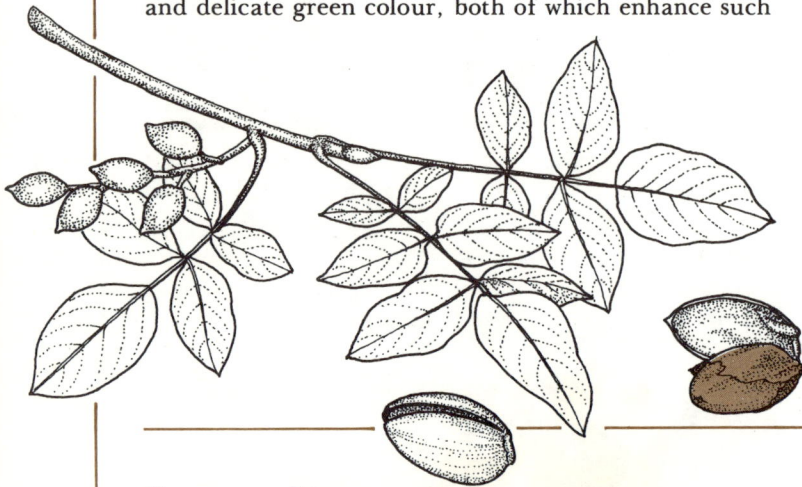

Nut custard

50 g (2 oz) nuts (pistachios, brazils, walnuts, hazelnuts, or any to hand) 3 eggs
350 ml (12 fl oz) or 1½ U.S. cups milk
1 tablespoon honey 1 vanilla pod
Grind or pound the nuts to a fine paste and beat into the milk. Whisk the eggs, add the honey and milk and beat again. Add the vanilla pod and cook in a *bain mairie* in a low oven, 130°C (275°F, Gas Mark 2), for 45 minutes or until it solidifies.

delicacies as halva or locoum (Turkish Delight). They are used to decorate many Western dishes, and also as the main ingredient of numerous Middle Eastern recipes.

Nutritional content

30 g (1 oz) shelled pistachio nuts: 5 g protein, 168 calories, 29 mg calcium, 156 mg phosphorus, 2.5 mg iron, 306 mg potassium, 65 U.I. vitamin A, 0.2 mg B1 (thiamine) and 0.4 mg niacin.

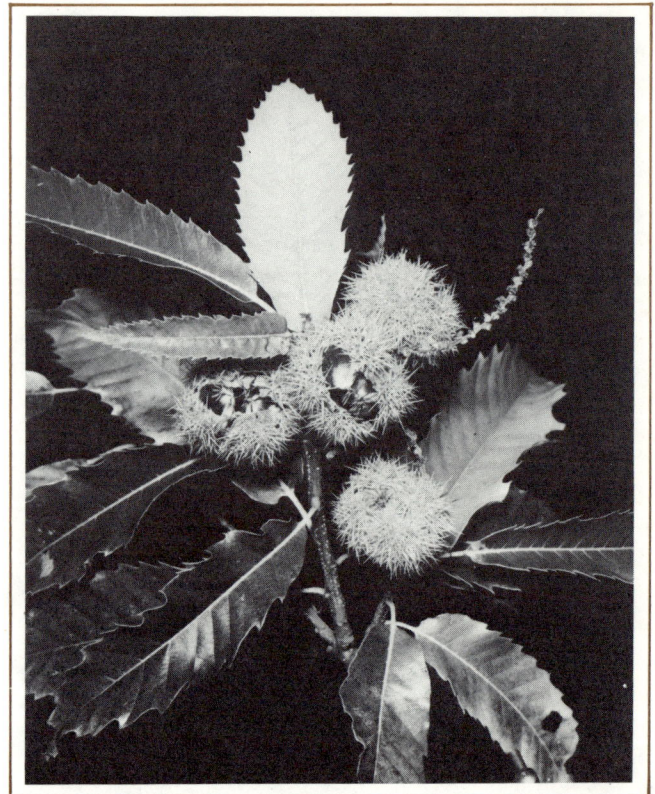

Sweet chestnuts

The sweet chestnut tree, *Castanea sativa*, is a native of the Mediterranean where many hundreds of different varieties grow wild. This chestnut tree belongs to the same family as the oak and beech but should not be confused with the horse chestnut tree, *Aesculus hippocastanum*, whose fruit is really only suitable for squirrels. However, in North America there are three edible varieties of horse chestnut.

The Roman legions carried sweet chestnuts with them beyond the Alps. The trees grow quite happily in colder climates but the fruit will not ripen.

In Britain the sweet chestnut is called the Spanish chestnut because Spain was the traditional source of supply. The quality of chestnuts varies quite considerably. France has developed the highest quality of sweet chestnut commercially, called *marron* (inferior chestnuts are called *châtaignes*). *Marrons* are used exclusively in all imported French chestnut products and *marron glacé*.

In many regions of southern Europe, especially Italy, chestnuts are treated as a daily staple rather than a luxury. The Italians grind them into a flour, *farina dolce*, which is used to make bread and a substantial gruel.

Nutritional content

56 g (2 oz) raw chestnuts contain: 1.5 g protein, 180 calories, 0.8 mg iron, 14 mg calcium, 44 mg phosphorus, 236 mg potassium, 50 I.U. vitamin A, 0.21 mg B1 (thiamine), 0.12 mg B2 (riboflavin), and 0.3 mg niacin.

Storing chestnuts

Chestnuts do not keep well at room temperature. They will keep for a few months in a refrigerator stored in a ventilated container. Whole, shelled chestnuts can be blanched and frozen.

Peeling chestnuts

Bring a pan of water to a rolling boil. Plunge the chestnuts in and immediately turn off the heat. Let the chestnuts stand in the boiling water for two or three minutes. Take them out and allow time for cooling. The skin can then be peeled off with a vegetable knife.

Roasting chestnuts

Slit the outer skin casing on the flat side. Spread each chestnut, flat side up, on a lightly greased baking tray and cook in a hot oven for about 20 minutes. Test for tenderness by prodding with a knife through the slit.

Walnuts

Walnuts are the stones inside the fruits of the *Juglans regia* tree which is of Middle Eastern origin. The Greeks called it 'The Persian tree' and described the nut as 'karyon' (kara meaning head) because it looked like the convolutions of the human brain.

Types of walnuts

European walnuts, also known in the U.S.A. as English walnuts. In Europe itself these walnuts are known as French or Italian walnuts. They are lightish brown nuts which grow all over the Northern Hemisphere. **Black walnuts** are native to North America. They have a pleasant flavour but very hard shells. The Indian tribes gathered the walnuts and stored them carefully as an important food source.

Walnuts are a popular addition to confectionery, or used as a flavouring or topping in many Western dishes. Middle Eastern cooks use walnuts in particularly imaginative ways, such as mature nuts made into delicate stuffings and sauces and the unripe nuts are pickled in vinegar and made into liqueurs. In Europe, walnuts are often incorporated into the local cooking. In Provence walnuts are used in salted cod dishes known as *raito,* and in Italian cooking, in *pesto.*

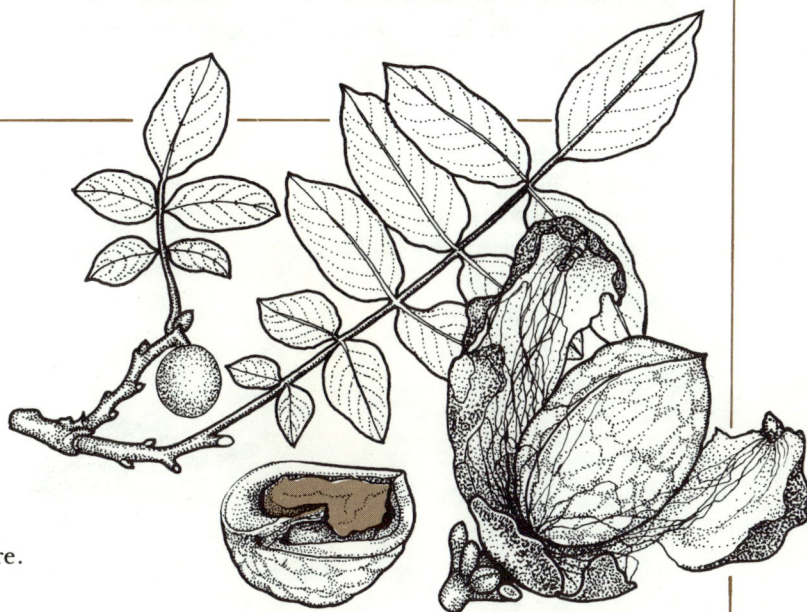

Nutritional content

100 g (3½ oz) English walnuts contain: 14.8 g protein, 586 calories, 2.1 g fibre, 99 mg calcium, 380 mg phosphorus, 3.1 mg iron, 450 mg potassium, 30 I.U. vitamin A, 0.33 mg B1 (thiamine), 0.13 mg B2 (riboflavin), 0.9 mg niacin, and 2 mg vitamin C.
100 g (3½ oz) Black walnuts contain: 20.5 g protein, 589 calories, 1.7 g fibre, traces of calcium, 570 mg phosphorus, 6 mg iron, 460 mg potassium, 300 I.U. vitamin A, 0.22 mg B1 (thiamine), 0.11 mg B2 (riboflavin), 0.9 mg niacin, and 2 mg vitamin C.

Oatmeal

The oat is one of the seven basic food grains and has been used for centuries in the form of oatmeal.

Oatmeal is whole grain that has been rolled or cut into flakes and it is this minimum of preparation without refining or processing that makes it nutritionally superior to the processed, puffed-up breakfast cereals.

Oatmeal marketed as 'instant' or quick cook has usually been pre-heated before being rolled. The larger flaked 'old fashioned' oatmeal which takes a longer time to cook has generally retained more of its value. Some experts consider that steelcut oatmeal has the highest nutritional value.

Nutritional content

Oatmeal is 16.7% protein. It is rich in inositol and has more B1 (thiamine) than any other breakfast cereal. It is rich in iron and phosphorus and has traces of copper, manganese, zinc and potassium.

235 g (8 oz) dry oatmeal contain: 5 g protein, 150 calories, 26 g carbohydrate, 1 g linoleic acid, 1.7 mg iron, 21 mg calcium, 140 mg phosphorus, 142 mg potassium, 508 mg sodium. It contains the following vitamins: 0.2 mg B1 (thiamine), 18 mg niacin, 30 mg inositol.

Particular value

Oatmeal is generally used as porridge or MUESLI in the morning when protein and nutrients are most needed according to some experts. It forms a good value protein when used with milk.

Types of oatmeal

There are three basic kinds of oatmeal: quick cook or rolled, which generally has small flakes; hulled or gritted oatmeal, and steelcut oatmeal. Steelcut oats have not undergone the high temperatures required when oats are rolled. Hulled or gritted oatmeal has not been heated at all during processing. Both these forms are considered superior.

Scots porridge

There is an old tradition on the west coast of Scotland that porridge is good for the eyes. The old crofter's diet consisted mainly of oats in porridge for breakfast and oats in oatbread with CHEESE for supper. It is now known that inositol, one of the B complex vitamins, is found in high concentration in the lens of the eye and heart. Oatmeal, together with MOLASSES, WHEAT and CORN, provides the richest source of this vitamin.

Oils

Fats are oils which are solid at room temperature. When fats are eaten they are broken down into glycerol and fatty acids. The body can manufacture all of the fatty acids from sugar, except linoleic acid, arachidonic acid and linolenic acid. These three acids are called the essential fatty acids. Linoleic acid is one of the most neglected items in our diets.

Corn oil (maize oil)

This grain has been pressed for its oil ever since the Peruvians began cultivation many thousands of years ago. Corn oil is semi-drying and is the softest, most unsaturated of all the grains.

The oil is high in linoleic acid containing up to 53% and also amounts of oleic, linolenic and arachidic acids too. Corn is also an excellent source of phosphorus and the fat-soluble vitamins A, D, and E.

Extraction of corn oil

It is relatively easy to extract. The oil is separated by centrifugal force with the help of water and during the process lecithin can be separated and sold alone as granules.

The oil has been found to correct the over-alkalinity of the body system and restore it to the correct acid balance. Dr Jarvis (*See* APPLE-CIDER VINEGAR *page* 62) and other doctors recommend it in cases of bad eczema type skin disorders. As a corrective, corn oil can be taken by the spoonful or applied directly to the skin.

Corn oil and medicine

Corn oil is a popular addition to margarine and other foods. As a cooking medium it is light and easily digested and stores well in a cool dark place.

Olive oil

The sunbaked olive groves of the Mediterranean countries have become woven into ancient literature. Homer and Pliny praised the virtues of olive oil and Hippocrates regarded it as a food and medicine. The Hebrews used olive oil in their sacred anointing ceremonies and regarded the olive as a symbol of prosperity.

Although olive oil comes low in the linoleic acid chart, it does have other benefits that make it important. The rich oleic acid content (80%) makes olive oil completely digestible. It has been found to increase the absorption of the fat soluble vitamins, A, D, E, and K.

Olives are also easy to press and release their oil without heat or chemical action. The finest grade olive oil therefore contains the fewest impurities of any vegetable oil.

Extraction of olive oil

Virgin oil is sometimes called lucca oil. The first cold pressing of the olives produces the best and most expensive oil. It may have a greenish tinge and a rich scent.

Grades 1 and 2 olive oil are the normal edible oils in which cold-pressed oil is blended with hydraulic extractions.

Sulfide The pulp that remains after the first few pressings is treated with chemical solvents to get this commercial grade.

Olive oil in cooking

Some nutritionists advise combining olive oil with one high in linoleic acid, such as safflower, to get a really beneficial salad oil and cooking medium.

97

Peanut oil

Known as arachis oil or ground nut oil.

Until about twenty years ago peanut oil was not rated high among the nutritious oils. Realizing that peanuts contain the essential amino acids and many valuable minerals and vitamins, botanists began to improve the species to obtain the best possible oil.

Peanut oil has a high content of oleic acid of up to 60%, and linoleic acid of 35%. It is non-drying and will keep liquid at room temperature. The more liquid oils like peanut and corn tend to have less linoleic acid.

How peanut oil is extracted

The method of extraction is particularly important to the value of peanut oil. The most beneficial oil comes from cold pressing. Another, sometimes cheaper way, is to use chemical solvents. The oil is then refined and heated and treated with anti-oxidants. At present the manufacturer is not obliged to state what method he uses. However, if the oil is cold pressed it is likely to state so on the bottle as this is both more expensive and more sought after.

Peanut oil in cooking

It has a bland taste and stores very well in cool conditions. Peanut does not cloud over like some other oils and may be clarified and used time and time again.

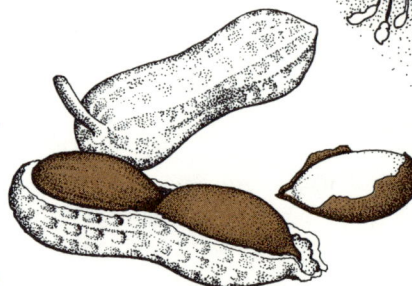

Peanut oil in medicine

Tests at the University of Vienna seem to indicate that peanut oil is an aid to the transportation of adrenalin around the body. It has laxative properties and may be safely used by diabetics. Research by the U.S. Department of Agriculture is now being carried out into the treatment of haemophilia with peanut oil.

Safflower oil

Many people confuse the safflower with the sunflower and regard the oils as interchangeable. In fact, the plants are quite different although they are both members of the *Compositae* family. Safflower oil tops the list of oils containing linoleic acid having up to 80%, sunflower coming second with up to 65%.

Safflowers were cultivated by ancient civilizations along the Nile and down into Ethiopia. The Arabs adopted the cultivation of this tall, thistle-like flower.

Extraction of safflower oil

Each seed contains up to half of its own weight in oil, and extraction should be an easy matter were it not for the hard shiny husk. The seed has therefore to be husked, or decorticated. It can then be pressed with powerful hydraulic machines and sometimes chemical solvents are used. Until the law on labelling is changed the only way to find out which method of pressing has been used is to check with the supplier.

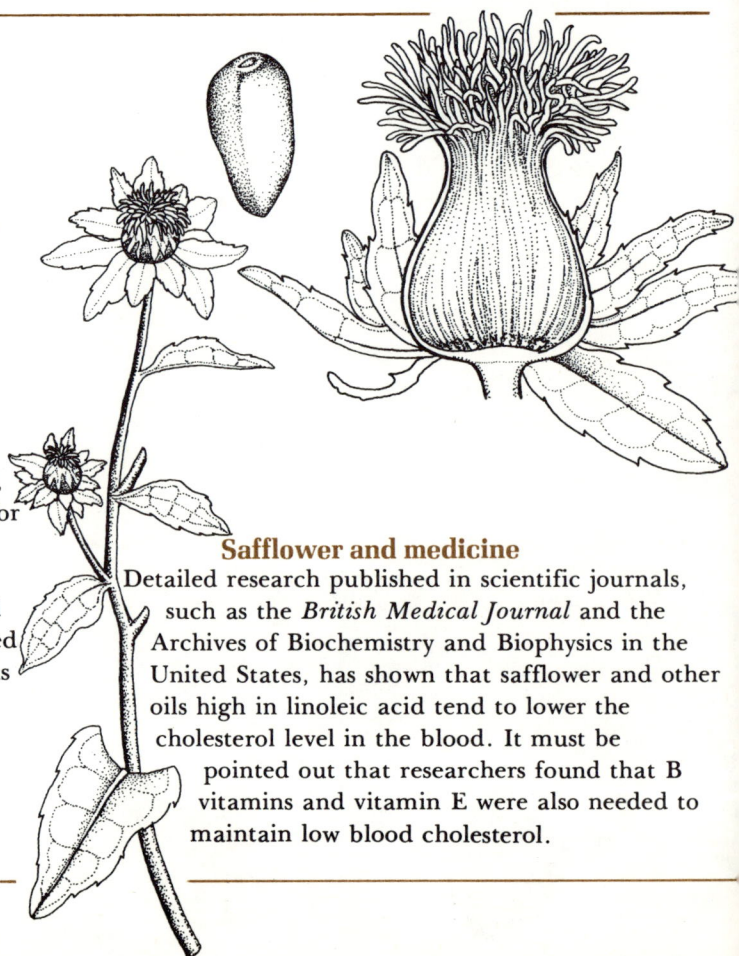

Safflower and medicine

Detailed research published in scientific journals, such as the *British Medical Journal* and the Archives of Biochemistry and Biophysics in the United States, has shown that safflower and other oils high in linoleic acid tend to lower the cholesterol level in the blood. It must be pointed out that researchers found that B vitamins and vitamin E were also needed to maintain low blood cholesterol.

Sesame oil

Sesame oil is also known as Gingelly oil or Benne oil and has been used in cooking in Africa and the Far East for many centuries. The main advantage of sesame over other oils is that it does not turn rancid, even in hot weather. For this reason it is very popular in tropical countries, Australia and the U.S.A.

It contains about 40% linoleic acid and 50% oleic acid, plus a good amount of lecithin.

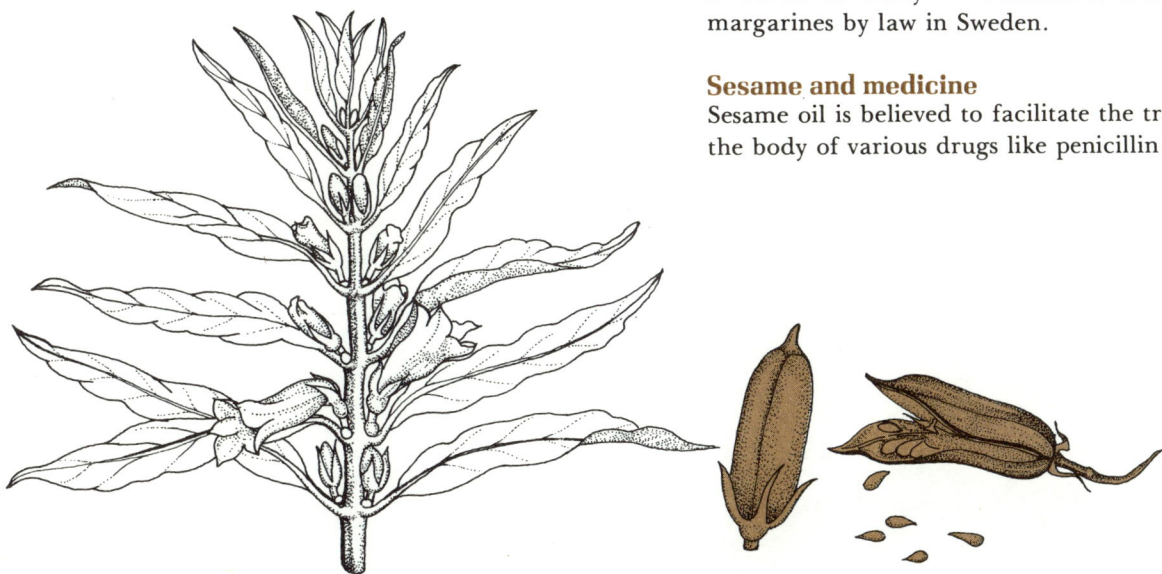

Grades and extraction of sesame

As there are no husks to be taken off sesame seeds, the extraction of the oil is extremely simple. Top grade oil is obtained in a single cold-pressing and is a clear, pale yellow colour.

The seed pulp is then heated and two further pressings are made under hydraulic pressure. This yields a much darker, inferior oil.

Analysis has revealed that an ingredient called sesamol is responsible for keeping the oil stable and free from rancidity. This substance is added to all margarines by law in Sweden.

Sesame and medicine

Sesame oil is believed to facilitate the transport through the body of various drugs like penicillin.

Sunflower oil

The sunflower seed has a linoleic acid content second only to safflower; almost half of the seed is made up of molecules of oil. It also contains oleic and palmitic acids.

Seeds grown in hot countries contain the least amount of linoleic acid. Those from Africa can have as little as 20% linoleic acid, while those from Russia can have up to 70%. An average amount would be 60% linoleic acid and 30% oleic acid. Sunflower oil is also rich in vitamin E — 25 g (1 oz) of seeds yields 10 mg tocopherols, — and components of vitamin E are present, as are good amounts of vitamins A and D.

Medicinal value

Like the other oils high in linoleic acid, sunflower can limit the risk of disorders from cholesterol deposits in the blood vessels. Many naturopathic doctors believe it also helps the formation of healthy tissue and generally aids resistance to disease. Sunflower oil is used also as a diuretic, and so benefits some kidney complaints.

Papaya

Biological name *Carica papaya*; popular names Pawpaw, The Medicine Tree, The Melon Tree.
The dusky melon-like papaya is the source of many tropical legends. This plant is such a powerful healer that it is known as The Medicine Tree in parts of Africa and the Caribbean.

The fruit hang under a crown of leaves on the *Carica papaya* tree which grows to about 6 m (20 ft). The leaves can grow to 60 cm (2 ft) wide and also have curative qualities.

Originally, male and female flowers were produced on separate plants, but now horticulturalists have produced a hermaphrodite variety. This has been introduced to the tropical parts of the United States.

In his book *Nature's Medicines* Richard Lucas describes how the early explorers were greatly impressed by the papaya fruit. Christopher Columbus observed that the natives of the Caribbean could eat exceptionally indigestible food without any distress if the meal included papaya. Marco Polo actually credited the fruit with saving his sailors' lives when they fell ill with scurvy — papaya does have a good vitamin C content. Magellan also recognized that papaya was a most important element of the diet and Vasco da Gama called it The Golden Tree of Life.

Many travellers have noticed that the toughest meat could be tenderized by being wrapped in papaya leaves and also that people from Africa and the Caribbean use the papaya fruit very much as a medicine chest: using it to treat wounds and sores, carbuncles and burns, stomach ailments, diarrhoea, earaches and enlarged livers.

Modern medical science has found many reasons why the papaya is so effective.

Nutritional content

Papaya is an excellent source of vitamin A, a good source of vitamin C and potassium, and contains amounts of calcium, iron, phosphorus, and niacin.

Half a medium fresh papaya (about 200 g or 7 oz) contains: 1 g protein, 75 calories, 18 g carbohydrate, 1.6 g fibre, 3500 I.U. vitamin A, 112 mg vitamin C, 0.6 mg niacin, 0.5 mg iron, 32 mg phosphorus, 470 mg potassium, 40 mg calcium, and 6 mg sodium.

Medical value of papaya

The unripe fruit contains a powerful enzyme called papain. This protein-digesting enzyme resembles pepsin in action and so has an excellent effect on digestion.

The juice is collected from the fruits while they are still on the tree and dried at low temperatures. It is made into tablets which are sold around the world for many stomach disorders.

Papain also has blood clotting properties and doctors have used it effectively to stop bleeding. For the actual medical application of papaya *See page* 17.

All parts of the fruit have curative qualities. The leaves contain an alkaloid called carpaine which has the same effect on the heart as digitalis. The seeds contain the glucoside caricin.

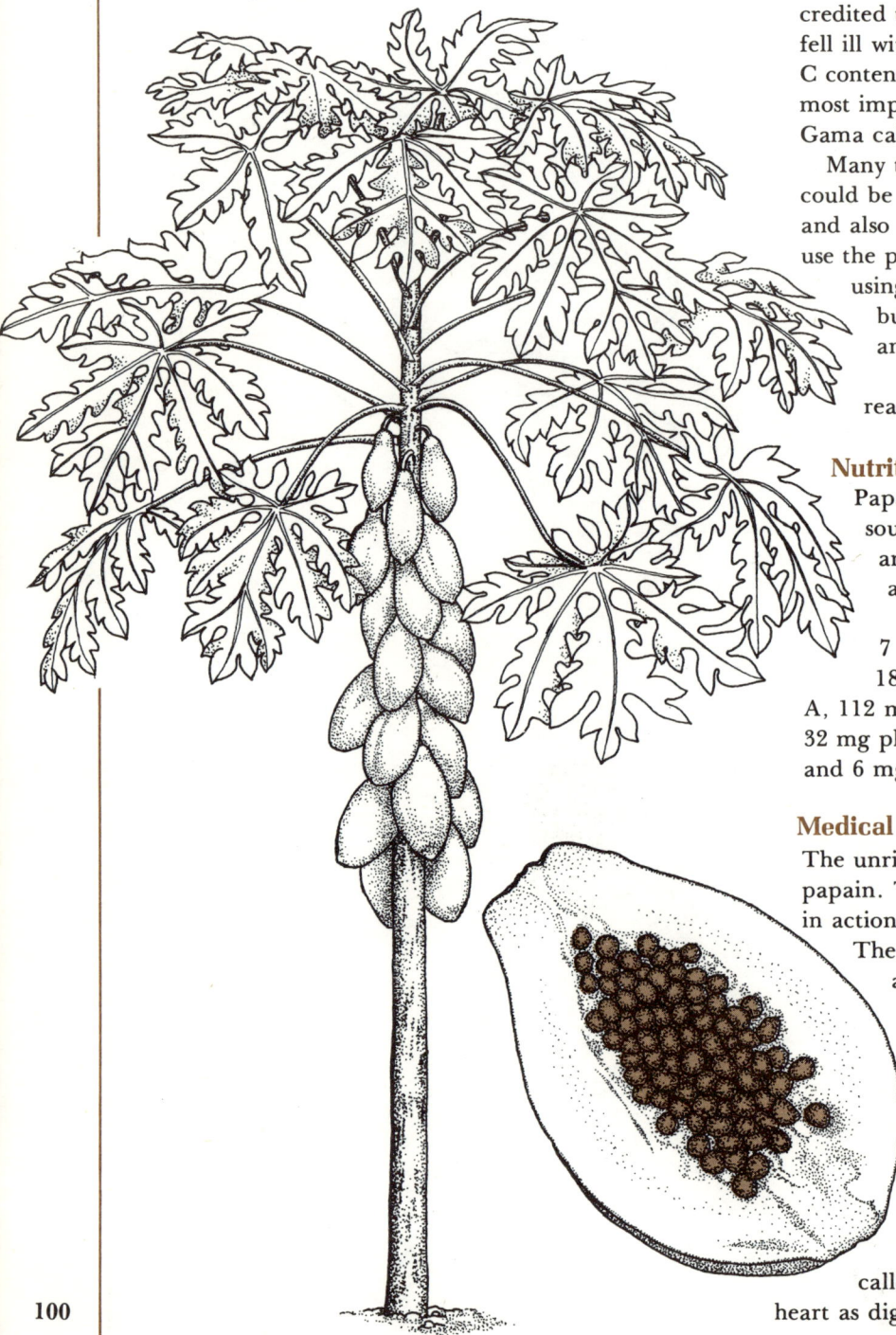

They dispel flatulence and aid menstrual disorders. Seed juice is prescribed by naturopaths for dyspepsia, piles and certain disorders of the liver. The seeds are ground into a paste for cases of ringworm. The ripe fruit also has a beneficial action on digestion. It is helpful in certain liver and spleen disorders and corrects both constipation and diarrhoea.

Papaya as a tenderizer

The enzyme papain also acts on meat tissues and makes them more tender. In the U.S.A. it is standard practice to inject animals in the slaughter house with this enzyme. Commercially, the latex or pulp of the fruit is sold as a tenderizer in powder or granule form, which can be sprinkled on meat.

How to use papaya

The papaya is a delicious fruit and should be served as often as possible. Although the ripe fruit contains only minute amounts of the enzyme papain it does act favourably on the digestion. In tropical countries papaya seeds are dried, ground and used as a spice. Many people chew the large black seeds to aid digestion and simply because they like the taste. The seeds have a mildly pungent taste rather like mustard and cress. Papaya can be liquidized and drunk as a juice. However, it does have a tendency to butyrye

Papaya plantation in Hawaii

fermentation, but this can be corrected by adding a small amount of glycerine.

Note: Papaya should not be confused with the custard apple *Asimina triloba* of the U.S.A. which is also called Pawpaw.

Pasta

There is a deep-seated tradition that Marco Polo introduced pasta to Italy after his journeys in China. Perhaps this is due to the similarity between pasta and noodles, as the Chinese had perfected the long, thin noodle many centuries before. Both noodles and pasta are basically made with a 'paste' of flour and water.

Marco Polo

There is another legend that an Italian sailor persuaded his Chinese mistress to show him how to make noodles. Then with Italian flair he rolled the paste into bigger and wider rolls, and pasta was born. Whatever the true story, by the Middle Ages Italian cooks were devoting much of their artistry to pasta in its various forms, especially macaroni.

In the sixteenth century a leading Genoese doctor denounced the over-eating of pasta and a hundred years later the French led a campaign against the 'gluttony of pasta'. The Italians took no notice whatsoever and soon Italian influence of pasta-type foods spread to England and France. The Renaissance made Italy the cultural centre of Europe and it became the most important stop on the Grand Tour for the English aristocracy. Young, rich popinjays who aped the Italian style and manners back in England were known as 'macaronis'.

Types of pasta

There are about 150 major varieties of pasta, cut in every imaginable shape. The most important sorts are macaroni, spaghetti, lasagne, tagliatelle, canneloni, vermicelli, tortellini, and rigatoni. Ravioli are squares of pasta stuffed with meat or other fillings. Traditionally, all pasta is made from durum wheat. The endosperm or starchy layer is ground into a fine flour. Semolina is made from the same wheat, but not so finely ground.

The addition of eggs to the basic mixture was originally a regional variation, but now, many factory-made pastas have eggs added as a matter of course. The packet of pasta states this clearly — *al uovo* (with egg).

Spinach is a popular ingredient to many types of pasta, particularly *lasagne*. The product is then sold as *lasagne verde* (green lasagne).

Wholewheat pasta

Many specialist wholefood manufacturers are now producing good ranges of pasta. The difference is that they take the entire grain and grind it to provide a fine flour. As a result, 100% wholewheat pasta contains more vitamins and minerals than regular pasta. The inclusion of the bran gives it five times as much cereal fibre as the usual pasta. Wholewheat products need cooking a little longer, but taste equally delicious.

How to cook pasta

Allow 75-100 g (3-4 oz) of pasta for each person. Always cook in plenty of boiling water — at least 1.2 litres (2 pints) or 5 U.S. cups of water for each 100 g (4 oz) of pasta. A teaspoon of vegetable oil added during the cooking process will help keep the strands of spaghetti separated.

Home-made pasta

Pasta is not very difficult to make at home. You need a long rolling pin and an extra large pastry board.

450 g (1 lb) wholemeal flour

2 or 3 eggs

1 teaspoon salt

4 tablespoons water

Elizabeth David, in her book *Italian Food*, gives the following very clear description of how to make pasta:

Pour the flour in a mound on the board, make a well in the middle, and break in the eggs. Add a good teaspoonful of salt and 4 tablespoonsful of water.

Fold the flour over the eggs and proceed to knead with your hands until the eggs and flour are amalgamated and the paste can be formed into a ball. Having obtained a fairly solid consistency, you continue to knead the paste on the board, holding it with one hand while you roll it away from you with the other, with the heel of the palm.

During the process, flour your hands and the board from time to time. After about 10 minutes the dough should have the right somewhat elastic consistency. Divide it into two halves. Now roll out the first half, wrapping it round the rolling pin, stretching it each time a little more. After each turn round the rolling pin sprinkle flour over the paste; if it is not quite dry it will stick to the board and the rolling pin and get torn. After the operation has been repeated nine or ten times the paste is very thin and greatly enlarged but when you think it is thin enough you will still have to roll it out two or three times more until it is transparent enough for the graining of the wooden board to be visible through it. It will be like a piece of material, and can be picked up exactly as if it were a cloth, laid on a table or over the back of a chair while the other half of the dough is being rolled. Having finished the second half of the dough, both sheets can be left for 30 minutes. Each one is then rolled up lightly, like a newspaper, and cut, with a sharp knife, across into strips rather less than $\frac{1}{2}$ cm ($\frac{1}{4}$ in) wide. Spread the strips all out on a cloth or a flat basket and leave them until it is time to cook them. All that has to be done is to drop them into a large deep pan full of boiling salted water. As soon as they rise to the top, in about 5-7 minutes, they are ready. Drain them, put them into a heated dish with a generous lump of butter, and serve them as hot as possible, either with more butter and plenty of Parmesan cheese or with any of the sauces for pasta.

Fibre-rich wholemeal pasta drying in an English factory

Rice

Rice has been a staple part of the diet for thousands of years in Asia, China, Africa, South America, Spain and Italy. It is now estimated that more rice is eaten than any other cereal.

Rice has a similar structure to WHEAT. When it is milled the outer layers are removed and valuable nutrients lost. It was through rice that the first clue to vitamin B was found. When the Japanese navy adopted polished rice on board ship thousands of sailors died of beri-beri. In 1897, in Java, Dr Eijkman proved that men who ate unpolished rice did not get beri-beri. He concluded that something in the outer layers of the grain prevented this. The American Dr Robert Runnels Williams was the first to extract vitamin B1 (thiamine) in an oil from the rice bran and he fed it to a child in Manila who was dying of beri-beri. The child revived quickly and Dr Williams was awarded the American Chemical Society's Gold Medal. He told the Society: 'Man commits a crime against nature when he eats the starch from the seed and throws away the mechanism necessary for the metabolism of that starch.'

Types of rice

Rice comes in many shapes and sizes, from the long grain of Patna to the chunky Carolina grain.
Brown rice Only the indigestible husks have been removed.

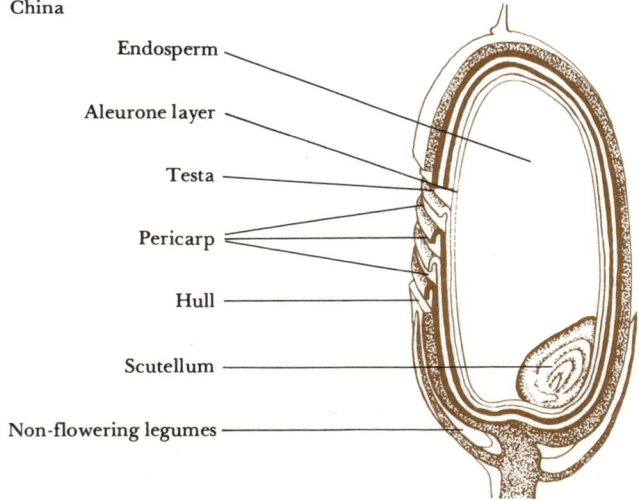

Rice terraces cut out of the hillside by the Tientai Commune in China

Endosperm
Aleurone layer
Testa
Pericarp
Hull
Scutellum
Non-flowering legumes

White rice has the husk, germ and outer layers removed. Often as a final part of the process the grains are passed between powerful rollers and polished with glucose or talc to a gleaming white. Sometimes this retails as *polished rice*. This process takes away much of the protein, almost all of the B vitamins, and most of the minerals.

Rice flakes are processed rice, power-flaked for quick and easy cooking.

Converted rice The unmilled grain is treated with steam under pressure which forces the vitamins to be carried to the centre of the grain. It can then be milled without loss of too many nutrients. Converted rice is recommended by the American nutritionist Adelle Davis.

Rice polish consists of the bran removed when the rice is milled. It is an outstanding source of the B vitamins and can be worked into cookies, muffins, rolls, waffles, pancakes, or used as an extender, for instance in meat loaf.

Rice flour is made from the by-products of the milling process, including some bran, ground into a fine powder. Rich in B vitamins.

Wild rice For centuries the North American Indians harvested the wild rice (sometimes called mahnomen) growing along the low lying Minnesota lakes area. Today, under a State Statute, the wild rice must still be hand harvested. Some firms now grow the grain commercially in artificial ponds. Wild rice is considered a gourmet's delight and retails at very high prices. In fact, it is not related at all to the other rice, being quite a different botanical species. Nutritionally, wild rice is superior, containing twice the protein of refined white rice, six times more B1 (thiamine), six times more B3, six times the amount of iron, and 20 times more B2 (riboflavin). The Gourmet Club of Britain describes wild rice as 'more filling and less fattening' than ordinary rice.

Nutritional content

The U.S. Department of Agriculture has listed these approximate values:

	grams	Protein mg	Calories	Iron mg	Calcium mg	Phosphorus mg	Potassium mg	B1 thiamine mg	Niacin mg
Brown rice	208	15	748	4	78	608	310	0.6	9.2
Converted	187	14	677	1.6	53	244	300	0.3	7.6
*White	191	14	692	1.6	46	258	247	t	1.6
*Rice flakes	30	2	115	0.5	9	44	60	0.1	1.7
Rice polish	50	6	132	8	35	553	357	0.9	14

*It is important to note that in these samples the white rice and flakes have been 'enriched' with vitamin B1 (thiamine), niacin and iron. Even so, it is clear that unprocessed rice is far richer in these nutrients.

To cook rice

Rice is enormously flexible and is a good base for imaginative meals. There is quite an art in cooking rice so that each grain is separate and firm, not a soggy mass.

A very simple method is to allow one cup of rice to one and a half cups of water. (Brown and wholegrain rice will need two cups of water.) Bring to the boil, add a pinch of salt, and immediately turn heat down to lowest possible and put a tight-fitting lid on. Depending on the type of rice, about 20 to 40 minutes later, all the water will be absorbed and the grains whole and ready to eat.

Salt (common salt)

Salt is of fundamental importance to animal life. All body fluids contain common salt (sodium chloride) which is a mineral essential for life. The valuable properties of salt were soon realized. Its white granules preserve meat and fish and disinfect wounds and sores.

Over the centuries, salt has assumed great importance. The ancient Egyptians and Chinese worshipped it as a 'giver of life'. Logically they reasoned that salt preserved food to sustain them when times were hard such as in winter when many would have died from starvation.

Salt fish was the standard food of the Greek workers, and the Romans became highly skilled at mining salt and evaporating it from the sea. The authorities often put high taxes on this valuable commodity and as a result salt was often adulterated with clay and chalk. This may have prompted the image in the Bible when Jesus says to the Disciples: 'Ye are the salt of the earth; but if the salt have lost his savour, wherewith shall it be salted?'

Salt has also become synonymous with worthiness and good faith. To clinch an agreement an Arab will say: 'There has been salt between us.' In the Middle Ages in England, where high ranking people sat at the top of the table, lower orders sat 'below the salt'. A

Salt lake in the Galapagos

thoroughly worthy person is still called 'salt of the earth'.

The vital balance of salt in the body

Sodium and potassium are finely balanced and act together in the body. Each person has precise requirements for sodium together with potassium and the balance between the two in the body fluids maintains the osmotic pressure in a state of equilibrium inside and outside the cells. Sodium and potassium are also required to assist in the working of the body's neuro-muscular system.

It is the concentration of the sodium salts in the body fluids that is vital and the kidneys act as the basic regulator excreting water or salt as required.

How much salt do you need?

The individual requirements for salt can be worked out largely by common sense.

According to *The Manual of Nutrition* published in London by H.M.S.O., the amount of salt needed by an adult each day is about 4 g in a temperate climate. 'Such an intake can be achieved from salt already in food, but most people add more and take in from five to twenty grams.'

A recent U.S. Senate Select Committee on Nutrition

A stockpile of salt at the salt lakes in the Camargue, France

and Human Needs advised the reduction of salt intake to 3 g a day. From this it becomes clear that many people perhaps unwittingly maintain a very high sodium intake. To a large extent this is determined by the food processors since salt and other sodium compounds are added to most processed food. The 3 or 4 g of salt recommended by the British and U.S. authorities is actually equivalent to a present day hospital low-sodium diet.

A person living in a very hot climate or doing heavy manual work in the blazing sun will obviously need more salt than an office worker in Norway but day to day adjustments have to be made, such as when the office worker is digging in his garden on a hot Saturday. He may then perspire 4 g of salt through his skin in three hours.

The effect of too much salt

Too much salt overloads the system with sodium, disturbing its balance with potassium and predisposing a person to high blood pressure and arthritis, among many disorders.

Research has established a correlation between high sodium diets and high blood pressure. In Japan the diet is high in salted fish and the major cause of death is from strokes caused by high blood pressure. In the U.S.A. Dr L.K. Dahl has for a long time researched the relationship of salt to high blood pressure. He has found that the greater the salt intake, the more numerous the deaths from hypertension.

Food manufacturers throughout the world had to reduce the sodium content of baby foods when it was proved that infant kidney failure resulted from the high salt levels.

Too much sodium can cause the displacement of potassium from the body. Without potassium, glucose cannot be changed into energy. Water retention and muscle damage can also result from this imbalance. Patients with certain kidney and liver disorders are recommended by their doctors to adopt a low-sodium diet.

Achieving the balance

In the light of the latest findings, eminent authorities are advising a much lower salt intake than previously. There is certainly a case for each person to monitor the daily intake of salt.

Some food itself contains a high salt level. If you happen to be fond of bacon and follow it up with a bowl of cornflakes, then spread some toast with YEAST EXTRACT, you have already consumed about 1500 mg of salt.

It is important to be aware of the amount of salt present in various foods. Look at the labels on cans and packets of processed food, most of which contain salt or other sodium compounds. So does drinking water and the four hundred or so additives in our food. It is easy to see how the average person achieves 20 g a day.

Types of salt

Table salt Usually water is pumped into underground salt mines and the resulting brine vacuum dried. Table salt is ground fine for smooth running and often starch, phosphate of lime and other substances are added.

Rock salt is another name for land salt as it occurs in rock veins below the ground.

Crystal salt can be either mined or sea salt in the form of largish crystals. It is generally salt only with no additives. Some gourmets think that crystal salt, ground the moment before eating, has a superior flavour.

Sea salt is obtained by evaporating sea water in enclosed areas. It has a distinctive flavour and is recommended by many health experts because it has a high iodine content. It is, however, becoming increasingly difficult to find unpolluted seas. For this reason, some health food suppliers such as Harmony are returning to mining the rock salt laid down when the prehistoric seas covered the earth.

Iodized salt is generally table salt to which potassium iodide has been added. Leading nutritionists recommend this for regular use.

Salt substitutes are readily available from all specialist stores.

Seeds

Pumpkin seeds

In China the pumpkin is called the 'Emperor of the Garden' and has become the symbol of fruitfulness. The name comes from the Greek word *pepon* which means 'cooked in the sun'.

The pumpkin is a member of the gourd family and native of Asia. It grows on a vine up to 6 m (20 ft) high and the gourd swells to 60-90 cm (2-3 ft) across.

Nutritional content

Pumpkins are richer in iron than any other seed and very high in phosphorus. They are a good source of many B vitamins and contain a small amount of calcium and vitamin A; they are also 30% protein and 40% fat which is rich in unsaturated fatty acids. 100 g (3½ oz) pumpkin seeds contain: 29 g protein, 387 calories, 190 I.U. vitamin A, 9 mg vitamin C, traces of B2, B3, and B6, and 11.2 mg iron.

Medicinal value

The use of pumpkin seeds is well documented in old herbals for the treatment of prostate disorders. Recently, Dr W. Devrient of Berlin researched the effect of pumpkin on the prostate gland. He concluded that it contains a native plant hormone 'which affects our own hormone production':

Dr Devrient here explains how the prostate gland becomes swollen with age.

My assertion of the androgen-hormonal (the male hormone) influence of pumpkin seeds is based on . . . my own personal observations throughout the years. This plant has scientifically determined effects on intermediary metabolism and diuresis (urination), but these are of secondary importance in relation to its regenerative, invigorative and vitalizing influence.

Tests by Dr G. Klein at the University of Vienna revealed the healing power of pumpkin seeds in many bladder and urinary disorders.

Pumpkin seed has been used for centuries as an effective taeniafuge — that is, a remedy that expels tapeworms and is noted for this according to the recent issue of Potter's *New Cyclopaedia of Botanical Drugs and Preparations*.

Hull-less pumpkin seeds

A new species of pumpkin seed has been developed by the U.S. Agricultural Research Service (ARS) that has no shells or husks. It has the delightful name of Lady Godiva. The flesh of these pumpkins is rather tough for use in pumpkin pie, but ARS states: 'further research is underway to combine the naked-seed characteristics with good eating quality found in the flesh of other pumpkin varieties'. These pumpkins are available in many seed catalogues. (*See* WHERE TO BUY *page* 152)

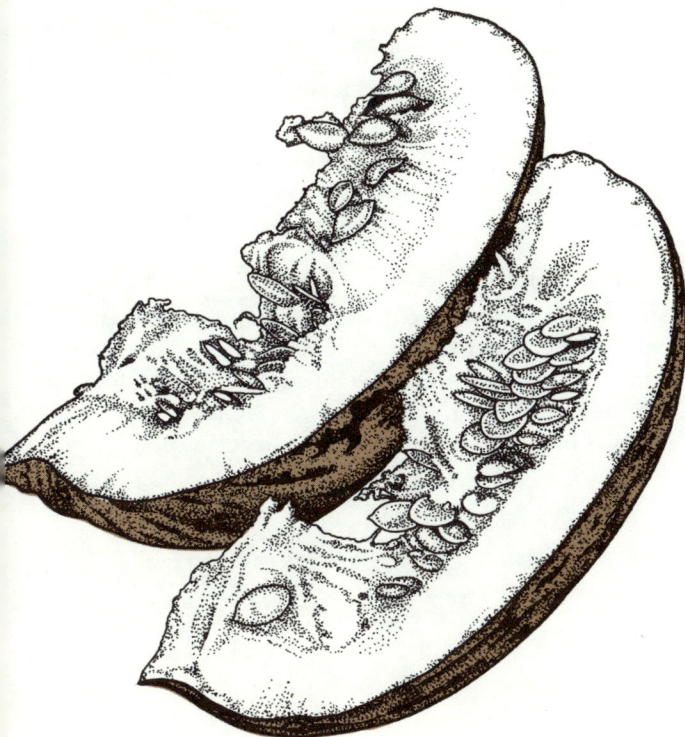

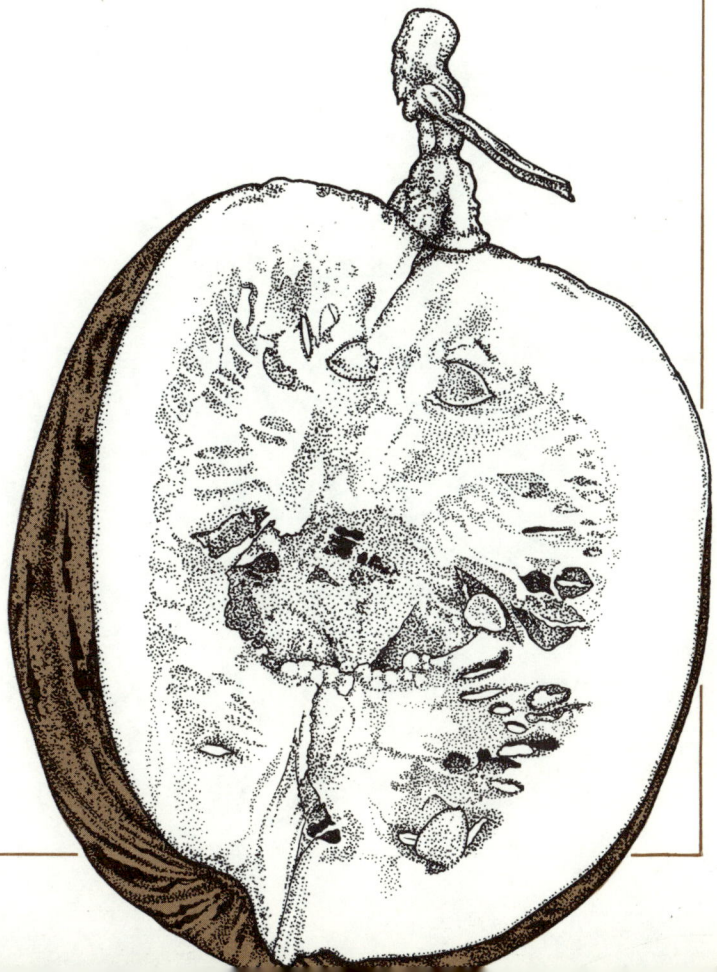

Sesame seeds

In Hindu mythology the god Yama blessed the sesame seed and it has since become regarded throughout the East as a symbol of immortality.

Sesame seeds come from an attractive annual plant which is not difficult to grow, but which until recently has been difficult to harvest as the plant literally broadcasts the seeds when they are ripe. Research has produced a non-scattering variety and sesame is now grown around the world as an important food crop.

Nutritional content

The seeds are packed with vitamins and minerals, calcium, iron and protein. The mucilage content provides soothing qualities, and the lecithin lowers the level of cholesterol.

50 g (2 oz) dry sesame seeds contain: 9 g protein, 280 calories, 10 g of linoleic acid, 5.2 mg iron, 580 mg calcium, 308 mg phosphorus, 360 mg potassium, 30 mg sodium, 15 I.U. vitamin A, 14 mg B1, 1 mg B2 (riboflavin), 2.7 mg niacin, plus good amounts of lecithin, inositol, and choline.

Tahini

Both Turkey and the Arab countries use this delicious creamy paste made from sesame seeds as part of their staple diet. It has the high nutritive value of the seeds and oil in concentrated form. It is quite easy to make with a blender:

Tahini

225 g (8 oz) or 1 U.S. cup sesame seeds
100 ml (4 fl oz) or ½ U.S. cup water
1 garlic clove
2 tablespoons sesame oil
sprinkle salt
juice of half a lemon

Put the seeds in the blender and grind to a powder fine. Add water, chopped garlic, and lemon juice. Blend again.

Add the salt and sesame oil and blend until quite smooth. The amount of water required will vary quite a lot depending on the age and type of seeds. Add the amount required to achieve a creamy consistency. Use tahini as a spread on sandwiches or a sauce with vegetables as the Arabs do.

Tahini butter

Blend the sesame seeds to the same consistency as peanut butter and add a few drops of sesame oil.

Halva is a traditional sweet made from sesame seeds. It is sold in delicatessens but may contain white sugar or preservative.

Sesame crunch

Nutritious sweet can be quickly blended with sesame seeds. Switch the blender on and off until the seeds are medium ground. Spread the powder and carefully mix in honey until a stiff consistency is obtained. Stir in sultanas or raisins and form into 'sweet' shapes.

Sunflower seeds

The great golden face of the tall sunflower turns on an axis to follow the sun around the sky from East to West, pivoting like a radio telescope. It became the mystic symbol of several primitive peoples, notably the Incas who worshipped the sun.

The North American Indians appreciated the medicinal value of the beautiful flower and they cultivated large crops, propagating the seed from wild sunflowers beyond the Mississippi. The Indians used the leaves as animal food; the petals were brewed into a distinctive yellow dye for their skin and clothes; and the seeds were ground into food and crushed into oil.

In Russia today sunflowers are a multi-million rouble crop. The Soviets make extensive use of the oil and seeds, the leaves being used to treat malaria. The stalks are burned, and the ash used as fertilizer.

Nutritional content

Sunflower seeds are remarkably rich in the B complex vitamins and are good source of phosphorus, magnesium, iron, calcium, potassium, protein, and vitamin E.

Sunflower seeds contain trace minerals, zinc, manganese, copper, chromium, and carotene. 100 g ($3\frac{1}{2}$ oz) sunflower seeds contain: 24 g protein, 267 calories, 47 g linoleic acid, (about half the daily requirements), 920 mg potassium, 837 mg phosphorus, 120 mg calcium, 38 mg magnesium, 31 mg vitamin E, 7 mg iron, 5.4 mg B3, 1.96 mg B1 (thiamine), 1.25 mg B6, 0.23 mg B2 (riboflavin).

Sunflower oil (*See* OILS *page* 99)
Sunflower meal When sunflower seeds are crushed to make oil the 'defatted meat' of the seed left is called meal. This is a traditional feed for animals and now packaged for human consumption in specialist shops.

Scientists at the Texas A & M University observed that the meal was highly valuable nutrition, containing practically no fat and 57% protein with rich amounts of B vitamins and minerals. The Texan group recommend using up to 5% sunflower meal in a wheat loaf for 'enhanced protein and a slightly nutty flavour.'

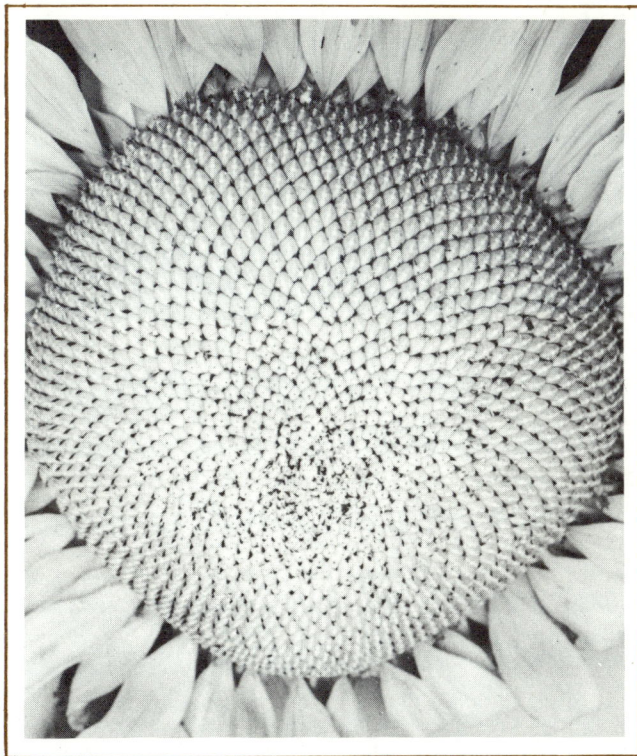

How to buy

Sunflower seeds are much cheaper to buy unhusked by the kilo, but there is no short cut to removing the husk. It must be cracked by the teeth in the time-honoured fashion. Seeds can be bought ready to eat, and are generally cheaper if bought in bulk.

How to grow sunflowers

Sunflowers are semi-hardy annuals and very easy to grow provided they are placed in the direct sun and given plenty of humus to support their tall growth. Sow 50 cm (20 in) apart with 60.9 cm (2-3 ft) between rows.

To harvest the seeds

As the flowers seed watch carefully to judge the moment of exact ripeness. Then snip the head off and rub gently over a clean cloth. The seeds will obligingly fall to be gathered and stored.

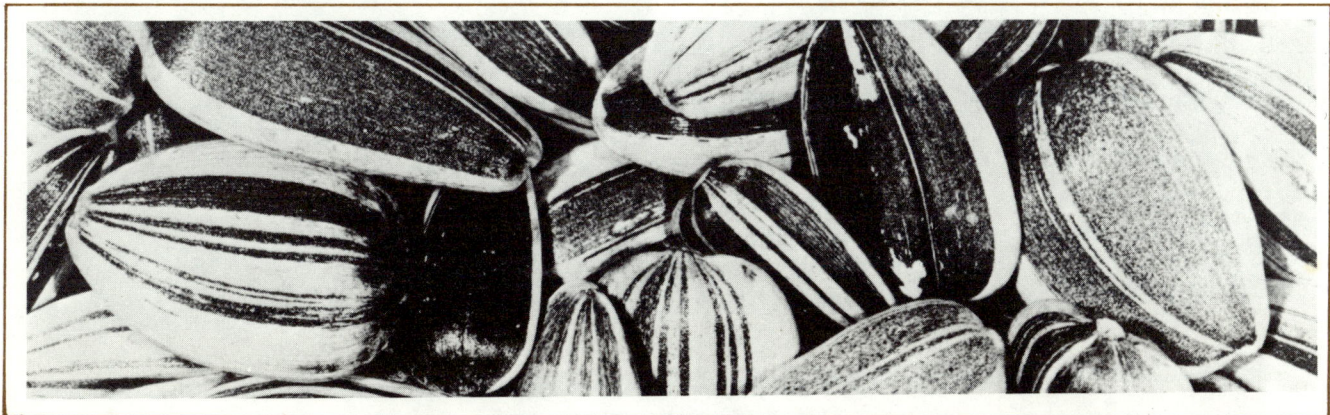

Slippery elm

Botanical name *Ulmus fulva*, popularly known as Indian elm or red elm

The early American pioneers noticed that the Indians stripped the bark of the red elm in spring and used it as a medicine and food. The Indians called it 'Oohooska' — it slips. The bark is so full of mucilage that it does indeed slip like a runny jelly.

The red elm is a smallish tree about 6 m (20 ft) high with rugged branches, pointed hairy leaves and yellow leaf buds. In the spring when the sap rises, essential nutrients are taken to every part of the living structure. The inner bark of the elm is then rich with valuable minerals including calcium.

Long, thin strips of the bark are taken from ten-year-old trees and ground into powder. This stripping limits the life of the tree, and the plantations are constantly replenished.

In the Indian tribes the slippery elm was valued as a powerful medicine. The braves rubbed their wounds and burns with the bark and infused it into a tea for all stomach ailments. They also discovered that the bark prevented animal fats from becoming rancid.

Slippery elm pudding

Use two level tablespoons of slippery elm powder to 275 ml ($\frac{1}{2}$ pint) or $1\frac{1}{4}$ U.S. cups of milk. Mix with enough cold milk to make a smooth paste. Bring the rest of the milk to the boil and pour it onto the paste in small quantities. Pour back into the saucepan and bring just to the boil, stirring as it thickens.

Add a spoonful of honey, or a dash of nutmeg, cinnamon or lemon rind. This makes a delicious dessert much appreciated by children and safe for small babies.

Milk shake

Use one teaspoon of slippery elm powder to 275 ml ($\frac{1}{2}$ pint) or $1\frac{1}{4}$ U.S. cups of milk to make a milk shake. Bring to the boil as above. Let it cool if necessary. Then whirl in the blender with vanilla and fruit pulp.

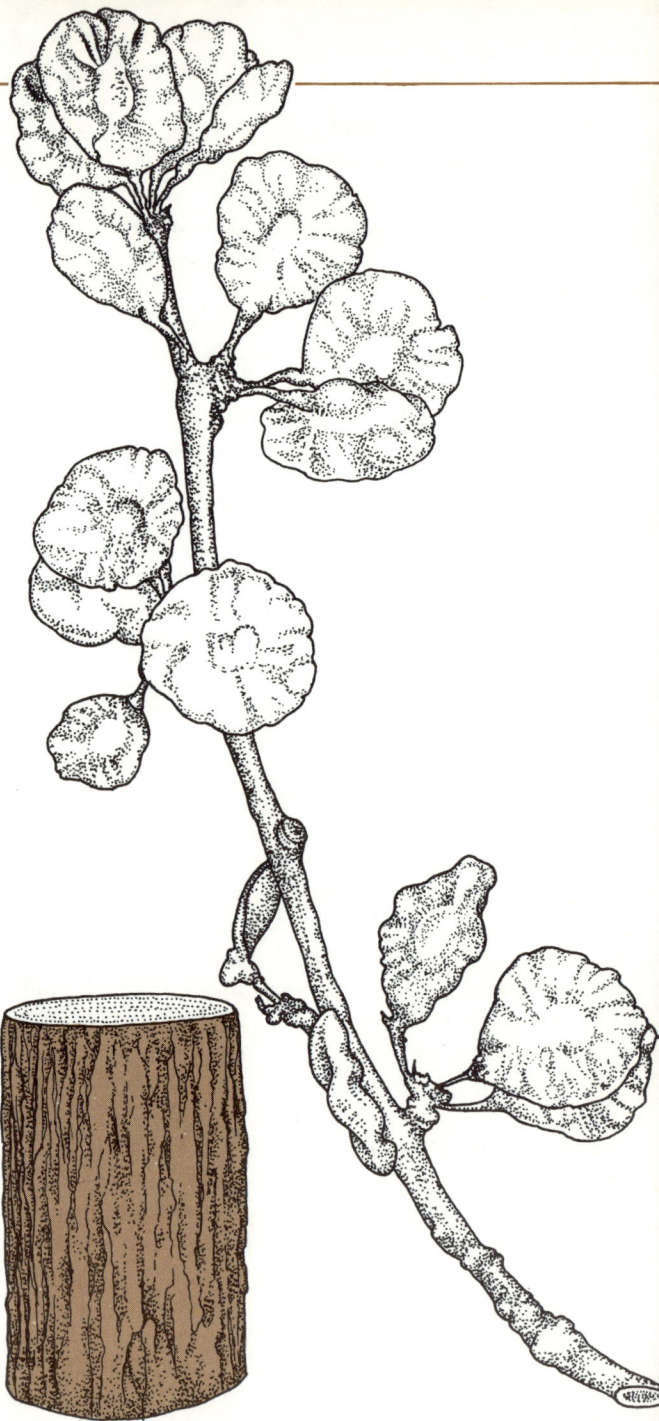

Particular value

The abundant mucilage of the slippery elm is particularly soothing and healing to all organs of the body. It is one of the finest demulcents of nature, and most effective in all gastric upsets. Sore stomachs will tolerate slippery elm when other food is rejected. It eases mucus in the bronchial tubes and so aids chest complaints. Any mucus producing complaint such as gastric catarrh responds to slippery elm.

How to use it

Slippery elm bark is sold as a white powder which is easy to make into a gruel. It is thickened rather like custard.

Sprouting seeds

Known also as bean sprouts and grain sprouts. To many people sprouting beans mean only mung beans, but almost any whole seed is capable of being sprouted. Sprouts are often produced from grains such as WHEAT, BARLEY, MAIZE, CORN, and OATS, and legumes such as SOYA BEANS, MUNG BEANS, LIMA BEANS, ALFALFA, PEAS, CHICK PEAS, LENTILS, FENUGREEK, and NAVY BEANS.

The history of sprouting seeds in the West is interesting because they have been 'discovered' several times during the last few centuries. In the East, sprouts have been an important part of the diet for about 5000 years.

In the eighteenth century, scurvy was the scourge of every ship. It was caused by the lack of vitamin C which is found mainly in fresh fruit and vegetables. Twenty years before the introduction of the lime or lemon to prevent scurvy on ships, Captain James Cook became interested in sprouting barley grains as a source of vitamin C. He had read a treatise on sea scurvy by Dr David MacBride in 1767 which contained a recipe for a wort or drink made from sprouting barley seeds. Captain Cook had the wort prepared punctiliously on board the *Endeavour* and during his three-year voyage from 1768 to 1771 not a single man was lost through scurvy. This was at a time when some vessels lost half of their crew from scurvy on long voyages. Although Captain Cook was awarded a Royal Society Medal for this experiment, the British Government did not make use of the knowledge. Instead it introduced the more expensive lemon cure for scurvy.

In the twentieth century, scientific research has proved that certain sprouts contain six times more vitamin C than the same amount of citrus fruit.

During the Second World War both the British and U.S. Governments recommended sprouted seeds as a

Captain James Cook and his ship, the Endeavour

valuable source of protein. In the U.S.A. a nationwide campaign was mounted to teach people how to sprout grains themselves.

Nutritional content

The accurate value of the sprout does vary with the species of seed, but all of them are especially rich in vitamin C and several of the B complex group. They also contain a high level of protein and amino acids. Some sprouts are good sources of the vitamins E, G, K, and U. (*See* INDIVIDUAL ENTRIES.) Legumes have generally a higher value of vitamin C than grains but grains contain more vitamin B.

How the sprout manufactures the vitamins and minerals

Every seed stores energy in the form of starch. When the seed's life force is activated by moisture and warmth it starts to manufacture the vitamins and elements it needs for growth. In this way the sprout becomes a rich store of vitamins, nutrients, trace elements, and amino acids. After a few hours of germination the seed develops vitamin C which was completely lacking when in its dried state. When the

sprouts are stored in the refrigerator the vitamin C content goes on increasing for about one week.

The B vitamins begin to appear after several days and then rapidly reach a peak within a day. This varies in different legumes or grains. For instance, B1 (thiamine) reaches its peak value in lentils after six days' germination. Some seeds do not reach the peak of B vitamin production until after the fourth day, by which time they have usually been consumed. Some research seems to indicate a marked increase in B2 (riboflavin) when the cotyledon or the first two leaves appear. Most sprouts are eaten before these leaves appear. Vitamin B12, which is notoriously hard to find in plant life, is found in many germinating seeds. One good serving of sprouts daily can furnish the body's needs of this vitamin.

1 Alfalfa sprouts

2 Soya sprouts

3 Aduki (dry)

4 Mung sprouts

5 Aduki sprouted

Alfalfa sprouts. Nutritionists throughout the world have become excited about the potential value of alfalfa, so the seeds for sprouting are becoming widely available. They contain 40% protein and are very high in vitamins A, B, and C with good amounts of D, E, G, K, and U. They are also a possible source of B12. Alfalfa sprouts are a good source of calcium and iron, and have amounts of sodium, potassium, sulphur, phosphorus, silicone, aluminium, magnesium. (*See* ALFALFA *page* 23)

Aduki sprouts Far Eastern countries such as China, Japan, and Korea have always sprouted as well as cooked this bean. The sprout contains 25% protein, and is a good source of vitamin C and many of the vitamin B complex. It has several amino acids, particularly the important one of lysine. Aduki is easy to sprout and has a crisp, nutty flavour.

Alphatoco sprouts The seed merchants Thompson and Morgan, U.K., (*See* WHERE TO BUY *page* 154) have recently introduced this seed especially for sprouting. They claim that the big advantage of alphatoco is its richness in vitamin E. It also contains amounts of vitamin C and the B complex.

Barley sprouts This grain has been traditionally used for centuries in brewing beer and its germinating value is well appreciated in the Western world. It is particularly high in vitamin C and the B complex group and contains several amino acids. Like most grain sprouts it should be eaten when less than 3 cm (1 in) long. Some authorities advise eating sprouting grain when the shoot is no longer than the seed itself. This is because the germinating grain weaves itself into a thick thatch. (*See* BARLEY *page* 47)

Fenugreek sprouts contain about 25% protein and large amounts of choline. They are rich in vitamins A and D as well as C and are also a good source of iron. Fenugreek has been used in medicine and healing for thousands of years. It has quite a spicy flavour and is best eaten when the sprouts are 4 cm ($1\frac{1}{2}$ in) long. Do not cook for more than three or four minutes as the sprouts become bitter with overcooking.

Lentil sprouts contain 25% protein and large amounts of vitamin C, and a good range of the B complex group except for folic acid. They are easy to sprout and have a slightly nutty flavour. Eat when the sprout is 3 cm (1 in) long. Never use split lentils for sprouting. (*See* LENTILS *page* 84)

Mung bean sprouts are often sold in shops as 'Chinese bean sprouts'. The mung sprout contains 37% protein and is a rich source of a wide variety of B vitamins. Vitamin B1 (thiamine) goes on doubling in content each day until the fourth day when it stops gaining any more nutritional value. Mung sprouts are a very rich source of vitamin C and they contain also a good range of available amino acids. Eat them when the shoot is between 4-6 cm (2-3 in) long.

Pea sprouts are a rich source of the vitamin B complex group, particularly B1 (thiamine), which reaches its peak after two days' sprouting. They are a reasonable source of vitamin C and have a good selection of amino acids. (*See* PEAS *page* 77)

Triticale sprouts are a cross between wheat and rye. Nobel Prize winner Dr Norman E. Borlaug is of the opinion that triticale is a very valuable nutrient — 'The protein level is better than wheat and the level of amino acids higher.' Triticale sprouts contain 19 amino acids and a good amount of vitamins B, C, D, E, and F. They are 30% protein and a source of natural fibre. (*See* BRAN *page* 26)

Soya bean sprouts The soya bean is a complete protein and of outstanding nutritional value. The sprout contains the wide range of vitamins and minerals present in the bean, plus, of course, vitamin C which it manufactures itself. The soya bean sprout is a good source of the B complex group, in particular B1 (thiamine), B2 (riboflavin) and B6. It is rich in vitamins C and E and contains vitamins U and K. There are excellent amounts of iron, calcium, plus potassium, phosphorus and zinc.

There are many types of soya beans and all may be sprouted. The green soya bean developed in the U.S.A. is excellent as a sprouting seed. The Chinese use blue, black and white soya beans. The most familiar variety on sale is the small, yellowish bean which sprouts well.

Soya beans need much more rinsing than the average sprouting seed. Some authorities advise rinsing six times a day and it is perhaps advisable to gain sprouting experience first on the mung bean. (*See* SOYA BEAN page 80)

Wheat sprouts are considered by some devotees to be the most delicious of the sprouting grains. They are a good source of B complex vitamins with some vitamin C. Spring wheat contains more vitamin C than winter wheat. Wheat sprouts very fast and does not slow down so much when refrigerated. It should be eaten when less than 2 cm ($\frac{1}{2}$ in) long before the sprouts become a dense mass. (*See* WHEAT *page* 56)

A word of caution All soya bean products contain a trypsin inhibitor and must be cooked. Cook the sprouts for two minutes before storing and then another six or ten minutes before eating.

This substance is present to some extent in all legumes and some experts therefore recommend that all legume sprouts should be cooked for at least three minutes. This applies to peas, chick peas, beans, fenugreek, alfalfa, clover, lentils and soya beans. Sprouts from grains such as wheat, rye, corn, barley, millet and oats can be eaten raw.

Steaming or stir frying in the Chinese manner does not destroy the vitamins and cooking can actually improve the nutritional value. Heating makes the amino acid methionine more available.

5

Fried rice and sprouts

2 tablespoons vegetable oil or bacon fat
350 g (12 oz) or 2 U.S. cups chopped onion
450 g (1 lb) or 2 U.S. cups cooked organic rice
125 g (4 oz) or 1 U.S. cup steamed alfalfa
sprouts
150 g (6 oz) or 1 U.S. cup cooked chicken
with bacon pieces (well diced)
2 eggs beaten with 2 tablespoons soy sauce
(Any sprout may be used but alfalfa forms a
very good protein with rice.)
Heat oil in the skillet and add the onion and
cook until golden. Add rice and stir well. Add
the egg mixture and stir gently. Add chicken
and sprouts and heat through.

In her book *Add a Few Sprouts*, Martha H.
Oliver has done much original research into
sprouting seeds. She gives the recipe for wort
devised by Dr David MacBride and used by
Captain Cook, which makes a non-alcoholic,
sweet and very nourishing drink:

Sweetwort

450 g (1 lb) or 2 U.S. cups barley sprouts
1.2 litres (2 pints) or 5 U.S. cups
boiling water
honey to taste
Grind the barley sprouts in a meat grinder, or
place in a blender with a third of the water
and liquefy. Add the rest of the boiling water
and allow the brew to stand for several hours
or until cool. Strain. A very refreshing
beverage, it may be reheated and served with
honey to taste. To preserve the antiscorbic
qualities, do not boil.

How to sprout

There are several sprouting utensils available (*See*
KITCHEN UTENSILS *page* 144) but by far the simplest
way is to use a glass jar. Place the dried seeds inside,
put muslin or cheesecloth over the top and secure with
a rubber band. Rinse several times a day with warm
water, and leave the jar on its side to drain, such as on
the sink draining board because the seeds do not need
the dark in order to sprout. Choose a largish jar as the
seeds can swell to about 10 times their size. 125 g (4 oz)
of seeds to a 1 k (2 lb) jar is a good proportion. To get
off to a quick start you can flood the seeds with water
and leave them for several hours or until they swell.
Drain this water off carefully and every time the seeds
are rinsed they must be carefully drained. If the seeds
are from an organic source this water can be reserved
and used in soups and stocks.

Different seeds obviously take different times to
sprout, but the longest time is about six days.

Keep the jar in a warm place, but not in direct
sunlight. The ideal temperature for germination is
between 13-21°C (55-70°F). Generally speaking, the
warmer the spot, the quicker germination takes place.

It is important to choose food quality seed. Much
commercial seed intended for germination under
ground has been treated with non-water soluble
herbicide and insecticide. Obtain seed intended
specifically for sprouting from specialist shops or
directly from the seed merchants. (*See* WHERE TO BUY
page 152) Mail order can sometimes be a little cheaper.

Always use whole seed. Split peas, cracked wheat and
husked rice will not sprout.

Light or dark?

Many books advise keeping the sprouting seeds in the
dark but this is not necessary. Seeds sprouted in
darkness have more vitamin B2 (riboflavin) and are of
a white colour. Seeds grown in the light turn green as
they make chlorophyll and they often have more
vitamin C. One advantage of sprouting seeds in the
light is that it is then possible to keep the jar in sight in
the kitchen. This makes it much easier to remember to
rinse the seeds several times a day.

A common cause of failure is insufficient rinsing or
draining. If any water is left standing in the container
the seeds will go mouldy and smell awful.

How to cook sprouts

Steaming or stir frying preserves the vitamins and
minerals present in the sprout and generally tastes
better than boiling. The Chinese traditionally use a
Wok (*See* KITCHEN UTENSILS *page* 144) but a heavy
frying pan or skillet will do just as well.

Finely chop the vegetables to be cooked with the
sprouts. Put one tablespoon of oil in the skillet and
heat gently and be careful not to boil. Slowly add the
vegetables, stirring all the time. Sprouts should be
added during the last two or three minutes of cooking.
Stir all the time with a large spoon and just before
serving add soy sauce or flavourings.

Wheat germ

In the germ or kernel of the wheat is a tiny embryo which nature has packed with nutrients needed for the future life of the plant. Before the introduction of the steel roller flour-milling process in 1879, the wheat was crushed between two flat stones, and so complete wheat was then eaten. The germ of the wheat is rich in natural oil and this was soon found to be clogging up the steel rollers as well as causing the flour to have a much shorter life as wheat germ is highly perishable. This did not suit the manufacturers who wished to package flour for export all over the world.

For many years, the wheat germ separated during the steel-rolling process was fed to animals. This was nearly 50 years before the discovery of vitamins in food and it was not realized then that the discarding of the wheat germ removed most of the valuable nutrients.

This process which stripped the wheat of many vitamins and minerals vital to the staple diet is of the utmost importance in the history of nutrition. For example, there is strong evidence to suppose that the reduction of vitamin E in the diet is linked with the growth of degenerative diseases.

The U.S. Bureau of Research has published figures to show that the average American diet today supplies approximately 15 mg of vitamin E daily. A hundred years ago, before the steel-milling process was introduced, the average intake of vitamin E was 150 mg daily. The brothers, Dr Evan and Dr Wilfred Shute, have had great success treating heart patients with wheat germ oil and large doses of vitamin E.

Nutritional content

Wheat germ is particularly rich in B complex vitamins and vitamin E. It is a good source of iron and calcium, and contains 12 amino acids which build into a good protein. 100 g (4 oz) wheat germ contain: 24 g of protein, approximately 230 calories, 400 I.U. vitamin A, 27 mg vitamin E, 2.6 mg B1 (thiamine), 0.75 mg B2 (riboflavin), 1050 mg phosphorus, 71 mg calcium, 7.5 mg iron, and good amounts of the B vitamins, pantothenic acid, niacin, paba, biotin, and inositol.

Wheat germ oil is a product of wheat germ which is very rich in alpha tocopherol, a component of vitamin E. Wheat germ oil should be refrigerated and never cooked. It may be taken by the spoonful as a supplement.

Rancidity in wheat germ Natural wheat germ is highly perishable and must be kept under refrigeration. Never buy it from shops that do not stock it under good, cold conditions. Rancid wheat germ has a characteristic sour smell.

Stabilized wheat germ To overcome this problem of rancidity, some manufacturers supply stabilized wheat

germ which has been treated to prolong its keeping qualities, but at the expense of the more fragile constituents. It will state clearly on the packet if the wheat germ has been stabilized.

How to add wheat germ to the diet

It is delicious as a cereal with YOGHURT and milk, either on its own, or mixed with MUESLI. Wheat germ can be added to any bread recipe; a good proportion is 50 g (2 oz) wheat germ to 400 g (14 oz) flour. A higher proportion will need extra moisture.

There are innumerable ways an imaginative cook can add wheat germ to the family's diet. Added to meat loaves and patties it improves not only the nutritional content but also the flavour. Mix it with granola for apple and fruit crumble; add a knob of butter and mix with cheese for a casserole topping. Add wheat germ to all meat and vegetable stuffings. Use it instead of breadcrumbs when coating is required in a recipe.

Adelle Davis' walnut torte

Line the bottoms of two 20 cm (8 in) layer cake pans with heavy paper and brush with soft margarine or butter.
Stir together thoroughly:
225 g (8 oz) or 1 U.S. cup brown sugar
3 egg yolks
225 g (8 oz) or 2 U.S. cups ground walnuts
75 g (3 oz) or $\frac{3}{4}$ U.S. cup wheat germ
Beat 6 egg whites until they have soft peaks and fold them into the above ingredients. Pour batter into pans, spread evenly to edges, and bake in slow oven at 160°C (325°F, Gas Mark 3) for 30 minutes. Turn out of pans and remove paper immediately. Prepare filling by mixing:
65 g ($2\frac{1}{2}$ oz) or $\frac{1}{3}$ U.S. cup brown sugar
65 g ($2\frac{1}{2}$ oz) or $\frac{1}{3}$ U.S. cup powdered milk
3 egg yolks
100 ml (4 fl oz) or $\frac{1}{2}$ U.S. cup top milk or cream
Cook slowly over low heat until thick, stirring constantly; do not boil. Remove from heat and add:
125 g (4 oz) or 1 U.S. cup ground walnuts or
125 g (4 oz) or 1 U.S. cup ground almonds
Spread between layers of the torte.

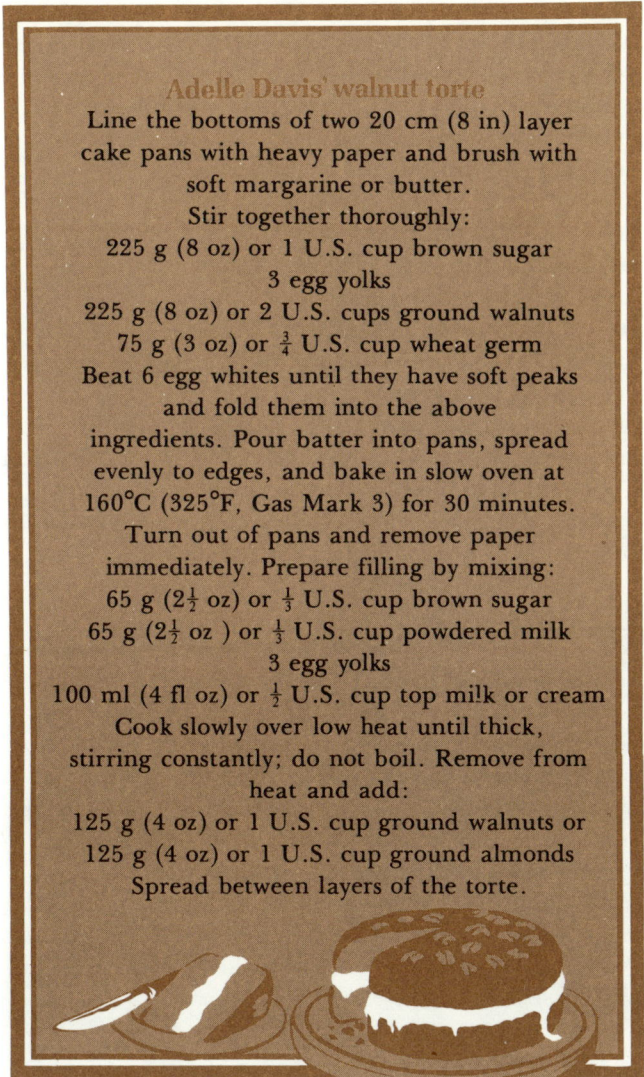

117

Yeast extracts

When fresh BREWER'S YEAST is mixed with salt it is broken down by its own enzymes. The soluble residue is evaporated under pressure to give the familiar sticky brown substance known as yeast extract. The process was invented in Germany in the 1890s, and is now used, with variations, in almost every country of the world. These extracts are known as hydrolysed or autolysed yeasts. They should not be confused with meat extracts which contain certain meat derivatives and MONOSODIUM GLUTAMATE. (*See page* 20).

Nutritional content
Yeast extracts are particularly rich in B vitamins. For instance 28 g (1 oz) Marmite (Savita) contain 1.5 mg of 16.5 mg niacin. Many special extracts aimed at the vegetarian market contain vegetable protein, iron and added B12. Check the labels for contents.

How to use
Yeast extracts are sold commercially under proprietary names such as Marmite (U.K.), Vegemite (Australia) and Savita (U.S.A.). They can easily be dissolved in water and make an excellent instant stock. A spoonful will give body to any casserole, broth or stew. Spread yeast extracts thinly on wholemeal bread and butter for a nutritious snack.

One disadvantage is that these handy extracts can sometimes be very high in salt content. 28 g (1 oz) of an average commercial brand contains 1300 mg of salt. Varieties with a low salt content will state so clearly on the label.

Welsh stew (cawl cymreig)
1 kg (2 lb) neck of lamb
2 large leeks
225 g ($\frac{1}{2}$ lb) swede (rutabaga)
225 g ($\frac{1}{2}$ lb) carrots
450 g (1 lb) potatoes
1 bayleaf
$\frac{1}{4}$ teaspoon dried thyme
15 g ($\frac{1}{2}$ oz) soya flour
1 tablespoon yeast extract
3 tablespoons unprocessed bran flakes

This traditional Welsh dish is made nutritionally excellent with wholefood additions.
Remove the fat from the meat and cover with water. Bring to the boil and simmer for $1\frac{1}{2}$ hours. Skim the top. Add the yeast extract, the cleaned and chopped vegetables, dried thyme, and bayleaf. Mix the soya flour with a little water and stir it in smoothly. Cover and simmer again for 35-40 minutes until the meat and vegetables are tender. About 5 or 10 minutes before serving add the bran flakes.

Yoghurt

According to an ancient tradition, an angel revealed to the prophet Abraham the method of making yoghurt. The Bible tells us that he lived to the age of one hundred and seventy-five and fathered a child when he was one hundred. This may have planted the idea that yoghurt is associated with longevity and fertility and the debate continues to the present day. A similar cultured milk drink, *kefir,* is known as 'The drink of the Prophet' in Islamic countries. Yoghurt, *kefir* and associated milk cultures have been used for centuries in the Balkans, Turkey, Greece, Egypt, Algeria, Arabia, India and China.

In 1904, Nobel Prize winner Ilya Metchnikoff of the Pasteur Institute of Paris, began to research into the properties of yoghurt. He had been impressed by the longevity of Bulgarian peasants who ate large amounts of milk soured with *Lactobacillus bulgaricus* — known as yoghurt. He discovered that the yoghurt produced friendly bacteria that killed disease bacteria in the large intestine. He published his findings in the *The Prolongation of Life* in 1908 and his research gave rise to a growing interest in yoghurt throughout the world.

Much research has since been done into the curative properties of yoghurt. (*See* NUTRITION AND MEDICINE *page* 80)

Nutritional content

175 ml (6 fl oz) yoghurt contain: 8 g protein, 120 calories, 295 mg calcium, 0.1 mg iron, 170 I.U. vitamin A, 0.09 mg vitamin B1 (thiamine), 0.43 mg vitamin B2 (riboflavin), 0.2 mg niacin.

Particular value

Modern research has confirmed that *lactobacillus* creates an environment in the large intestine which is unfavourable to the harmful bacteria such as *B. coli.* One reason for this is that yoghurt bacteria break down milk sugar into lactic acid, and bacteria which cause putrefaction and gas cannot live in lactic acid. Yoghurt bacteria is able to manufacture the entire group of B vitamins in the intestine, via the intestinal flora. This is an important factor since so many modern drugs can destroy valuable intestinal flora. Sulpha drugs and antibiotics such as penicillin, streptomycin and aureomycin can therefore cause multiple B complex vitamin deficiencies. Many doctors in Italy prescribe yoghurt when they prescribe antibiotics.

Yoghurt must be eaten regularly to produce a healthy intestinal environment. Dr Harry Seneca, writing in the *Journal of the American Geriatrics Association*, says: '*Yoghurt contains some antibiotic principle which reaches its peak in 48 hours of growth and then gradually disappears over the next few weeks. All types of pathogenic bacteria and protozoa (harmful germs) are killed within five hours.*' This powerful ability to kill germs has also been noted by Dr David B. Sabine of the U.S. Vitamin and Pharmaceutical Corporation. Under controlled conditions Dr Sabine grew harmful bacteria such as staphylococcus and *E. coli*. He added *lactobacillus* and *acidophilus* yoghurt bacteria and observed that the harmful bacteria began to gradually disappear. Further tests by Dr Seneca at Columbia University, U.S.A., have shown that when yoghurt is eaten over a long period, no other bacteria except the friendly ones appear in the stools. Another advantage of yoghurt is that people who are allergic or sensitive to milk are able to tolerate it.

Much of the commercial yoghurt contains preservative and colour, but it is both easy and cheap to make your own. It is a good idea to start with yoghurt culture, such as *lactobacillus bulgaricus*. Provided the yoghurt is refrigerated as soon as it thickens, this can be used indefinitely as a starter. Simply reserve two tablespoons to start the next batch.

How to make your own yoghurt

The easiest way is with a yoghurt maker which plugs in and stays at the correct temperature (*See* KITCHEN UTENSILS *page* 144); or you can use a thermos flask or an airing cupboard. The idea is to keep the milk and the friendly yoghurt bacteria at a temperature of 43°C, (110°F). Bring 575 ml (1 pint) or 2½ U.S. cups of milk to the boil and hold for about 5 seconds. Let it cool down to 43°C (110°F) — just above body temperature. It should feel comfortable if you test it with a clean finger. Pour the milk into the yoghurt maker or other

container. Stir in the culture or two tablespoons of plain yoghurt and leave it to thicken. It should take between 3 and 8 hours, depending on whether you have used culture powder or not.

Refrigerate as soon as it has thickened to a good consistency. Do not shake the container as this causes curds to form. Skimmed milk, soya bean milk, goat's milk or cream may all be used. Sterilized milk is also good.

A common cause of failure when making yoghurt is using fresh milk and not boiling it first. Animals are often given antibiotics which appear in the milk and 'fight' the yoghurt bacteria.

Herbs and Spices

Angelica

Botanical name — *Angelica archangelica*.
This plant is a native of the Baltic and was supposed to have been blessed by St Michael the Archangel, hence its name. Despite angelica's northerly origins it will flourish in most climates and withstand the cold.

Medicinal use

The roots, rhizomes, plant and seeds all possess stimulant and tonic activants. Their use is valuable for stimulating appetite, aiding digestion, producing perspiration and relieving troublesome coughs and colds.

Angelica's complex constituents combine oils, resins and acids. It is a popular ingredient for herb teas. Angelica *should not* be taken by diabetics as it raises the level of sugar in the blood.

How to grow

Angelica is not a strict perennial as it only lives for two to four years. However, once established, it readily self-seeds; or if the plant is cut down before maturity, it will be sure to produce leaves the next year.

Angelica should be sown in partial shade in spring or autumn and needs a rich, well drained soil. Allow plenty of room because this aromatic plant quickly develops to 2.5 m (10 ft) high with a 1.3 m (5 ft) spread. During the first and second years it will produce attractive divided leaves and thick stalks. Afterwards come the large round greenish-white flower heads and finally a profusion of seeds.

In cooking

The roots are an essential ingredient of famous liqueurs such as green Chartreuse and Bénédictine. The crystallized stalks are well known as flavouring for cakes and creams. They are also delicious in marmalades and marrow preserve and good with rhubarb dishes, ice creams and apricot puddings.

Angelica

Anise

Botanical name — *Pimpinella anisum*
This delicate herb originated from Asia Minor and was referred to in St Matthew: 'Ye pay tithe of Mint, Anise and Cumin.' In Roman times rich meals were rounded off with *mustacae* which was a spiced cake flavoured with anise seeds (aniseed) to prevent indigestion. This thought to be the origin of our wedding cakes at the end of a bridal feast.

Medicinal use

The seeds make a soothing tea which ancient users thought an effective aid against the Evil Eye! Nowadays, anise infusions are added to hot milk to make an excellent sleep-inducing drink that is safe for children. Anise is also used in the mixing of many cough medicines and lozenges. The volatile oil constituent makes it a powerful antiseptic. This is particularly useful when digestion is weak or slow and can stop the fermentation of food in the stomach. Anise can correct the balance of acidity in the digestion.

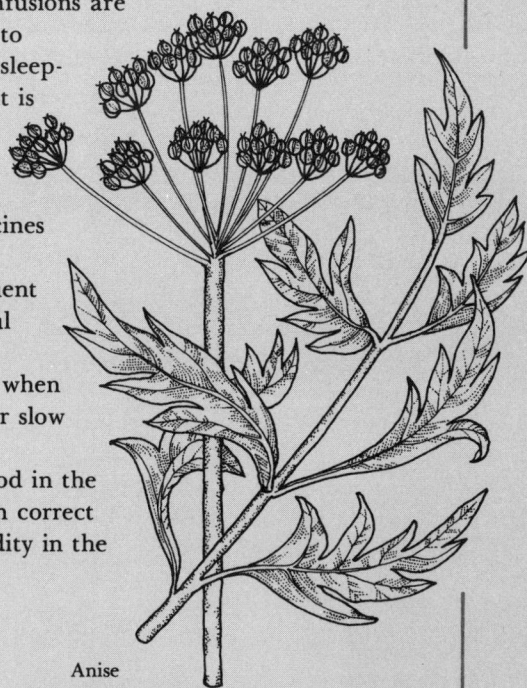

Anise

How to grow

Anise is a slender annual growing to 45 cm (18 in) high, with a cluster of whitish flowers which appear in mid-summer on its umbrella-like head. Sow the seeds during spring in well drained fertile soil in full sun. Thin the seedlings to 23-30 cm (9-12 in) apart. Anise is grown for its seeds which need a good warm summer to ripen.

In cooking

Anise seeds are popular sprinkled on cakes and breads. They are good on fish, veal and pork as a counter to their richness.

The seeds are also an important ingredient of liqueurs. The French add the crushed seeds to vegetables such as carrots and also cream puddings. The torn leaves are a useful garnish, used sparingly, for curries, salads, potatoes, and pickles.

121

Basil

Botanical names — Sweet Basil — *Ocimum basilicum*
Bush Basil — *Ocimum minimum*

This delicate, fragrant herb has been popular in cooking and perfumes for over two thousand years. Some authorities say that the name basil comes from the Greek word for king; others that it is linked with the fabled creature Basilisk. A charming Tudor custom was to present visitors with a pot of bush basil when they were leaving.

Medicinal use

Its camphoraceous oil is principally an aromatic and digestive agent. Herbalists rate basil highly for calming the nerves and it aids the digestion as well as having definite cooling properties.

How to grow

Basil is an erect, branched, half-hardy annual and bears small white flowers in late summer. It needs a sheltered spot in full sun and well drained fertile soil. Sow the seeds in late spring or earlier under glass, and save the seed heads of the flowers for the following year.

In cooking

The sweet, clove-scented leaves can be used generously. Basil is a great favourite with French cooks. Before the Fire of London in 1666, basil was the flavouring in the famous Fetter Lane sausages which drew people from all over the capital.

It goes very well with sausage and minced meats and is the perfect herb for all tomato dishes and courgettes. Use chopped leaves in salads, stuffings, herb butters and rice dishes.

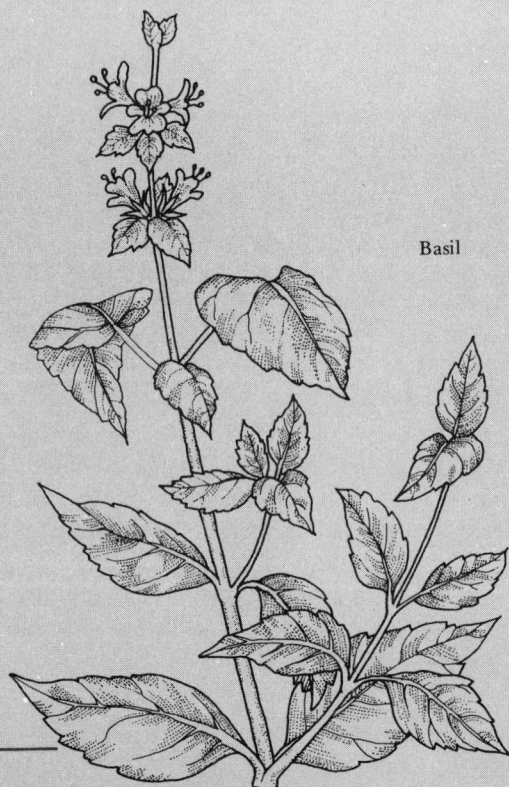

Basil

To preserve basil

The leaves will freeze, and will also keep for a short time in polythene bags in the refrigerator. The best way to keep the flavour is to preserve the leaves in oil. Pack clean leaves in a jar in layers, sprinkle on salt, fill the jar with olive oil and seal. This will keep in a refrigerator for several months.

Buchu

Botanical name — *Barosma betulina*

This small shrubby plant grows chiefly on the hillsides around Cape Town in South Africa. The Africans have used it for centuries and place a very high value on the herb they call 'bucku'. So far, all efforts to establish this plant in other parts of the world have failed. Buchu is included in this herb section because it is outstandingly effective for kidney, bladder and urinary complaints. It is used not only by herbalists but by orthodox medicine as well. The dried leaves and tablets of buchu are readily available from specialist shops.

Medicinal use

Buchu was introduced into European medicine in about 1790. The herb's constituents include a powerful antiseptic called diosphenol, plus volatile oils, resin, albumen, mucilage and gum. These constituents act in concert together and have a powerfully restorative effect on the kidneys and bladder. Buchu will adjust the flow of urine and reduce prostate swellings and can deal with cases of gravel and inflammation. It is prescribed by registered medical herbalists for mild cystitis and urethritis.

How to use

Make an infusion by pouring 600 ml (1 pint) or $2\frac{1}{2}$ U.S. cups of boiling water onto 25 g (1 oz) of leaves. Let it cool and drink a wineglassful three or four times a day. Buchu tablets and pills are easy to take. A preparation called Barosmin contains buchu. A buchu brandy is also manufactured.

Chives

Botanical name — *Allium schoenoprasum*

This tufted perennial is a native of Britain and is popular throughout the world.

Medicinal use

As a member of the *Allium* or onion family chives have all the health-giving properties of this group but in milder form. Chives contain a variation of the pungent volatile oil, allyl disulphate, found in garlic. They are rich in sulphur and have antiseptic qualities, and aid the digestion.

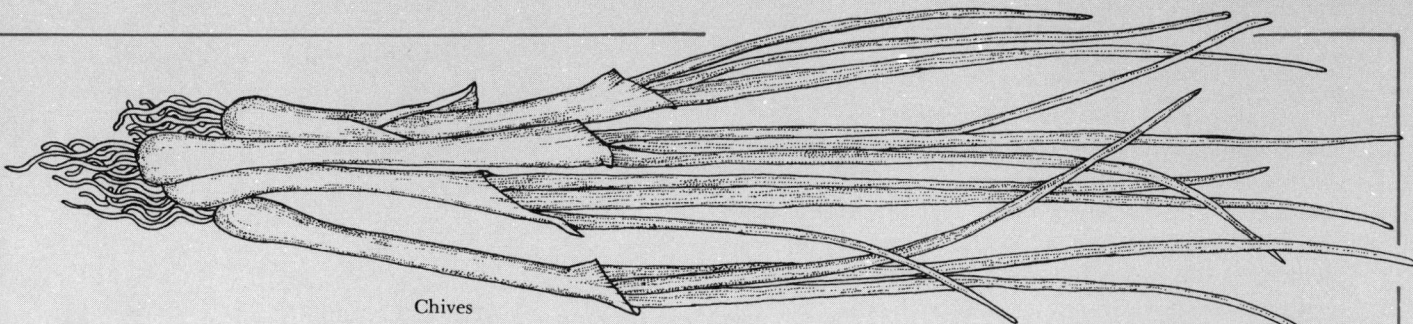

Chives

How to grow
Chives are easy to grow, either from seed or separation of the bulbs. They prefer a sunny situation but will thrive anywhere. Plant either in autumn or in spring when the soil is warm. The hollow leaves will grow to about 38 cm (15 in) and produce mauve flowers in high summer. The flowers must be snipped off before they develop or the quality of the leaves will deteriorate. Chives may be cut close to the ground so that the bulbs will quickly throw up new growth.

In cooking
The volatile oil in chives makes them a poor subject for drying but they freeze well. Chop them into an ice-cube tray, top up with water; use the frozen 'chive cubes' when required.

Chives make an ideal savoury garnish, and add zest to any salad, casserole, or omelette. Chive butter is delicious with cheese dishes.

Dandelion
Botanical name — *Taraxacum officinale*
The powers accredited to this herb are reflected in its name which is a corruption of the French *dent de lion*. The early herbalists honoured dandelion and likened its virtues to a lion's tooth.

Medicinal value
Dandelion has a very high vitamin A and C content, more iron than spinach and a good supply of potassium, potash and gluten. The active principles are still being studied by herb experts but the constituents insulin and latex are known to be valuable.

Dandelions act as a tonic, are slightly laxative and astringent. They act on the liver, kidneys and bladder in a beneficial way. Dandelion tea is prescribed by naturopaths for liver complaints.

How to grow
With these nutrients and benefits it is a shame that dandelions are often yanked out as a weed and thrown away. In French kitchen gardens the golden faced herbs have a respected place. There is now a widely available cultivated dandelion that should do much to restore the plant to its rightful place.

Obtain culinary dandelion seeds from a seed merchant and sow in spring. There is a thick-leaved improved variety available which makes an excellent vegetable.

The young plants can be covered with an upturned flower pot to blanch the leaves. This makes them less bitter and taste rather like chicory.

In cooking
Wash the leaves and cook them in a pan with only the water clinging to their leaves and a knob of butter. Or use a combination of half dandelion leaves and half spinach or young nettles. The most tender leaves can be added to salads.
Dandelion tea and coffee (*See* BEVERAGES *page* 136)

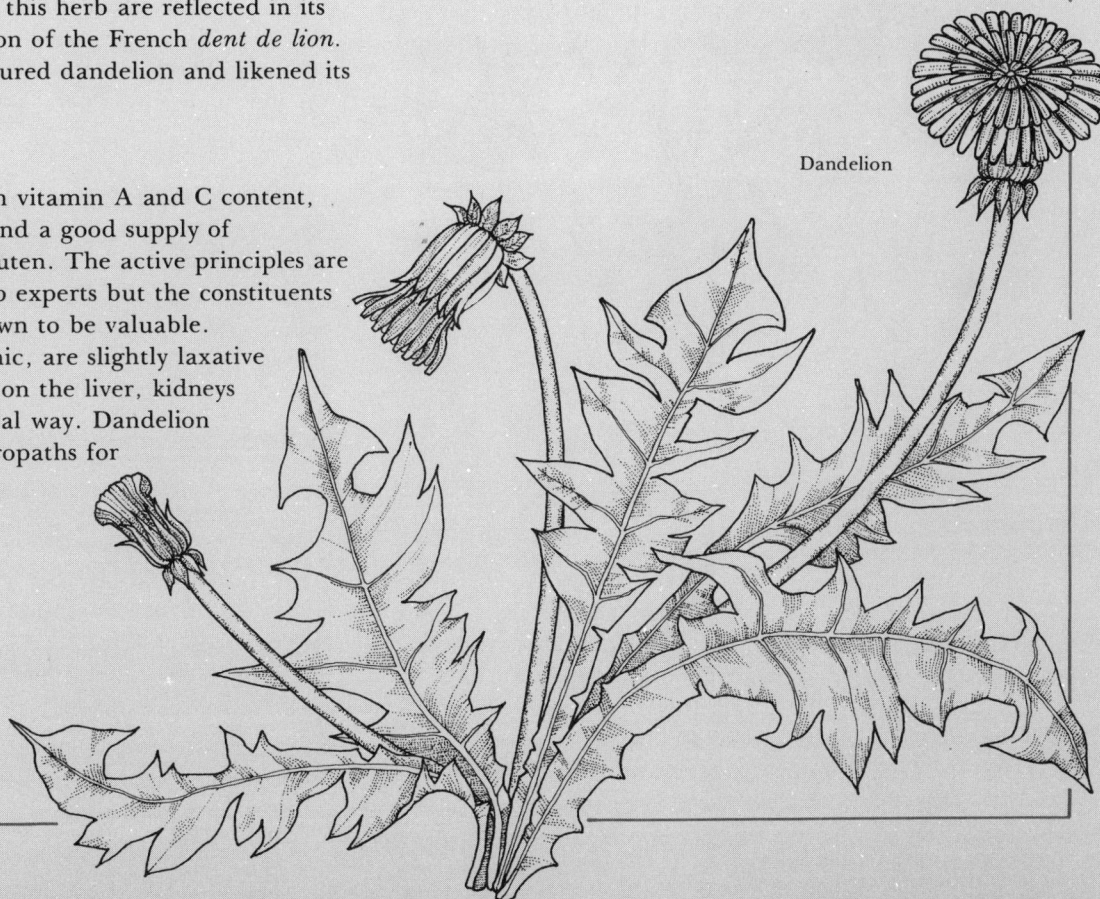

Dandelion

Dill

Botanical name — *Anethum graveolens*

The Anglo-Saxons discovered that dill would cure flatulence and also bring peaceful sleep. The name comes from the Norse word *dilla* meaning to lull to sleep. It is often used today in children's carminative medicines. Dill was popularly called 'meeting-house seed' because it was eaten by hungry churchgoers during long Sunday-morning sermons.

Medicinal use

Dill contains the same volatile oils as caraway (limonene and carvone) but in different quantities. It has a considerable effect on the digestion, soothes upset stomachs, and is alleged to stimulate the brain. It is a safe flavouring for diabetics and those on a low salt diet. Rich in minerals it is often recommended to nursing mothers as a milk stimulant.

In cooking

The leaves can be used to great effect in pickled cucumbers and gherkins. Freshly chopped dill leaves are good with Scandinavian-style fish mousses and in dill sauce as an accompaniment to mutton.

The seeds are gathered when the plant begins to turn a purplish-red and can be added to vegetable cooking water to improve the taste, especially of cabbage and cauliflower. Half a teaspoon of dill seed cooked in an apple pie is quite delicious.

The seeds can be infused into a tea. (*See* BEVERAGES *page* 137)

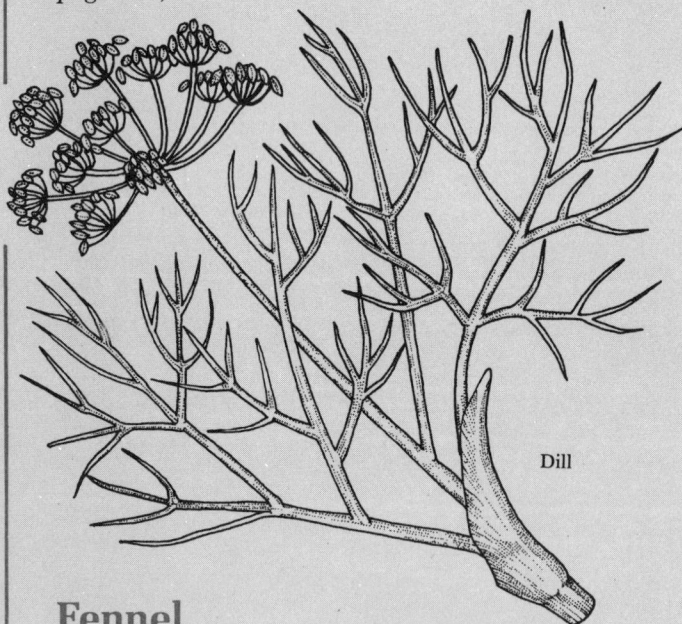

Dill

Fennel

Botanical name — *Foeniculum vulgare*

The Romans brought fennel to Britain and the herb became popular in medicine and cooking. Perhaps the native Britons did not care to see the fennel woven into the victory wreaths of their Roman conquerors. Later on, the English hung the herb over their doors on

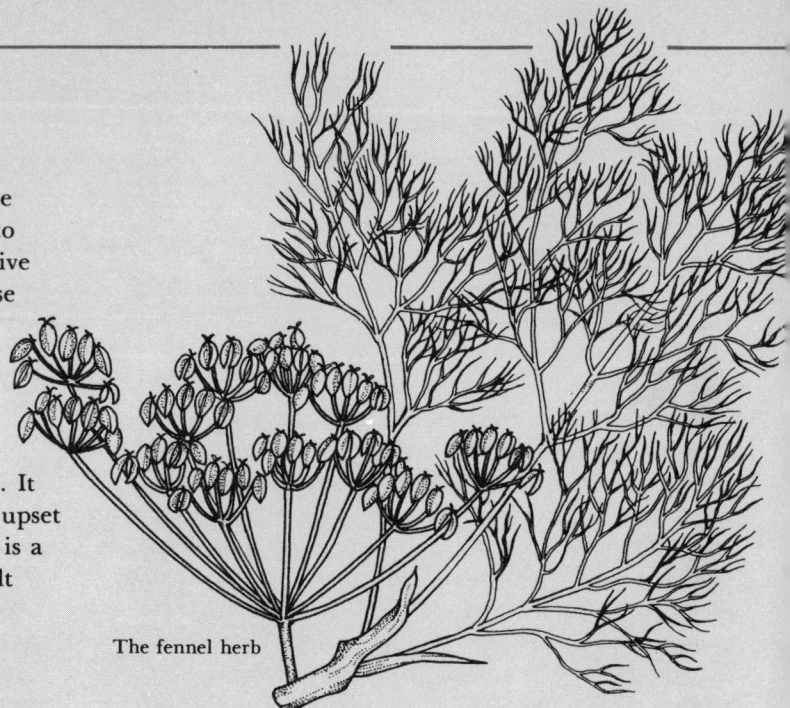

The fennel herb

Midsummer's Eve to protect them from witches and evildoers.

Modern pharmacy has a much more down-to-earth use for fennel. It is added as an ingredient to infant gripe water. The seeds are crushed and used in many medicines which aid the digestion.

In cooking

Fennel is an aid to digestion in the culinary as well as medicinal sense. The natural oils and acids make a good counter to any rich food, such as veal, pork, and fish. In Denmark fennel leaves are sprinkled raw on food in the same way that other countries use parsley. Fennel seeds are sprinkled on bread in Germany and Holland. The roots, leaves, and seeds can be chopped up and made into a good soup with a faint licorice flavour.

Florence fennel (fennel dulce)

This looks completely different to the fennel just described as it has stems rather like celery, but with a more bulbous base. Use it raw, chopped into strips for salad. Florence fennel is very popular in Europe. The licorice flavour adds zest to any green salad. Try this fennel on its own with chopped walnuts.

Fennel sauce

Prepare a white sauce in the proportion of 50 g (2 oz) of fat to 50 g (2 oz) flour. Add milk to the required consistency and bring to the boil, stirring constantly. Turn heat down and add chopped, washed fennel leaves until the sauce turns green. Do not boil again. Serve with rich meat and oily fish.

Garlic

Botanical name — *Allium sativum*

The pungent bulb of garlic has been used as a food and a medicine for five thousand years. The ancient Egyptians fed garlic to the slaves toiling on the pyramids to keep them strong and healthy. The first recorded strike in history was when the slaves downed tools as a protest when the garlic failed to appear one day. The Greeks pressed the juice from garlic and drank great quantities in training for the Olympic games.

The Roman armies marched and conquered on a wave of garlic. Their army doctors prescribed garlic for all intestinal and chest complaints among the soldiers. They rubbed cloves of garlic on wounds to stop them becoming septic. The antiseptic qualities of the herb were much valued in the Middle Ages when plagues were raging.

Important herbalists such as Culpeper recommended garlic for its powerful anti-germ qualities. So the bush grew in importance until it became known as 'The Prince of herbs' by Victorian herbalists who invaded the sickroom with strong smelling potions and unguents.

Garlic is perhaps the one herb that has been constantly valued throughout the ages. Early in this century scientific research began into the reasons why it is so potent and as a result garlic is now used by doctors throughout the world. It is prescribed for complaints ranging from high blood pressure, and high cholesterol to chest and stomach disorders. (*See* NUTRITION AND MEDICINE *page* 16)

Content of garlic

Garlic is rich in potassium and phosphorus and has a supply of vitamins B and C. Reasonable amounts of calcium and protein are present in the bulb and oil.

Scientists believe that one of garlic's volatile oils called allyl disulphate is the reason why it is such a powerful antiseptic. Oils of garlic are composed of sulphides and disulphides which can unite with a virus and make it inactive. This was shown by Dr J. Klosa in lengthy experiments in Germany in 1950. The Japanese scientist Fujiwara has proved the ability of garlic to increase the assimilation of vitamin B.

Garlic and bacteria

The ancient reputation for killing germs has proved accurate in the light of modern analysis. A leading Russian scientist, T. Yanovich, reported that he had introduced garlic oil into colonies of bacteria. All movement of the germs stopped in four minutes. The Russians use a garlic vapour in most of their hospitals.

Old uses of garlic

Herbalists and doctors in previous centuries made a very effective medicine by boiling cloves of garlic with vinegar and sugar. This was stored in an earthenware jar and used for asthma, bronchitis, colds, tuberculosis,

---

Aïoli (garlic mayonnaise)

Pound two large cloves of garlic in a mortar and gradually stir in the beaten yolks of two eggs. Add olive oil (or combination of other vegetable oils) drop by drop, until it reaches the required consistency. Aïoli is served traditionally in France with baked potatoes instead of butter. It is also delicious with cold meats and salads

---

and whooping cough. The combination of vinegar and garlic formed a powerful disinfectant.

The Victorian Dr Bowles also prescribed a garlic poultice for the feet when his patients had weak stomachs. That this went rapidly into the blood stream was proved by the smell of garlic on the breath some hours later. On a more basic level, farm workers have worn a clove of garlic inside their socks to ward off colds for many centuries.

Types of garlic

Four main species are generally used: white garlic, the most common kind; pink and red varieties which have fewer but bigger cloves; and giant garlic or Rocambole which is a native of Denmark. This has all the attributes of garlic but a less powerful smell.

Garlic pearles

Garlic pearles are an easy way to get the benefits of the pungent herb. In 1920 a German doctor, J.A. Höfels, discovered a way of putting the essential oils in capsule form. This he called a pearle. It dissolved in the stomach and caused no smell on the breath. The company he founded, Höfels Pure Food, is still one of the leading suppliers and deal in mail order. (*See* WHERE TO BUY *page* 154)

Garlic in cooking

A clove or two of crushed garlic will enhance practically any dish. Rubbing a clove around the salad bowl will not do much, as garlic needs the heat of the oven to bring out the taste. There is evidence to suppose that breath only smells offensively of garlic when the digestion is faulty.

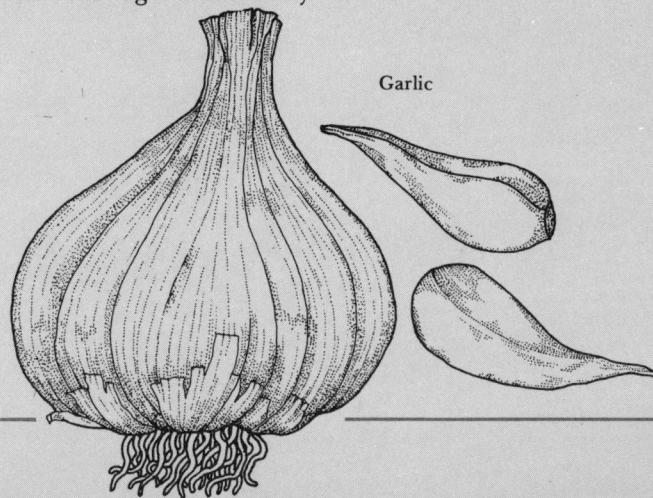

Garlic

125

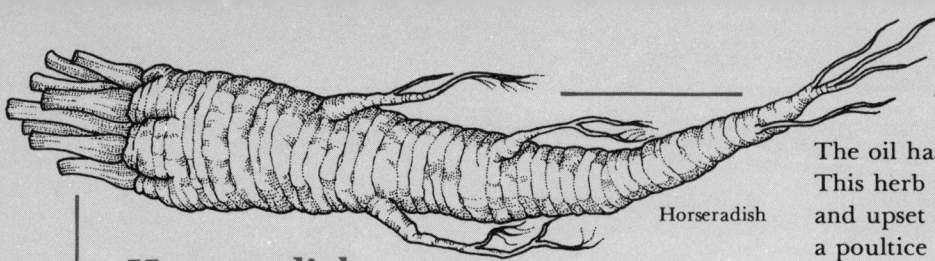
Horseradish

Horseradish

Botanical name — *Cochlearia armoracia*
Horseradish has been cultivated in the temperate zones
of the Old World since earliest history and was one of
the Five Bitter Herbs eaten at Passover. It has many
therapeutic qualities even when used as a condiment.

Medicinal use

Horseradish has powerful natural properties. it contains
a pungent, volatile oil, a natural antibiotic, an
antiseptic and very high levels of vitamin C.
Medicinally, horseradish acts on the kidneys and is a
stimulant to the body. It is gently laxative, and the
antiseptic elements can kill many germs. The volatile
oil has an effect on the mucuous, which is why noses
and eyes stream when strong horseradish is eaten.
These properties exist only in the fresh state. The root's
strength becomes inert on boiling.

In cooking

Old fashioned horseradish relish has become a
connoisseur's delight. It adds vitamin content to white
meats and stimulates complete digestion of rich fish
dishes. Traditionally horseradish is used in Sauce
Raifort, Kren, and *Moutarde des allemandes,* where it
combines a mixture of vinegar, wine, cream, spiced
mustard, and seasoning.

Hyssop

Botanical name — *Hyssopus officinalis*
'Purge me with hyssop and I shall be clean,' said the
psalmist in the Bible. Throughout the ages hyssop has
been used as a cleanser both inside and out. The
Greeks called it 'the holy herb' and used it in their
purification ceremonies.

Medicinal use

Hyssop contains flavanoids, the pro-vitamin C agent,
and a volatile oil, resin, plus a small amount of tannin.

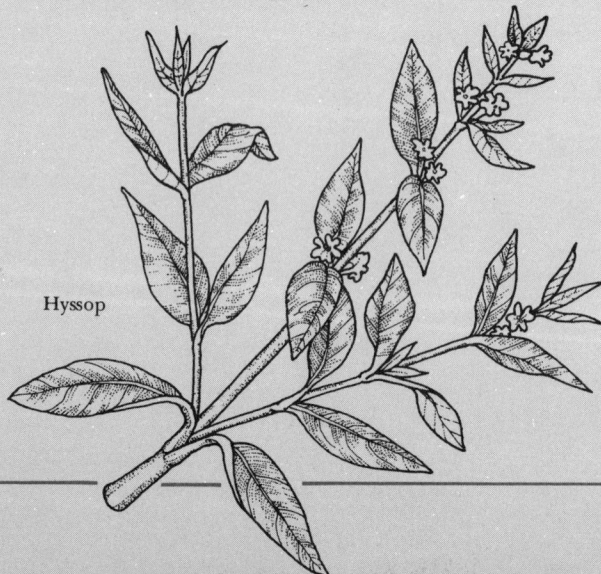
Hyssop

The oil has been found to have antiseptic qualities.
This herb is also a useful remedy for coughs, catarrh
and upset stomachs. It can also be applied externally as
a poultice of bruised leaves to heal bruises and certain
types of muscular rheumatism.

In cooking

Hyssop leaves are very good in a cranberry sauce, or
with a rich pâté such as duck, goose or game. Use a
few chopped leaves in any pulse-type dish using beans,
peas or lentils.

Laurel

Laurel

Botanical name — *Laurus nobilis*
Known also as bay laurel or sweet bay.
Once the highest acclaim for a hero was to have his
brow wreathed in laurel leaves. The French
baccalauréat degree comes directly from the word
bacc-laureus, or laurel berry.

Medicinal use

Laurel contains a powerful oil which can have a
vigorous effect on the system. The Romans thought it
lifted depressions and gave feelings of elation. It
promotes perspiration and so aids feverish colds, and
acts as an aid to digestion. Large doses are emetic.

How to grow

The bay tree is a worthy addition to any garden with
its glossy, pointed dark green leaves. It will grow and
spread to 3 m (10 ft) and double in warmer climates.
Cuttings take easily but are difficult to grow over
winter in cold areas. The shrub will grow in some
shade if it is protected from cold winter winds. It needs
a good, well drained soil and an occasional feed of
compost. Do not confuse this laurel with cherry laurel
of the *Rosaceae* family or mountain laurel grown in the
U.S.A. which are definitely poisonous. It is far better to
get a laurel plant from a good nursery than to try to
take cuttings of wild laurel trees.

In cooking

The bruised leaves are an excellent flavouring and an essential element of bouquet garni. Laurel adds a subtle flavour to meats, fish, soups and casseroles. It adds a distinctive flavour to milk and custard puddings. Always remove bay leaves when serving food — they should never be eaten.

Lemon balm

Botanical name — *Melissa officinalis*
The Greeks always grew lemon balm near bee hives because they thought it enhanced the value of the honey; the botanical name *Melissa* is the Greek for bee.

Medicinal use

Lemon balm dispels flatulence and is generally a good aid for stomach gas. It is diaphoretic, that is, promotes a mild perspiration and so aids feverish colds and influenza. Like other balsams, the volatile oils help clean and heal sores and wounds.

The old herbalists were keen on lemon balm infusions for lifting depressions. Carmelite water was a very popular drink in Europe. This is a blend of distilled lemon balm, angelica root and lemon peel spiced with nutmeg which was alleged to 'renew vigour, strengthen the memory and chase away melancholy'!

In cooking

The flavour of lemon balm is less strong than its scent. A few sprigs of bruised balm improves citrus drinks and claret cups. Torn leaves are a pleasing addition to

Lemon balm

cooked apple, marrow jam and teas served without milk. Used generously, it is an excellent addition to rice and raisin savoury dishes, and as a stuffing for fish and white meats. Lemon balm is a non-intrusive addition to omelettes.

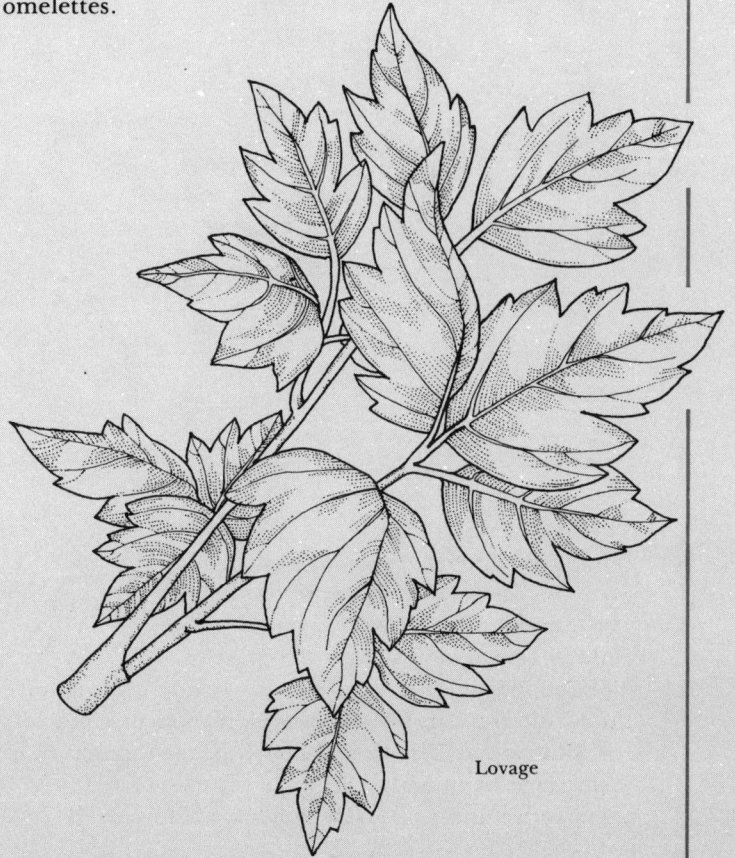

Lovage

Lovage

Botanical name — *Levisticum officinale*
Often called the 'Magi herb' because of the connection with the Three Wise Men, who sought the plant on their search for the Messiah. Lovage, for all its benefits, seems to have gone out of fashion since Elizabethan times.

Medicinal use

Lovage contains a volatile oil called angelic acid which has antiseptic qualities, plus strong resin and oils. These act on the kidneys and bladder and relieve menstrual disorders.

How to grow

Lovage is a perennial plant with mid-green leaves and small whitish flowers during midsummer. Remove the flowering stems to promote further young leaves. Sow the seeds in autumn.

In cooking

The leaves, seeds, stems, and roots are all used. The flavour is musky with a sharp tang. Chopped leaves go well with tomato and potato salads. The crushed seeds can be added to breads and crackers.

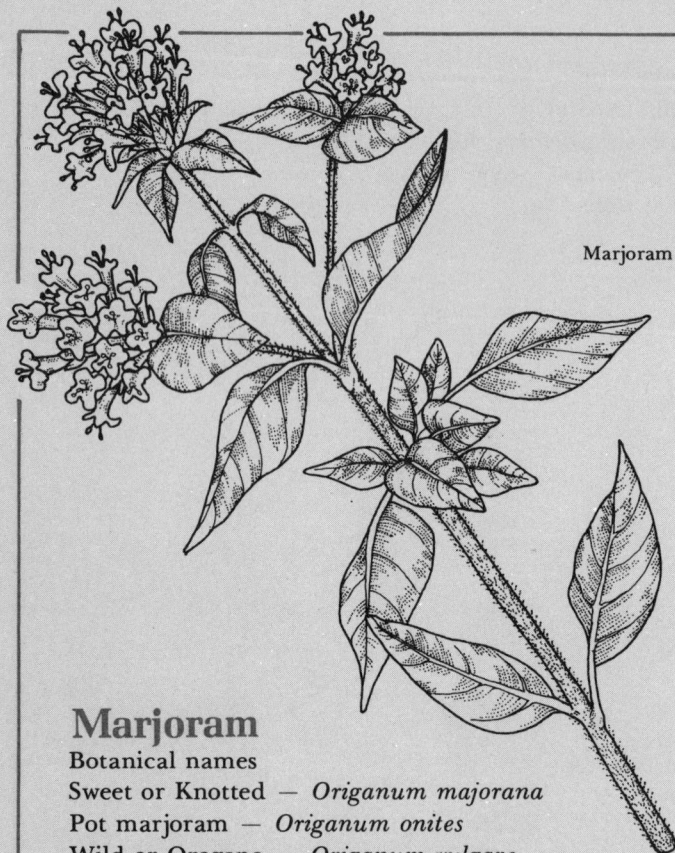

Marjoram

Marjoram

Botanical names
Sweet or Knotted — *Origanum majorana*
Pot marjoram — *Origanum onites*
Wild or Oregano — *Origanum vulgare*
The rose-purple flowers of wild marjoram growing on the Mediterranean hill slopes gave it the name 'Joy of the Mountains'. The Greeks and Romans thought that it presaged happiness. The herb was used as a preservative and as a lovely hued dye for wool.

Medicinal use
Marjoram is antiseptic and stimulant. It helps dispel flatulence and promotes perspiration. Recent research would seem to indicate that this herb aids healing by increasing the white blood cells to fight infection.

The fragrant, balsamic aroma was used in 'swete bags' in Tudor times. For centuries muslin bags containing marjoram have been put in bath water to soothe stiff and aching limbs and rheumatism.

The essential oil of marjoram, called *Oleum origanum*, is recommended for rubbing on stiff or paralytic limbs.

How to grow
Pot marjoram is easier to grow, but it is worthwhile making the effort to nurture sweet marjoram because it is, as its name suggests, sweeter. Treat sweet marjoram as a half hardy annual. Sow the seeds under glass in early spring and plant out when the weather is warm enough.

Pot marjoram is full hardy. The leaves can be used throughout the year. Marjoram plants grow to 60 cm (2 ft) and spread 45 cm (18 in).

Wild marjoram, or oregano, is much more pungent and scented. The seeds of all marjoram are slow to germinate.

In cooking
Marjoram is an essential ingredient in the seasoning of meat, poultry, soups, stews, and stuffings. It is excellent for red meats, as well as pizzas, liver and poultry. It can be added to scones, breads or cheese pastries for flavour and to aid digestion.

All marjorams blend well to obtain mixed herbs, and can be used with breadcrumbs for coating.

The Mints
(Spearmint, Peppermint and Pennyroyal)
Botanical name — *Mentha labiatae*
According to the Greek legend Menthe was a nymph beloved by Pluto. Proserpine was jealous and changed her into Mint, a gentle herb now universally loved.

The Romans had a fine appreciation of the digestive qualities of mint. In the Middle Ages mints flourished in monastic gardens and soothed many an ailment. The great herbalist, Nicholas Culpeper, listed forty maladies for which mint was 'singularly good'. The Pilgrim Fathers took spearmint with them to America, where it 'escaped' and now flourishes all over the continent.

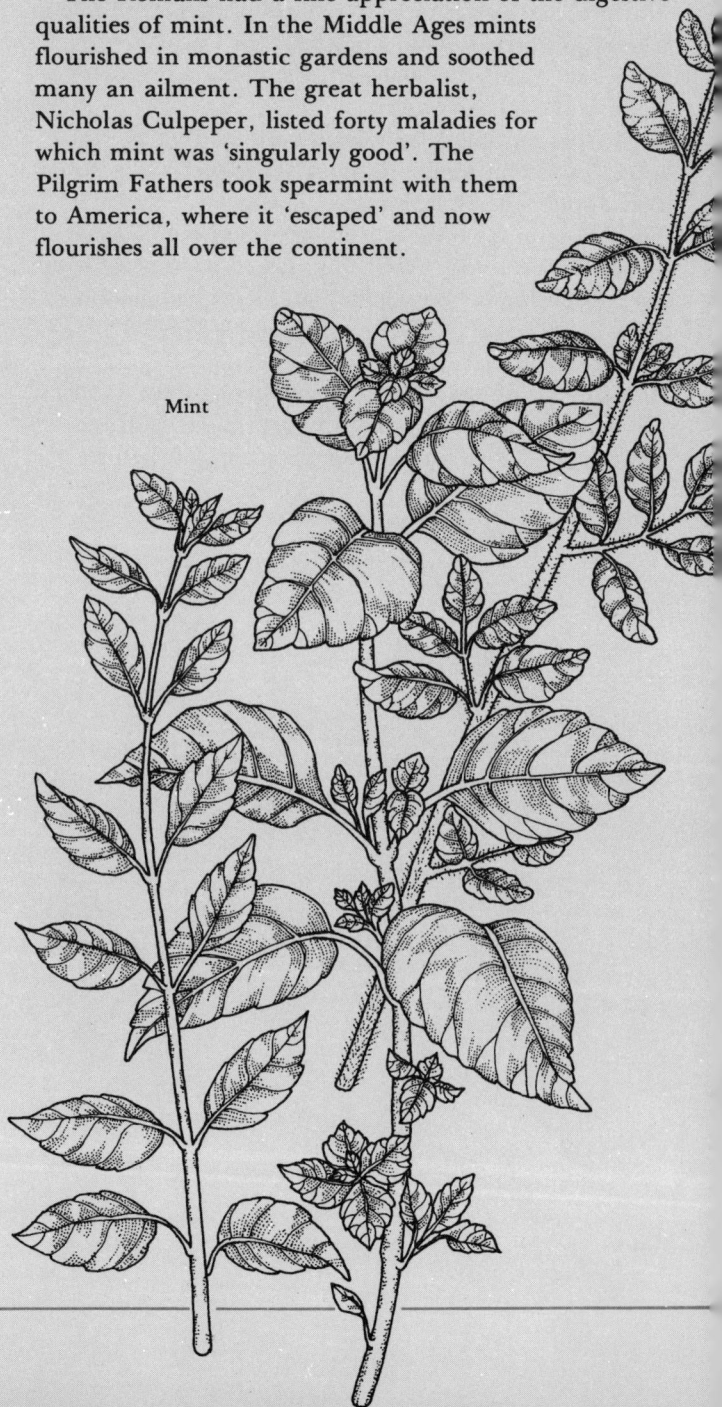

Mint

Medicinal use

The constituents of mint are a fine balance of oils and acids and work in a beneficial way on the digestive organs. It also has cooling properties. It stimulates the appetite, relieves flatulence and alleviates nausea, cramps and spasm of the alimentary tract. Mint is useful against colic and wind in infant feeding.

In cooking

Traditionally mint is used with lamb where its digestive properties come into full light. Make mint sauce by chopping the leaves very finely. For every tablespoon of leaves add ¼ teaspoon honey. Moisten with cider vinegar or lemon juice.

Mint makes delicious jellies and blends well with crushed garlic and cucumber when added to cheese and yoghurt mixtures. Chop the leaves over salads and all young spring vegetables. A cooling leaf of mint is an essential addition to long summer drinks.

Parsley

Botanical name — *Petroselinum crispum*
Parsley has one of the longest recorded herbal histories. The Greeks and Romans wove it into the crowning garlands for their heroes. The Romans thought so highly of its nutritional benefits that their soldiers and horses ate it daily. More legends and folk tales surround this herb than most others; and it is said to thrive in the garden only if the woman is boss of the household.

Medicinal use

Parsley is one of the richest sources of vitamin C and A, with good amounts of B, D, and E. It has as much vitamin A as cod liver oil and more vitamin C than oranges. It is also rich in iron and calcium with amounts of potassium, sulphur, and phosphorus. Its high nutritional content has meant that parsley has been long valued for its health-giving properties. Herb expert Audrey Wynne Hatfield comments that too often parsley is used as a garnish and set aside when it is likely to be richer in value than the food it decorates.

Another constituent is the volatile oil, apiol, which is used in the treatment of malaria. Parsley is used as a diuretic and is helpful in kidney and bladder disorders.
A word of caution Large doses must never be taken, particularly during pregnancy.

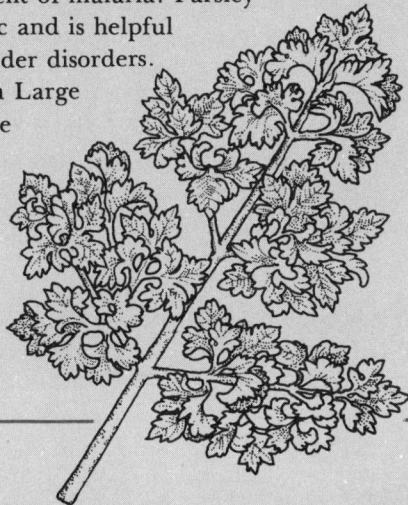

Parsley

In cooking

As well as being a traditional garnish, parsley can be used lavishly in *maître d'hôtel* butter, in parsley sauce, and as an ingredient in *fines herbes*.

Radish

Radish

Botanical name — *Raphanus sativus*
This valuable little salad plant is an excellent source of vitamin C. It was very popular in ancient Egypt and was cultivated along the Mediterranean shores. The name 'radish' comes from the Anglo-Saxon *rude* or *reod* (meaning red) but it did not become popular in Britain until Tudor times.

Medicinal use

Radish contains a pungent volatile oil and amylclytic enzyme. It is useful in urinary ailments and is said to prevent the formation of gallstones and gravel.

How to grow

As soon as the soil is frost free make regular sowings in ½ cm (¼ in) and 1 cm (½ in) drills allowing about 13 cm (5 in) between each seed. Water well to promote quick growth as radishes are sweet and crisp if harvested quickly. Light, fairly rich soil suits them best. They will thrive in the shade of asparagus and potatoes, fennel or parsley but never plant radishes anywhere near hyssop.

In cooking

Radish is excellent in all salads and with cheeses. Make several cuts stopping almost at the base of the bulb. Put in iced water for a few minutes and the radish will then open up like a flower.

Rosemary

Botanical name — *Rosmarinus officinalis*

This sweet scented bush with its spiky leaves is the emblem of everlasting love and remembrance. Rosemary is traditionally woven into bridal garlands and a few sprigs are chopped into Christmas puddings and birthday cakes.

Sir Thomas More wrote, 'As for Rosmarine . . . not only my bees love it . . . it is the herb sacred to remembrance and therefore, to friendship.' Rosemary's sea-green slender leaves have prompted the name 'dew of the sea'. It was burned frequently in sick rooms to purify the air.

In medicine

Oil of rosemary is distilled from the flowering tops of the plant. The pungent, pointed leaves are much used in medicine and perfumery. Rosemary's constituents are a combination of oils and acids, with astringent qualities, and it is used as a tonic. It also promotes perspiration and since Elizabethan times it has been held to ease nervous depressions. This ancient reputation for stimulating the brain and helping nervous disorders has some basis in fact because rosemary has a definite effect on the blood vessels.

The oil or infused leaves of rosemary are very effective for hair and scalp health. The oil will stimulate the scalp follicles and also darken the hair. **A word of warning** Strong infusions of this herb act on the heart and blood vessels. Heart patients should perhaps be cautious about drinking rosemary tea too often.

How to grow

Rosemary will grow to about 2 m (6-7 ft) and have a similar spread in the right conditions. It produces light blue flowers in summer. It may not grow so high on chalky soils, but it is supposed to be more aromatic. Ideal conditions would be a south-facing wall in light soil. Rosemary will grow even in northern borders of the garden if it is provided with protection from the wind. More inclement conditions may prevent the bush from flowering. The stems of rosemary can be easily pegged and layered in summer to raise new plants; it is easily propagated by seed, layering, and cuttings.

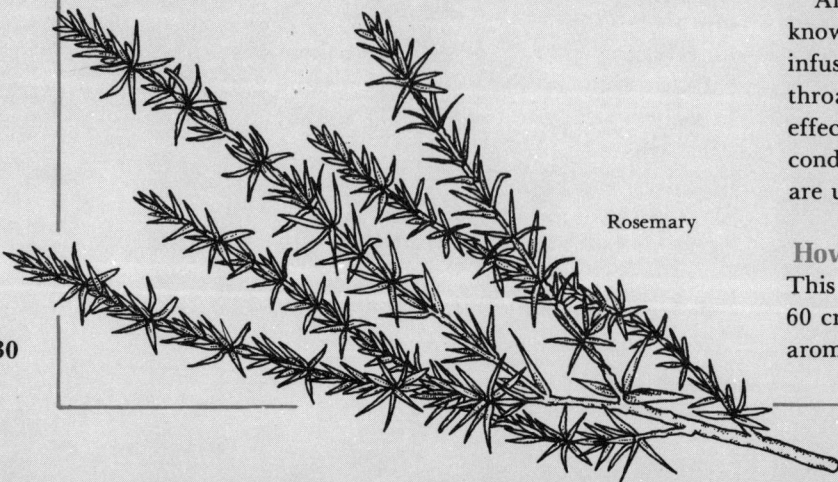

Rosemary

In cooking

The leaves are most useful sprinkled over rich meat such as lamb, pork and rabbit, or grilled fish. Rosemary conserve makes a good sweetmeat or accompaniment to meat instead of currant jelly.

Lamb spiked with rosemary

This dish is typical of Mediterranean countries. The rosemary adds a distinctive flavour to the meat and smells delicious.

1 leg lamb
6 cloves garlic
6 leaves rosemary
freshly ground black pepper
1 tablespoon olive or safflower oil
175 ml (6 fl oz) or 1 U.S. cup white wine

Prick the meat sharply with a knife and insert a rosemary leaf in the slot. 'Plug' with a clove of garlic. Repeat at judicious points around the meat. Rub olive oil over the joint, sprinkle with freshly ground black pepper. Wrap in foil and cook in medium oven for about one hour. Remove the foil. At this stage you can pluck out some of the rosemary sprigs if the meat is to be only lightly flavoured. Pour the wine over the meat and continue to cook until well done.

Sage

Botanical name — *Salvia officinalis*

In country districts throughout Europe, older people still chew a few leaves of sage every morning, perhaps heeding the motto: 'Who has sage in his garden, he would live for aye'.

The official name for this evergreen sub-shrub is translated variously as 'To save', 'to heal', or 'I am well'. Certainly its benefits have been well appreciated since the Romans.

Medicinal use

The constituents of sage are volatile oils, tannin and resin which are stimulating and astringent. It also has a substance called ketone thujone which helps animal tissues to resist putrefaction.

All parts of sage are of value. Sage tea has been known to lower blood sugar in diabetics. A similar infusion makes an excellent gargle for sore or relaxed throats and bleeding gums. Small doses of sage are effective in fevers, biliousness, fatigue, ovarian conditions, liver and kidney disorders. Sage infusions are used to restore fading dark hair.

How to grow

This hardy evergreen shrub will grow and spread up to 60 cm (2 ft). It has oblong-ovate, greyish green aromatic leaves which smell rather like eucalyptus and

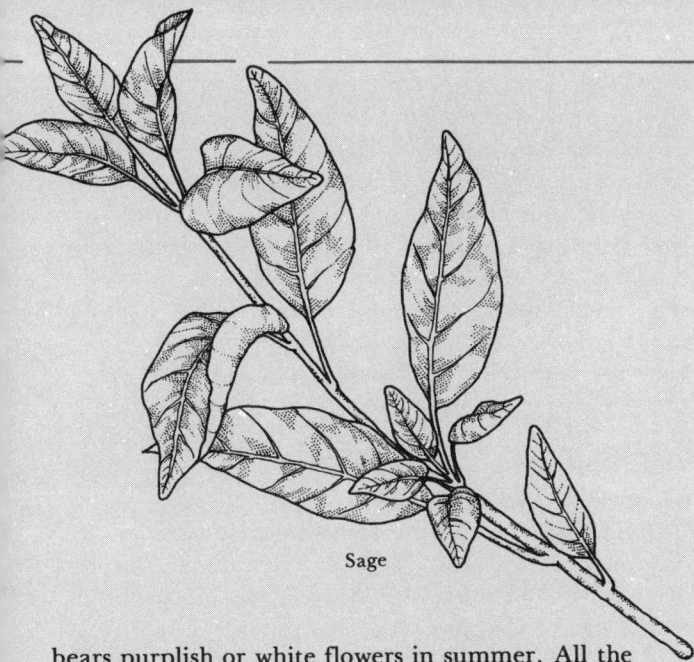
Sage

bears purplish or white flowers in summer. All the sages grow well in good, rather dry soils in sunny positions. After four or five years the plants tend to grow rather woody, so propagate by cuttings or divisions from two-year old plants to keep up a good supply.

In cooking

Sage's volatile oils aid digestion and help dispel flatulence. It has rather a strong taste so use sparingly. This herb is superb with cheese, especially home-made ones. Add a few chopped leaves to soya beans, split peas or any of the pulses; mix with almonds and other nuts when adding to savory rice dishes. Chop a few fresh leaves over cooked spinach, onions, potatoes, aubergines and beetroot. Use carefully with any rich meats or fish, such as goose, liver, pork, hare and beef. Sage is a good addition to herb butters.

L'aigo boulido (Traditional French sage soup)
1 large sprig sage
1 sprig thyme
1 bay leaf
2 tablespoons mayonnaise
1.2 litres (2 pints) or 5 U.S. cups water
freshly ground black pepper
pinch salt
6 cloves garlic
Crush the cloves of garlic. Bring the water to the boil and add the garlic; simmer for five minutes. Take off the heat and add the chopped sage, thyme and bay leaf. Allow to infuse for four minutes and strain out the herbs. Add a little of the liquid to mayonnaise in a bowl and mix. Gradually add to the herbed water. Put back on heat but do not boil, stirring all the time until it thickens. Serve with garlic bread.

Savory

Botanical names — Summer savory — *Satureia hortensis*
Winter savory — *Satureia montana*

Early American settlers took these two sweet herbs with them as a reminder of the scents of the Old World. Today, market gardeners plant summer savory between the rows of bean crops to ward off black fly. (*See* GARDENING ON A HEALTHY SOIL, *page* 148). The savory must be in flower before the black fly start attacking. Savory has an affinity with beans, both in growing, and as an accompaniment in eating them.

Medicinal use

Summer savory is the medicinally valuable one; winter savory merely pleases the taste buds and aids digestion. Summer savory eases colic and dispels flatulence. It is warming and easing for catarrh and coughs and is often added to cough medicines as a warming aromatic agent.

According to folk lore, savory is a great soother of sore eyes. An infusion may be made of one teaspoon of the dried herb to 275 ml ($\frac{1}{2}$ pint) or $1\frac{3}{4}$ U.S. cups of boiling water. When the mixture has cooled, strain and bathe the eyes.

In cooking

Savory's warm, rather spicy taste is an excellent addition in all bean, pea and lentil dishes. It is good in stuffings, and mince meat recipes and many cooks choose savory for their trout dishes. Put a sprig of savory in with beans (including soya) while cooking. Sprinkle the dried herb over salads.

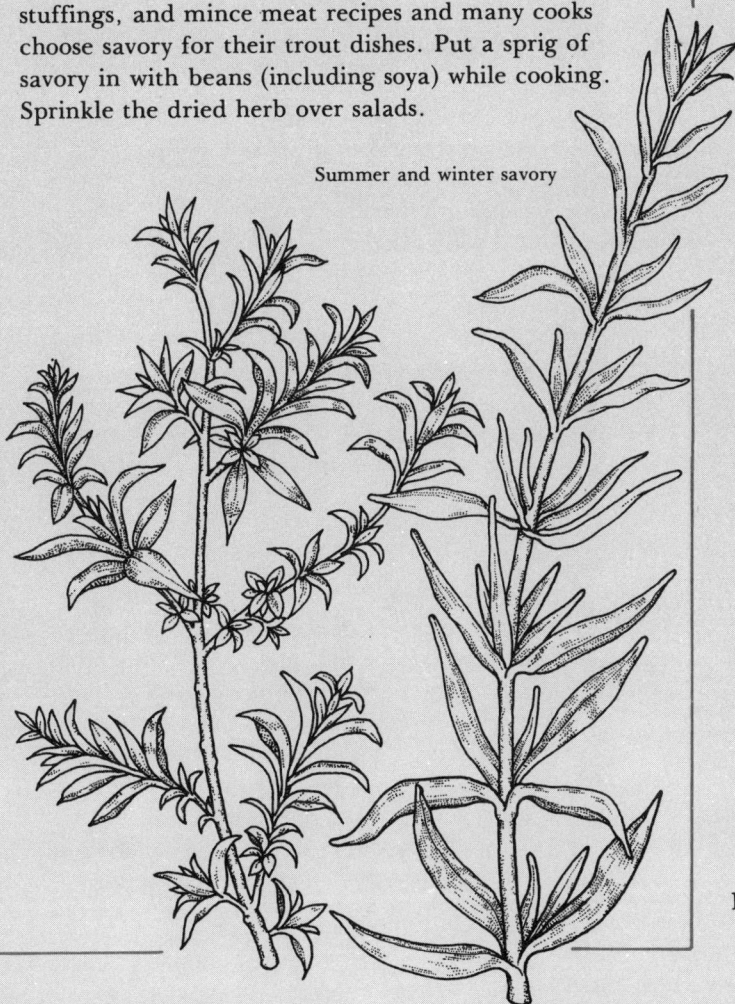
Summer and winter savory

131

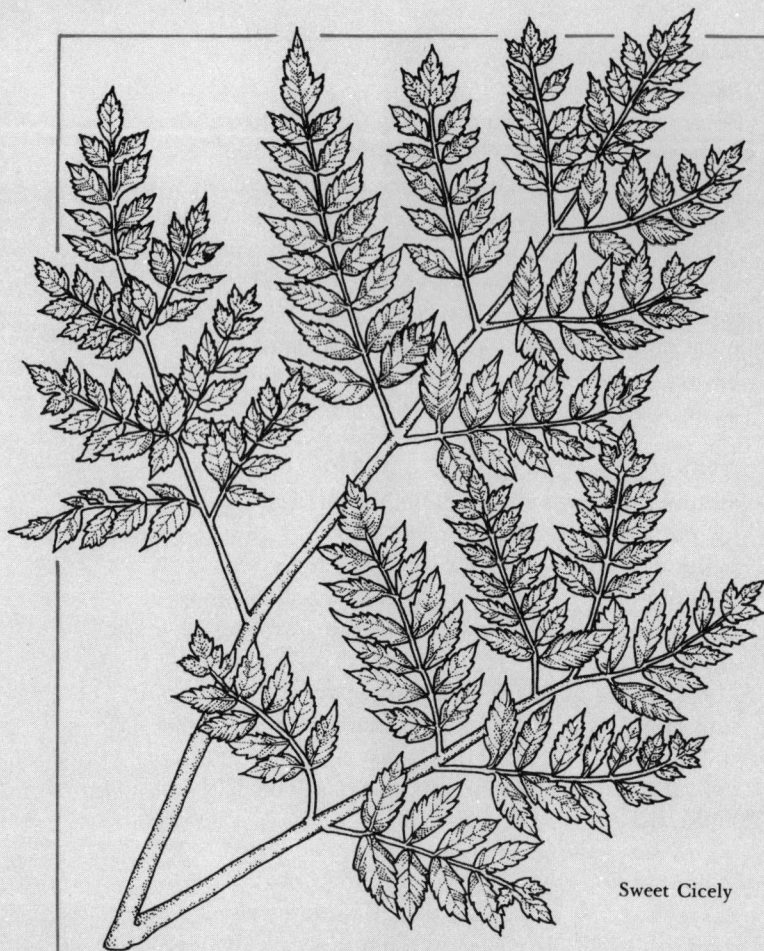

Sweet Cicely

Sweet Cicely

Botanical name — *Myrrhis odorata*
This delicate fern-like herb bears ruffles of white
flowers in summer and will grace any herb garden. It
has a slightly anise flavour and its large, dark, brown
seeds were popularly blended into a wax polish to
perfume old wooden floors.

Medicinal use
The whole plant and seed possess useful properties.
The fresh roots are antiseptic and are prescribed by
herbalists for girls during puberty. The distilled water
of cicely is diuretic and acts on the kidneys. Essence of
cicely is believed to be aphrodisiac. Ointment of the
herb is soothing in gout.

How to grow
Sweet cicely will obligingly thrive in almost any good
soil and does not object to a damp, shady site. Plant
the seed when the frost is past and thin out seedlings to
allow for full 1.5 m (5 ft) of spread for each plant.

In cooking
This herb is ideal for slimmers. A tablespoonful or two
of chopped cicely leaves and stalk will flavour and
sweeten any tart fruits and vegetables. It counteracts
the acidity of gooseberries and plums. The anise
flavour is excellent with cabbage dishes and parsnips.

Chopped leaves are good with salad dressings and as a
flavour for fruit juice cocktails.
  The fresh roots make a tasty vegetable chopped into
salads, or boiled and sprinkled with oil and vinegar.
The green seeds are good in salads as flavouring. When
the seeds are ripe, store them for flavouring winter
stews and soups. In Germany the ripe seeds are ground
up like pepper and used as a tasty condiment. Cicely
seeds are popular in all Middle European cooking.

Tarragon

Botanical name — *Artemisia dracunculus*
'The little dragon' is the translation of tarragon's
botanical name and it is a good description of the
slender leaf with a big bite. Ancient herbalists noted
that it was 'a friend to head, heart and liver'.

Medicinal use
Chemically, tarragon contains the same volatile oil as
anise. It promotes digestion and stimulates appetite,
and its stimulating properties also act on the heart and
liver.

How to grow
It is important to grow French tarragon as the Russian
tarragon is very much inferior. French tarragon has
smooth dark leaves set alternately around a dainty
stem. Russian tarragon (*Artemisia dracunculoides*) is
paler and often has a pronged leaf; its flavour is only
minimal.
  Tarragon can be difficult to grow. It needs a fertile,
well drained soil in full sun. Under good conditions, it
will spread 60 cm (2 ft) and make a delicate bush. The
yellow flowers of summer seldom mature, so it is
advisable to take shoots from the tangle of roots each
year for continuity.

Tarragon

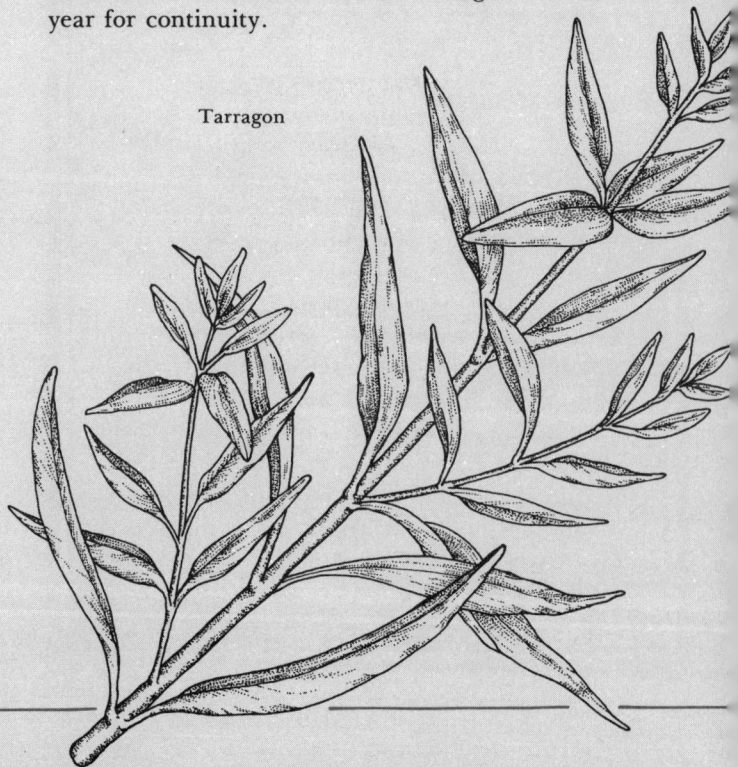

In cooking

Tarragon vinegar is one of the great flavourings of French cuisine. It can be made simply by putting 50 g (2 oz) of tarragon leaves in a bottle and pouring on 575 ml (1 pint) or 2½ U.S. cups of wine vinegar. Cap the bottle and strain after about four weeks. Use the vinegar in salad dressings, mayonnaise and mustards. It is the correct ingredient for sauce Béarnaise.

Tarragon has an affinity with chicken, as in the classic *poulet à l'estragon*. Serve tarragon butter with artichokes, broccoli spears, and asparagus. Sprinkle tarragon over mixed salads.

Thyme

Botanical name — *Thymus vulgaris*
In the days of Chivalry, ladies embroidered a symbolic sprig of thyme and a honey-bee on their scarves, which they gave as 'favours' to the bravest knights.

Originally, thyme took its name from the Greek for fumigate. Its powerful antiseptic qualities were appreciated in the ancient world for purification. This sweet-smelling, creeping plant is beloved by the bees and the many varieties of thyme give a variety of delicious honeys. The famous Hymettus honey comes from the thyme-clothed slopes of Mount Hymettus, near Athens.

Medicinal use

Thyme's constituents include phenol, thymol and carvacrol which are antiseptic and have antibiotic properties. It is a most beneficial herb and has an invigorating effect on the system.

Medical herbalists prescribe solutions of thyme for many female complaints, for it is especially beneficial to the womb. Thyme is also very effective as a gargle for sore throats and catarrh. As such it is included in many medications for those complaints. Thyme tea promotes perspiration and eases bronchitis.

In cooking

Thyme is one of the great herbs in cooking. It has the quality of being pungent and warming, yet subtle. No bouquet garni would be complete without it. Thyme can be added to many soups; adds distinction to court bouillon and many stuffings; gives zest to vegetarian dishes with peppers, courgettes and aubergines. Thyme's great culinary asset is its affinity with the traditional meat dishes cooked slowly with wine and garlic. *Boeuf en daube* and *boeuf bourguignon,* for instance, are greatly enhanced by a sprinkling of thyme.

Types of thyme

The most common type is the *Thymus vulgaris* often called garden thyme. Lemon thyme *(Thymus citriodorus)* is popular with many cooks. So is caraway thyme *(Thymus herba-barona)* which was traditionally used with baron of beef. Wild thyme *(Thymus serpyllum),* often called Shepherd's thyme, can be used in cooking but has less taste.

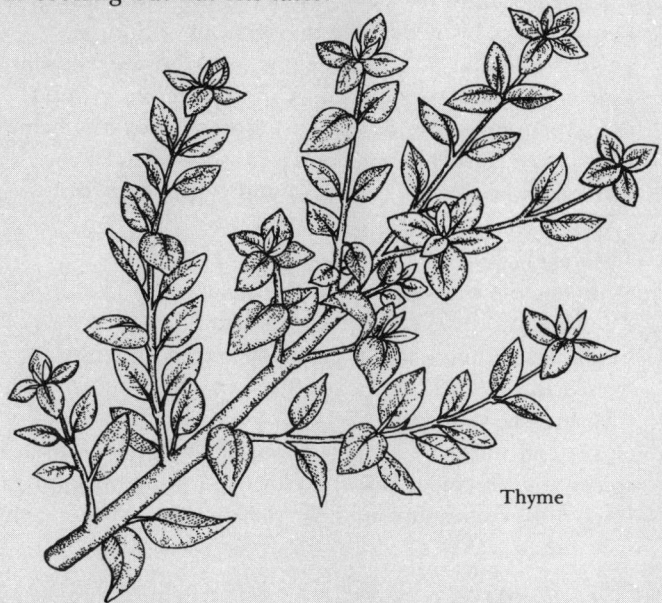

Thyme

How to dry herbs

Gather herbs for drying in the morning when the sun has dried the dew. Plants grown mainly for their leaves should be picked when they are young and fresh. Flowers should be picked in full bloom, and seeds gathered in late summer when they are ripe.

All parts of the plant are dried in the same way. If washing is really required, use cool water and pat dry with kitchen paper. It is better to let the leaves stay on the stem for drying unless they are very large.

Put the herbs on flat trays or cheesecloth and put in a dry, airy place such as an airing cupboard. Turn them carefully at least once a day. Most plants will become brittle and dry after five days.

Test to see if the herbs are dry enough by putting them in a glass jar for a few days. If any moisture gathers on the sides of the glass, more drying is needed.

The English Herb Society recommends opaque containers to store dried herbs. Tightly close the lids and keep them out of direct sunlight.

An alternative way of drying plants is to tie stems together into loose bunches and hang tip downwards. Hook the bunches in a warmish place where the air can circulate. These bunches of drying herbs are a delightful and aromatic part of many French kitchens. Bunches generally take longer to dry than the leaves on their own. Strip the leaves off when they are brittle and store in the recommended containers.

Some herbs, such as PARSLEY, chervil and CHIVES, do not dry well but make excellent subjects for freezing. Blanch the leaves for one minute, then plunge into chilled water until cold. Drain well and pack into small polythene freezer bags or foil.

Spices

All spices should be stored whole, and ground just before use. This is because they contain a highly volatile essential oil which begins to evaporate as soon as it is ground. A recipe that calls for freshly ground black pepper or freshly grated nutmeg is not just being finicky. As freshly ground spice can really make the difference between a mediocre and a first class dish.

Allspice (Jamaica pepper)

Many people buy allspice on the assumption that it is a combination of several spices. In fact, allspice is a small purple berry which grows on a tree native to the West Indies. The berries are dried in the sun until they turn brown; they taste like a mixture of cinnamon, cloves and nutmeg. Allspice is one of the most useful spices and enhances cakes, curries and pilau. It is the spice most commonly used for marinating Scandinavian fish dishes.

Cinnamon

Cinnamon is the bark of a small evergreen tree which is a native of Sri Lanka. Cassia also comes from the same family and is often sold instead of cinnamon. True cinnamon has a lighter and more delicate flavour than cassia. To obtain the best quality, the outer layers of the tree are taken off and the fine inner sheaf rolled into spills. These are sold as 'cinnamon sticks'.

Cinnamon is very popular in Western cookery in many cakes and delicacies. In Eastern dishes cinnamon sticks are often put in with meat dishes such as lamb to give a lingering flavour. Many curries use cinnamon as an ingredient. It contains the powerful antiseptic oil, phenol.

Cloves

Cloves actually came from Spice Island. They were taken to China and spread, via the Caravanserai, to the Middle East and Europe. The cloves that we buy are the dried berries of the clove tree. Ideally, they should be round and oily when they reach the shops, not dry and wrinkled.

Cloves have a particularly pungent taste that goes well with long-cooked meat, such as the French *pot-au-feu*. It has become traditional in the West to stick cloves in apples and hams and recipes for many

pickles recommend them. They add a distinctive flavour to spiced wines and liqueurs.

In the East, cloves are used in all varieties of curries, where their essential oil, phenol, prevents putrefaction of the meat.

Ginger

Ginger is the root of a tropical plant which is now grown in many hot countries such as Australia. The root looks like a swollen fist, and is actually called a 'hand' of ginger. It is easy to buy the root fresh, peel it and pulp it to add to curries as cooks do in the Middle and Near East.

The dried root is bruised before chopping and adding to recipes. It can be ground in a coffee mill just before using. Unfortunately, most ginger is bought in finely ground form, where it quickly loses its lovely aroma. Dried ginger is immensely popular in the West for ginger breads and biscuits, beers and cordials, puddings and sweets.

in mortar: whole allspice
in pots: black pepper, whole cloves, white peppercorns, ginger root cinnamon sticks
in dishes: ground allspice, ground ginger, ground nutmeg, mace
in the foreground: vanilla pods, whole nutmegs, nutmegs with their covering of mace

The most delicate parts of the root are made into crystallized or 'stem' ginger, a favourite delicacy.

Mace

This is the inner case or aril of the nutmeg. The delicate red webbing is dried into blades of mace. It has a more delicate flavour than nutmeg and is more expensive.

Nutmeg

The nutmeg is the inner part of a yellowish fruit which grows on the nutmeg tree. When the fruit is ripe it splits and the hard, black nutmeg is taken out and dried. Sometimes the nutmeg is coated with lime as an insect deterrent.

Nutmeg is a particularly useful spice which flavours a wide variety of dishes. It goes into cakes and custards, haggis and sausages, ravioli and spinach. Although nutmeg is not an essential flavouring in curries, it is popular in Middle Eastern dishes.

Mulled and spiced wine drinks often contain nutmeg. Never use large quantities of this spice as it is poisonous in overdosage.

Pepper (vine peppers)

Both black and white pepper come from a vigorous tropical vine. Clusters of red berries hang among the dark leaves. For black pepper, the berries are picked green and dried in the sun until they turn darkish brown or black. For white pepper, the berries are allowed to ripen on the plant to the full bright red colour. These are dried and then the outer skin is removed.

All pepper contains piperine, an alkaloid which acts as a stimulant on the digestion and promotes perspiration. Black pepper is more pungent than white. During cooking this pungency is dispelled but the essential oils remain.

Pepper is one of the great spices and was the reason for the long search for a sea route to the East. Today it retains its importance and adds an indefinable zest to so many dishes.

Vanilla

Vanilla is the pod of an exotic climbing orchid which is native to Central America. The pods are picked before they ripen and develop the vanilla flavour by enzyme activity during a long curing process.

The curing makes the pods tough yet flexible, rather like leather hide. Serious cooks buy the pods rather than vanilla essence in bottles. The essence is often extracted chemically and may have added preservatives. Apart from this reason, the vanilla pod itself tastes so much better and can be used time and time again. Scoop the pod out of a dish just before serving, rinse under cool water and pat dry with kitchen paper. Store the pods in an airtight jar.

Why not just drink tea and coffee?

Common beverages such as coffee, tea and cola contain caffeine, a powerful stimulant belonging to the bitter alkaloids family.

Caffeine can increase the basic metabolic rate (known as B.M.R.) by 10%. Regular large doses then mask the attendant symptoms — high blood pressure, hyperacidity, nausea, increased pulse rate, and anxiety. *The Lancet*, a leading British medical journal, advised doctors in 1977 to look out for these symptoms of caffeine addiction among patients seeking help for many ailments including headaches and anxiety state.

Freshly ground coffee can contain 100 mg of caffeine per cup; instant coffee has 80 mg of caffeine per cup; tea contains 60 mg, and cola 40 mg. So it is easy to see how a person drinking a reasonable six or eight cups of coffee each day consumes about 600 mg of caffeine and is likely to be clinically addicted.

This beverage section deals with the many delicious alternative beverages many of which have positive health benefits.

Coffee substitutes

Dandelion coffee is one of the most delicious of the coffee substitutes. It can be bought as an instant powder, but why not make it yourself? Dig up the roots of two-year-old dandelion plants in autumn when they are stocked with essential food reserves. Snip off the crowns, wash the roots gently and pat dry with kitchen paper. Bake them in a cool oven until quite dry; to crisp the outsides turn up the heat when they are nearly dry before removing them from the oven. Store the dandelion roots in an airtight tin and only grind them just before use.

Many different blends of dandelion coffee, all varying in taste, are now widely available and some manufacturers add lactose or other natural sweeteners

Grain coffees There are many ingenious mixtures of 'coffees' based on toasted grains. One contains RYE, OATS, MILLET, BARLEY, figs and chicory. Another, equally popular, is made from toasted BRAN, WHEAT and MOLASSES. These grain beverages need gentle boiling to bring out the flavour, and actually improve with reheating.

Postum is the original coffee substitute and deserves a special mention. It cannot be made at home and is manufactured by mixing molasses and bran and roasting them to a high temperature. Red wheat is then blended in, and the ingredients finely ground. Add boiling water to make a tasty drink.

Swiss coffee substitutes The main difference is that these drinks contain fruits and roots as well as grains and cereals.

What about decaffeinated coffee? If regular intake of caffeine is to be avoided, it might reasonably be supposed that decaffeinated coffee is a good substitute. Unfortunately, American tests have revealed that the chemical used to take out the caffeine often remains in the coffee.

China tea

Mint tea

Chamomile tea

Orange juice

High protein drink

Tomato juice

Herb teas

Drinking a herb tea is a delicious way to absorb the health-giving qualities of the plants. Such has been the increase in popularity of herbal beverages that many flavours are now available in quick and easy tea bags.

An introduction to herb teas might best be made with one of the great favourites — CHAMOMILE, LIME or MINT. Over a hundred varieties are available on sale, so there is great scope for developing a taste for herbal drinks. ALFALFA, ANISE, celery seed, COMFREY, FENNEL, FENUGREEK SEED, mullein, PAPAYA, raspberry, sarsaparilla, SAGE and yerba santa are just a few of the health-giving teas.

Mixing your own herb tea

It is easy to buy or dry a variety of herbs and mix them to fit your own needs and tastes. Stronger leaves can be balanced with milder flavours, or a blend can be mixed to aid a specific complaint. For instance, a commercial herb tea which acts on the kidneys and liver contains buchu, couch grass, fennel, marshmallow, senna leaf and yarrow. A popular traditional English herb tea contains agrimony, dandelion, meadowsweet, melilot, nettles and logwood.

Some of the major herbs which can be infused or decocted as a tea and which aid specific ailments are listed below:

Infusion

arthritis — COMFREY, DANDELION, BUCKWHEAT.
asthma — nettle, coltsfoot, MARJORAM.
bladder disorders — BUCHU, couch grass,
 DANDELION, PARSLEY.
bronchitis — ANISE, BORAGE, CICELY, coltsfoot,
 COMFREY, elder.
catarrh — BALM, CICELY, coltsfoot, elder, THYME.
colds — elderflower, PEPPERMINT, tansy, THYME,
 SAGE coltsfoot.
cystitis — BUCHU, couch grass, marshmallow.
digestive complaints — ANISE, BASIL, CHAMOMILE,
 CICELY, DANDELION, FENNEL, HYSSOP, MINT,
 PARSLEY, tansy, THYME.
fatigue — DANDELION, nettle, ANGELICA, DILL, SAGE.
insomnia — CHAMOMILE, lime, cowslip.
menstrual disorders — meadowsweet, CICELY,
 tansy, THYME, BUCKWHEAT.
rheumatism — COMFREY, couch grass, cowslip, HYSSOP.
sprains — COMFREY, BUCKWHEAT, mallow.
varicose veins — BUCKWHEAT, lime.

Decoction

arthritis and rheumatism — celery seeds.
eczema and skin complaints — DANDELION roots.
general vitality — sarsaparilla root.
slimming and gastric troubles — fenugreek seed.
There are two ways of making herb teas —

How to infuse

Boiling water is poured on the leaves rather like ordinary tea. Most dried herbs, flowers and leaves are infused. Use only stainless steel or ceramic containers, *never* aluminium or iron. Use one teaspoon of leaves for each cup of water. Pour on the boiling water and allow to steep for five or ten minutes. (Herb tea bags are perforated to steep faster.) Do not allow the steam to escape while steeping. Cover up the lid and spout tightly; then strain and flavour with a slice of lemon or a spoonful of honey.

How to Decoct

In this method the herbs are gently boiled. Seeds, roots, barks and chips are decocted. Use about two tablespoons of seeds, roots etc. for each 600 ml (1 pint) or $2\frac{1}{2}$ U.S. cups of water. Use slightly more water if so desired in order to allow for evaporation. Bring to the boil, cover and simmer for about 15 minutes. Use only stainless steel or ceramic containers. Strain into a teapot or jug, cover and steep a few more minutes before pouring.

Bancha tea is a macrobiotic tea made from herbs and twigs. George Ohsawa, who introduced macrobiotics to the U.S.A. recommends ten parts of bancha tea to one part of soy sauce for an invigorating 'pick-me-up'.

Green buckwheat tea is made from natural dried buckwheat leaf and flower and contains all the benefits of the plant itself. Buckwheat is rich in rutin which has an excellent effect on the arteries and circulation. It is also rich in iron and B vitamins. (*See page 30*) Buckwheat tea is free from caffeine and tannin which can cause digestive imbalances.

Gossip tea is made from rose hips, cloves, orange peel, and hibiscus, and thus has a spicy taste. It is rich in vitamin C and caffeine and tannin free.

Luaka tea comes from the high mountainous areas in the east of Sri Lanka. It is lower in tannin and caffeine than other 'ordinary' teas.

Mu tea is the great Japanese tea which contains GINSENG and fifteen other herbs. The word 'mu' is Japanese for space or infinity. Macrobiotics consider this tea to be the most yang or alkaline of all beverages. Constituent herbs in mu tea include ligusticum, paonia root, rehmannia, coptis, licorice root, atractylis, and hoelen. Mu tea has a full, spicy taste and is a powerful stimulant and astringent which induces perspiration.

Rooibosch tea comes from the *Aspalathus linearis* plant which grows on the mountains of the west Cape of South Africa. It contains no caffeine or tannin and many claims are made for its health-giving properties, especially as an anti-allergy factor. Rooibosch contains vitamin C, iron, manganese, calcium, magnesium, potassium and sulphate. The plant was first used by the Hottentots who ascribed many healing powers to it. This tea has a pleasant taste, not unlike Earl Grey and is distributed world wide. (*See* WHERE TO BUY *page* 152).

High protein drinks

High protein drinks are made by mixing natural food protein powders with milk or water. These powders contain a wide variety of ingredients. Typical constituents are LECITHIN granules, BREWER'S YEAST, essential oils such as WHEAT GERM and SAFFLOWER, cooked SOYA flour (See LEGUMES page 80), CAROB. dried YOGHURT or papain, and skimmed milk powder. It is generally cheaper to buy the ingredients and mix the drinks yourself.

The value of high protein drinks lies in their concentration and balance of essential nutrients. Each item of the drink can be carefully chosen for its specific nutritive quality. These concentrated drinks can take the place of a meal and nutritious liquid 'food' is a great asset in times of illness, stress, or simply when time is short at breakfast.

The following recipes are easier to blend in a liquidizer. The optional ingredients can be chosen according to their respective nutritive value or as the imagination dictates. For instance, postum could replace carob, or molasses could be used instead of honey.

Carob milk shake
700 ml (24 fl. oz) or 3 U.S. cups milk
1 or 2 tablespoons carob powder
1 tablespoon honey
2 teaspoons granular lecithin or
1 teaspoon brewer's yeast

High protein booster
700 ml (24 fl oz) or 3 U.S. cups milk
100 ml (4 fl oz) or ½ U.S. cup fresh yoghurt
2 teaspoons brewer's yeast
1 tablespoon vegetable oil ' 2 egg yolks
The following are optional —
1 teaspoon bone meal
2 teaspoons cooked soya flour
100 ml (4 fl oz) or ½ U.S. cup
frozen orange juice or
100 ml (4 fl oz) or ½ U.S. cup chopped papaya
1 teaspoon natural vanilla
100 ml (4 fl oz) or ½ U.S. cup
skimmed milk powder

Juices

Making your own juices is an excellent way of obtaining the nutrients of the fruit or vegetable in a convenient and palatable form. In addition, juices concentrate the goodness of the natural product. It takes four cups of raw chopped carrots to obtain one cup of juice. Juices provide everything contained in the raw substance, except fibre, which is lost in the juicing process. Carrots, not normally considered a good source of protein, contain more protein than an egg when used as carrot juice.

Pineapple pol
Half a fresh pineapple
4 lettuce leaves
juice of 2 oranges
Put the chopped up pineapple in a blender, add the diced lettuce leaves and the orange juice. Buzz until smooth. If you like, leave a few pineapple chunks whole.

Tomato sun up
100 g (¼ lb) skinned tomatoes or
100 ml (4 fl oz) or ½ U.S. cup tinned juice
2 cups diced carrots
a dash of Worcester or soy sauce
100 g (4 oz) yoghurt
Put the tomatoes and carrots in the blender with the yoghurt.
Buzz two or three times.
Add Worcester or soy sauce to taste.

Nutritional content
225 ml (8 fl oz) or 1 U.S. cup of carrot juice contain: 35,000 I.U. vitamin A. 0.56 mg vitamin B1 (thiamine), 0.66 mg B2 (riboflavin), 40 mg vitamin C, 360 mg calcium, 328 mg phosphorus, 4.8 mg iron, and provide 8 g of protein.

The very concentrated character of juices gives cause for alarm in some quarters. This is especially so following the bizarre case of the Englishman, reported in the *New Scientist* in 1974, who drank himself to death on carrot juice while taking massive doses of vitamin A.

The recommended daily dietary allowance for an adult is approximately 5000 I.U. of vitamin A. Most people could possibly take 50,000 I.U. a day for very short periods without harm. Since the vitamin is stored in the body, amounts taken by the misguided carrot freak reached 70,000,000 I.U. a day. This does illustrate the fact that juices, like whisky and other powerful drinks, should be treated with respect. Parsley, for example, contains apiol and other constituents which should not be used in highly concentrated form.

Most ordinary imbibers of fruit juice drink enough only to obtain the health-giving benefits. Juices are far preferable to soft drinks with their high levels of permitted colours and other additives, and caffeine loaded drinks such as colas.

Try experimenting with unusual juice combinations such as Apricot juice (*See* DRIED FRUITS *page* 37) and MOLASSES, or orange and watercress. Some ideas are given in the recipes.

Certain juices contain positive medical values. Beet juice, for example, contains butaine, a powerful liver detoxifier. Cabbage juice is a rich source of vitamin U, which is widely used in Russia in treatment of stomach ulcers.

PAPAYA juice from unripe fruit contains a protein-digesting enzyme which benefits the digestion and has other properties. Pineapple juice contains the meat-digesting enzyme bromelin. This enzyme is unusual in that it is not affected by ripening or heating and is the reason why pineapple cannot 'jel' in gelatin preparations.

Nutritional content
225 ml (8 fl oz) fresh, home-squeezed orange juice contain: 460 I.U. vitamin A, 0.2 mg B1 (thiamine), 0.2 mg B2 (riboflavin), 120 mg vitamin C 90 mg calcium, 50 mg phosphorus, 1 mg iron, 0.9 g protein.

Juice drinks
The following combinations are particularly successful: tomato and carrot juice, carrot and celery juice, pineapple and papaya juice, orange and pineapple juice, cranberry and orange juice, clam juice and tomato juice. Always try to combine a strong tasting partner like spinach with larger amounts of a sweeter one like orange or cranberry.

Water

Bottled waters
A recent survey showed that one in five Californians use bottled water. With increased public education about water pollution this trend is growing. Sales of water filters are also rising. (*See* WHERE TO BUY *page* 152). There are many factors involved — chlorine and fluoride and other chemicals present in the water, danger from lead in the pipes, and the controversy about disease-causing factors in soft and hard waters.

In 1970, a Federal Community Water Supply Study in the U.S.A. published findings that caused water authorities around the world to start their own surveys. The Study found that ten million people were drinking potentially harmful water — 56% of water systems showed basic plant deficiencies; 36% of tap water samples did not comply with Federal drinking water standards; and 79% of local authority systems had nott been inspected for over one year.

In the Greater London area water is recycled six times and a spokesman for the Greater London Council said that it is virtually impossible to meet the pure water standards laid down by the Government.

Bottled water is defined as 'water that is sealed in bottles or other containers and intended for human consumption'. It is distinct from MINERAL WATERS: but can come from spring sources. In the United States, bottled water to F.D.A. standards, is subjected to high standards of control. There is no guarantee that it contains no chlorine. Some suppliers can honestly make this claim but it is a question of checking the labels.

Distilled water
This is pure H_2O. Distilled water is free from bacteria and also free from minerals. It has however a curiously flat taste.

St Anne's Well at Malvern in the west of England

Mineral waters
Mineral waters from recognized sources are the most beneficial of all waters. These can be positively healthful since many natural springs contain calcium, iron and other trace minerals. Several countries have outstandingly good springs which are strictly checked and controlled by government authorities. France has Vichy, Volvic and Perrier. Medicinal claims have been made for these waters, and it is probable that they aid digestion and stomach troubles. Volvic is said to be so pure that it can be given to babies direct from the bottle.

Queen Elizabeth II drinks only Malvern water which is bottled at the pure spring found at Malvern in the west of England. Several crates of this mineral water accompany her on trips abroad.

Each bottle of mineral water will state quite clearly any trace mineral content, and whether it has been approved by a goverment body.

Kitchen Utensils

The most important question to ask is what type of utensil is best and safest to cook in?

Stainless steel pans have been highly polished by the manufacturers to form an inert film. If this film is scoured only once with steel wool or abrasive powder, small amounts of highly toxic metallic elements dissolve afterwards into every meal cooked in these pans. Tests in the U.S.A. have discovered small amounts of chromium and nickel in meals cooked in a well-scoured stainless stainless steel pan.

The manufacturer may well say that the utensils leave his factory in a safe condition and that all is the fault of the housewife who scours off burns and food stuck to the bottom of the pan. With so much money at stake, it is unlikely that manufacturers will want to place a red triangle warning against the use of steel wool or abrasive powders on utensils.

Aluminium has the same tendency to dissolve into meals after being scoured. It has, however, a safety factor in that it combines with phosphorus in the body and is excreted as aluminium phosphate.

Non-stick pans are good if they are never subjected to very high temperatures. If once allowed to sear or burn, non-stick pans will give off toxic sodium fluoride gas. Lecithin sprays are now available which make utensils non-stick in a safe way.

Ceramic and enamel have an uneven heat distribution and are more likely to burn or stick.

Glassware based pots and pans allow the destruction of B2 (riboflavin) because of exposure to light.

Cast iron is the best of all materials. It distributes heat so evenly that food rarely sticks. It is easier to keep in a good condition without abrasive washing and actually improves with age. Many French cooks would never dream of washing their cast iron pots. They simply rinse them out or wipe with kitchen paper and lightly oil them before putting away.

Choosing the equipment

A natural foods cook does not need to buy any special equipment. It is sensible to choose the particular kitchen aids to suit your individual needs. If you decide to have a fruit juice every day an electric juicer would be a sound investment (*See* BEVERAGES *page* 138). A

Blender

Casseroles

elect

yoghurt maker is a must for those who appreciate the virtues of YOGHURT. A mouli or electric grater will save time and the fingertips of cooks who put raw vegetables on the daily menu. To quote the cookery writer Elizabeth David — 'Don't hamper your cooking and waste time and materials through lack of the right tools for the job.'

The right tools

Earthenware casseroles Every kitchen should have earthenware casseroles and terrines. Earthenware is a superb medium for keeping the flavour during the long cooking of casseroled meats or legumes. Elizabeth David says: 'Many recipes . . . lose something of their flavour and a good deal of their charm if cooked in an ordinary saucepan.'

The classic French tall-sided stewpot is called a marmite. Its shape causes minimum evaporation and equal distribution of heat. In the English-speaking countries every earthenware vessel used for casseroling food is called a casserole, and there are as many shapes as potters' wheels.

Blender A good blender is a great asset to any serious cook, but especially to a wholefood *aficionado*. There are a wide variety of blenders available; simple one or two speed machines; blenders with grinder attachments, and the latest models which actually cook the food while you blend it.

A blender can whirl up soups, purées, milk shakes, high protein drinks, mayonnaise, vegetable dressings, and many other recipes. The grinding attachment is usually intended for coffee beans but is excellent for small quantities of NUTS, SEEDS and BEANS *(See* LEGUMES *page* 66*)*. Peanut and other nut butters can be made easily in a blender.

Grain mill You do not have to be a dedicated wholefooder to realize that grains bought direct from

Juicer

Grain mill

the mill and ground just before use are the ultimate in freshness and vitamin content.

There are two main types of grain mill: stone grinding or steel blade. Exactly the same problem applies to home grinders as it does to the grinders used in flour mills. Some stone buhrs grind more finely than others and are able to release more of the seed embryo into the flour. Steel mills are often easier to use and have a greater range.

Several enterprising manufacturers are now making convertible grain mills for home use. These have both stone buhrs and steel blades, thus solving the problem. (See WHERE TO BUY page 152)

Hand or electric grain mills Most low cost grain mills are hand operated. There are several varieties of electric-powered mills but when choosing one, make sure it has adjustable speed. Some high powered (and high cost) mills operate at between 1600 and 1800 rpm which is really too fast for volatile grains. Maximum nutritional content is retained at speeds below 500 rpm.

Whichever grain mill is used, it must always be dismantled and well cleaned after each use. Any particles left in the joints will quickly turn rancid and affect the next batch of grains.

Wash the stainless steel mill in warm water and dry thoroughly to prevent rusting. Avoid washing the stone buhrs. Wipe well with a damp cloth and dry immediately.

A weekly grinding session is more efficient and the flours can be stored in airtight containers.

Graters Nutritionists such as Dr Bircher-Benner (See MUESLI page 86) and Adelle Davis (See BREWER'S YEAST page 28) advise eating at least one raw vegetable daily. It is often easier to fulfil this ideal if the vegetables are grated. For instance, those who would not dream of eating raw turnip find it easy and quite delicious finely grated in a mixed salad.

More and more wholefood and vegetarian recipes require grated produce, such as the following recipe which calls for a large grated onion, four large grated carrots, and 450 g (1 lb) of grated potatoes. By the time all these vegetables have been grated on a conventional rectangular grater the result is an aching arm, streaming eyes, and a strong conviction that a grating aid is a good investment.

Hand or power graters? A grater need not be an expensive item. The old fashioned model that clamps to the table is still very useful, although many

Griddle

Mouli-légumes

Grater

Hachinette

Meat thermometer

Knives

improved varieties with suction hold are now available. Hand operated *Mouli-légumes* are deservedly popular. Like other hand graters, these come with a selection of grating rings and can cope with anything from CHEESE to baby foods.

A large family fond of raw foods could well decide that an electric grater is essential. Moulinex make an outstanding model that grates, grinds, blends and minces.

Griddle pan is a ribbed pan usually made of cast iron. The raised ribs keep the meat out of the fat that drips from it. A griddle pan is good for any meat that is grilled (broiled) and especially for steak or chops. This useful pan produces tender, striped meat without any of the hard patches caused by direct top heat.

Hachoir is a crescent-shaped chopping knife with a double handle. The fine chopping of vegetables, meat and onions becomes a quick and efficient task with a *hachoir*. Cordon Bleu cooks use a multi-blade *hachoir* to chop meat into a fine mince which retains all its juices.

Hachinette is a smaller single-handled crescent blade complete with its small wooden bowl. It is ideal for chopping herbs and small amounts of vegetables.

Juicer Fresh fruit and vegetable juices are such nutritional assets that most food-conscious people try to put them on the menu as often as possible. A good electric juicer is an expensive item, but so is pure, unprocessed juice. The big advantage about an electric juicer is that drinks can be invented to suit personal tastes and nutritional requirements. When the produce comes straight out of the garden or in bulk from an organic supplier, these juices will be much cheaper.

A juicer gets one away from the old familiar carrot or orange-juice rut. What about lettuce, squash and tomato juice? Or celery, pears and peanut juice?

More complicated juicers will remove the pips, pith and skin if necessary. These machines neatly unclip, so that the contents of the waste compartment can be tipped straight into the compost bin.

If juices are made when fruit and vegetables are plentiful and frozen for the rest of the year, an electric juicer will soon pay for itself.

Knives When Escoffier was asked what culinary utensil he would not be without, he replied with a fearsome look: 'A really sharp knife.'

All good cooks should try to buy the best quality knives and keep them sharp. It is as well to remember to wipe the blade carefully after sharpening, or else minute particles of metal will enter the food. The range of kitchen knives available is vast — basic straight-edged pointed knives for slicing and trimming; saw-edge blades for cutting bread, vegetables and fruit; and carving and boning knives.

The very best knives are made from carbon steel. Some experts advise drying thoroughly and lightly oiling these knives before putting them away.

Mandolin is a solid, wooden, rectangular frame inset with adjustable steel blades. It is indispensable for the quick slicing of potatoes, carrots, celeriac and cabbage. It gives perfect even slices, and is easy to clean.

Meat thermometer Using a meat thermometer is really the only accurate way to produce tender roasted meat from the oven. The principle of roasting is to heat the inside of the meat above 49°C (120°F) at which temperature the tough, connecting tissues break down. The heat must not be allowed to rise above 77°C (170°F) which will cause the protein content to shrivel and toughen.

A meat thermometer takes the guesswork out of this timing. Push the spike of the thermometer through the centre of the raw meat making sure it does not touch a bone.

Salt and pepper mills

Mandoline

Hachoir

Mortar and pestle

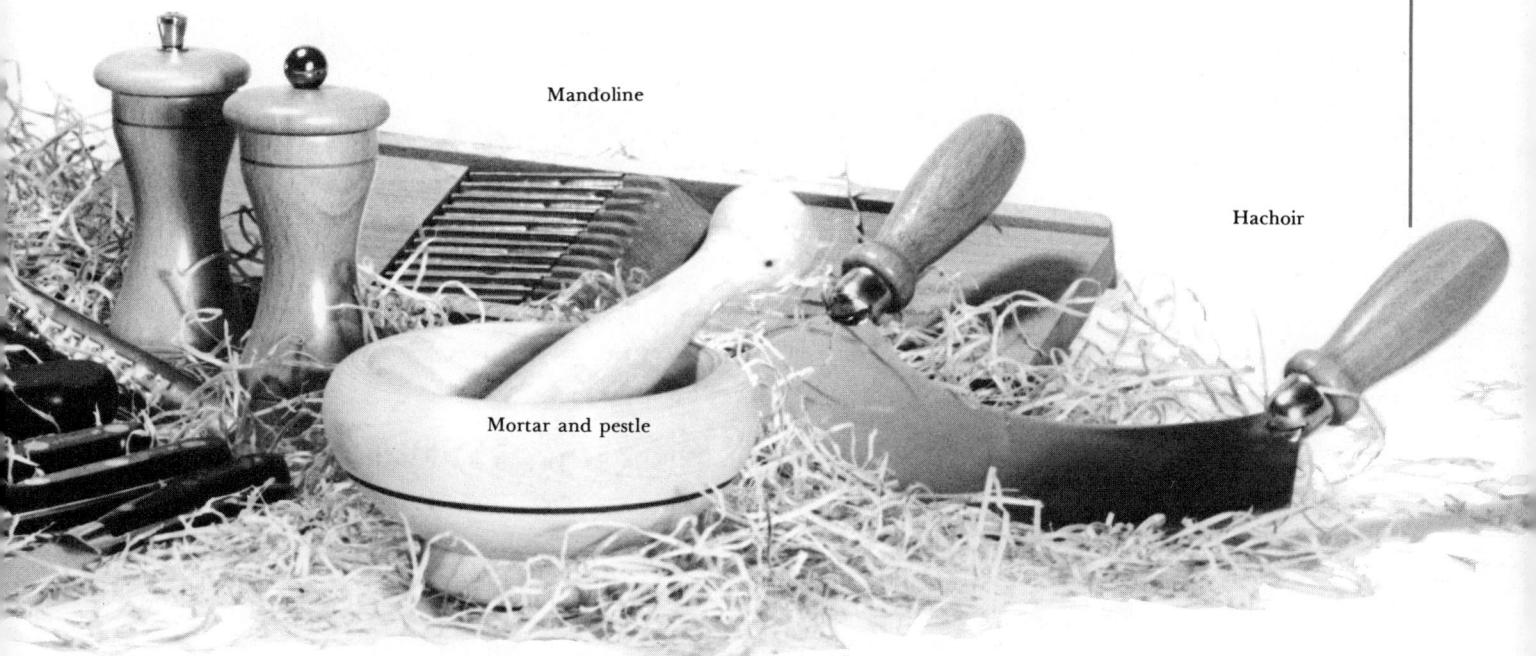

Mortar and pestle In spite of all the sophisticated kitchen aids, a mortar and pestle is still a useful implement. It was originally made in marble but is now more often found in quality wood. The bowl is the mortar, and the round-headed pestle smoothly sweeps against its sides crushing seeds, garlic, and herbs to a creamy paste.

Salt and pepper mills Pepper in particular contains volatile oils which rapidly diminish when the seeds are ground. It makes a tremendous difference to a dish to have freshly ground pepper added at the last moment. These mills are produced in many attractive designs.

Seed sprouters are supposed to take the guesswork and labour out of SPROUTING SEEDS. One popular variety is shaped like a small spaceship, with two domes that unclip in the middle. The centre holds the seed trays. Water is poured through the top half and flows onto the seeds and down the trays to the lower half. In this way, the seeds never sit in stagnant water and the sprouts develop evenly. The top half of the dome is often coloured to exclude light.

Yoghurt makers will make 600 ml (1 pint) or $2\frac{1}{2}$ U.S. cups of yoghurt for less than the price of a small shop-bought carton. Cost, however, is not the only factor. With home-made yoghurt the correct culture can be used to produce a superior product. Home-made yoghurt will also be free from colourings and preservatives.

The big advantage of yoghurt makers is that they keep the culture at exactly the right temperature of 43°C (110°F). You simply plug in and let the culture develop for 6-8 hours.

The two main types of yoghurt makers are: a cylindrical shape holding about 600-850 ml (1-1$\frac{1}{2}$ pints) or 2$\frac{1}{2}$-4 U.S. cups; or a tray shape containing six or more small cups. (*See* WHERE TO BUY *page* 152).

Water filters are invaluable items attached to a tap to filter out many of the impurities in the water supply. A water filter will remove up to 90% of the chlorine, between 70% and 98% of the lead, 95-98% of the mercury, and 50-90% of the cadmium. Growing public awareness of the pollution of ordinary tap water has led to huge increases in the sales of filters. (*See* BOTTLED WATER *page* 139).

Check the carton for the filtering agent. One successful and safe filter is finely divided carbon in the form of charcoal which absorbs and attracts the pollutants.

Wok is an ancient Chinese utensil which is perfectly shaped for quick-cooking vegetables. The wide circumference concentrates all the heat in the bottom of the pan. It is excellent for frying rice, sautéing vegetables, or steaming and braising in the Chinese fashion. Eastern cooks claim that the Wok is the secret of their superb quick-cooked vegetables.

Wok

Yoghurt maker

Seed sprouter

Water filter

Why organic?

Mr Colin Fisher is the director of the Pye Research Centre at Suffolk, U.K., which researches in a detailed scientific way methods of cultivation and animal husbandry. According to Mr Fisher, *'The case for organic gardening is overwhelming. For a start, organic growing represents an efficient use of resources and we live in a world of declining resources. An organic gardener is much more sensitive to the delicate balance of requirements that the soil needs, and much more likely to get the balance right.*

Organic growing is more aesthetically satisfying than using a great deal of chemicals. If a man uses a powerful chemical spray he may have to keep his kids away from the area for days. It is not a nice feeling that your kids can't run free in your garden.

The soil is an enormously complex physical entity. The use of compost and organic matter is much more likely to achieve the correct physical balance between the inter-related molecules. If an equilibrium is maintained, then the soil will give greater yields and have greater resistance.

If the soil is deficient in an essential nutrient you are much more likely to correct it with compost than applying various chemicals.'

Another important factor is the way in which plants choose not to take up available chemicals from the soil. Tests have shown that up to 90% of a chemical fertilizer can be rejected by a plant. This could lie in the soil and alter the balance of the soil bacteria.

Why grow your own

Food can only be as good as the soil in which it is grown. Adelle Davis in *Let's Eat Right to Keep Fit* tells of carrots which have been analysed and found to contain no carotene whatsoever. Research in Berkeley, California, has shown that produce grown on deficient soil cannot provide the daily vitamin requirements. It might look all right, but such food can be misleading. 225 ml (8 fl oz) or 1 U.S. cup of fresh juice from a recently picked orange does provide 130 mg vitamin C. However, the orange is picked when green, packed in the hold of the ship, marketed, and often stored on a warm table. The vitamin C content may be no more than one third of a freshly picked orange.

The other great loss of nutrients occurs in shipping, canning, storing, freezing, and cooking the plant. If you pick it yourself and eat it the same day (or quick-freeze it) you gain the greatest possible value from food. From the moment it is picked, a plant will begin to lose some of its nutrients. If stored in a warm room, the loss accelerates.

As an example, many people think that a glass of fresh orange juice provides a good amount of vitamin C

(*See* BEVERAGES). 225 ml (8 fl oz) or 1 U.S. cup of fresh juice from a recently picked orange does provide 130 mg vitamin C. However, the orange is picked when green, packed in the hold of a ship, marketed, and often stored on a warm table. The vitamin C content may be no more than one third of a freshly picked orange.

The great boom in gardening has a definite link with growing ecological awareness. When we grow our own vegetables and fruit we ourselves control the environment. Nobody is going to spray, colour, wax or inhibit the produce of our own garden. At the same time, the organic grower is not adding to the pollution of our rivers and countryside.

Compost and humus are vital

Compost is one of the essential weapons in the organic armoury. Many experts assert that a regular dressing of compost is vital for a healthy soil. The terms humus and compost are often used synonymously. Indeed, to all intents and purposes well decayed, friable compost becomes humus.

Humus is the biologically active part of the soil. It adds to the soil structure the all-important organic matter which produces the mucilage or colloid gum where the true nutrients lie. Sedge peat, leaf mould, and forest bark also provide organic matter.

Recent research using radioactive isotopes in both the U.S.A. and the U.K. has shown that plants are selective about the nutrients they take from the soil. In one experiment in the U.S.A. a crop of wheat took only 2% of available chemical phosphate fertilizer. Yet when the straw from the crop was used to make dung, the next crop took up almost all the available nutrients.

It is as well to remember this when analysis of the nutrients in organic manures seems low compared to chemical fertilizers. Many research stations around the world are now working on exactly why plants should choose nutrients from organic matter and sometimes reject those from chemicals.

Other tests have shown that long-term composting produces higher yields and greater resistance. The taste is better too. In blindfold tests done by the Henry Doubleday Research Association, (HDRA), compost-grown produce came out overwhelmingly on top.

In really warm climates such as Australia and some parts of the U.S.A. humus is essential for its water-holding properties. Even in dry weather, humus enriched soil will give good yields.

How to make your own compost

'Compost is rather like home-made wine — you start by following the book and add your own variations. But you must stick to a few simple principles.' So says Lawrence D. Hills, director of the HDRA. 'The few simple principles' are outlined in his excellent book *Fertility Without Fertilizers* and his advice is outlined here.

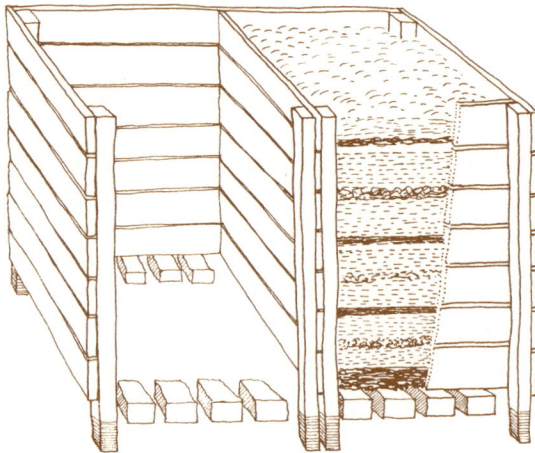

The container HDRA experts believe that a simple wooden 'box' structure which you can buy (*See* WHERE TO BUY *page* 154) or make yourself is far more effective than plastic composters. Mr Hills recommends the New Zealand box as the best small-scale system.

Choose a sheltered site For the bottom of the box, place two double rows of bricks 2.5 cm (1 in) apart and with 60 cm (2 ft) between the rows. On this erect the box. The ends of the bricks stick out under the front and provide the draught that keeps the 'bacterial bonfire' burning.

The layers To start, cover the bricks with tough, stemmy waste like hedge clippings to stop finer material blocking the air channels. The first layer should be 20 cm (8 in) of weeds, lawnmowings, or garden waste with kitchen refuse in the middle. On top of this, scatter enough dried blood, dried poultry

manure or fish meal to colour the surface or 1 cm ($\frac{1}{2}$ in) layer of other available manure. Add another 20 cm (8 in) layer of waste as before. Whiten it with slaked lime. Add a third layer and manure or 'activate' it. Go on adding layers in this way until the bin is filled. Most heaps take weeks to fill.

Activators make the bacteria work faster. There is now general agreement among organic writers about the system of layering and air venting, but there are as many favourite activators as there are experts. All types of manure can be classed as activators. Many commercial activators do not need the lime layers. A popular one is seaweed powder or jelly (*See* KELP *page* 63). The cheapest of all is the one euphemistically called 'bedroom slops'. These can be poured on every morning. Mr Hills advocates 'bedroom slops' for heaps that have dried out or failed to heat.

What can go in the compost heap?

A good rule of thumb is that anything that has once lived can enrich the compost heap, including wool, paper, tea-leaves, grass mowings, vegetable peelings and all kitchen wastes, and vacuum cleaner dusts.

Never use more than 10% paper and rip it up well. Spread really tough weeds out in the sun to dry before putting them in the heap. Smash thick brussels and cabbage stems up first. Many people invest in compost grinders which effectively shred waste and allegedly produce 'quick return' compost.

Leave out all meat wastes and cooked foods as these attract rats. Nylon and man-made fibres will not rot, neither will china, polythene or plastic, except when it is biodegradable.

When is the compost ready?

The worms will tell you when the compost is ready! They are very choosy and will not inhabit a heap that is not properly rotted. Compost should be a dark brown, blackish colour, with a crumbly texture and only a faint earthy smell.

How to use compost

Apply compost as a top dressing once or twice a year. Spread it about 3 cm (1 in) thick.

Compost can be dug in before planting or sowing and does not cause root crops to fork as manure does. Humus in planting holes gives the roots a good start.

Use well-rotted compost as a mulch, that is, a layer of organic matter kept all the year round on the soil to protect the roots from cold or heat, and to prevent the evaporation of moisture.

Common causes of compost failure

Putting too much soil in the heap Always shake the soil from weeds or plants before adding them. Mr Hills says: 'To expect the average heap to warm cold soil lumps to between 54-71°C (130-160°F) that will kill weed seeds in two to four days is like trying to boil a kettle with matches.'

Moisture amounts are important The average heap will get enough water via the ventilation holes generally except in very hot climates or prolonged dry weather. It is a question of judgment exactly how much water to add. Too much moisture gives a distinctive sodden smell.

Too many grass clippings and summer weeds are high in water content but low in fuel. To reach the necessary temperature stick to the 20 cm (8 in) layers and activate or lime well.

The no-digging way of organic gardening

The no-digging approach is based on not disturbing the structure of the earth while allowing earth worms to carry humus down through the soil layers.

Dr W.E. Shewell-Cooper is a leading exponent of the no-digging method. He is the founder of the International Association of Organic Gardeners (the Good Gardeners' Association) and at the headquarters at Arkley Manor, Hertfordshire, U.K., the soil has not been dug for sixteen years and the plants positively thrive.

'Digging is quite contrary to nature's plan', says Dr Shewell-Cooper. *'Think of the layers of the soil; the top soil is the litter layer which acts as a warming blanket; the next layer is the microbiological layer which is 13-15 cm (5-6 in) thick; beneath that is the anchorage layer where the roots anchor and stabilize themselves and get water.'* He believes that constant digging brings to the surface weeds which were deposited years ago. *'If you simply add a layer of compost or sedge peat you may get weeds for about a year, after that you'll have seen the back of them. A regular top dressing of compost gets the worms active. They rush to the surface and drag the valuable humus down with them.'* The worm tunnels allow air and water to go down to the soil in a natural way.

Dr Shewell-Cooper has this advice to anyone wanting to garden organically his way: 'The first thing is to lightly rake or rotovate the soil — don't go more than 5 cm (2 in) deep. Then spread a layer of compost or sedge peat 3 cm (1 in) thick over the area to be planted. Plant your seeds and deal with any problems that occur organically.'

Organic and biological control of pests

A good attack of black fly or leaf curl has knocked many a gardener off the organic platform and sent him reeling towards the nearest chemical spray. There are many effective organic sprays which can be bought locally or directly from leading research stations. (*See* WHERE TO BUY *page* 152)

Organic sprays Many of these are based on derris and pyrethrum. Some mixtures combine them both and are effective against a wide variety of pests which are listed on the labels. Quassia is the safest pesticide of all. Boil 100 g (4 oz) of quassia chips in 4.5 litres (1 gal) or 10 U.S. pints of water for two hours for a good all round garden spray against caterpillars and aphids. Rhubarb leaves can be chopped and boiled in water for a spray against green fly. Oil of garlic makes a powerful spray against a host of bugs.

Biological control A 'biological' gardener will try to encourage the predators of the pests he wants to destroy. For example, the large hover fly (chalcide wasp) devours about fifty green fly an hour. Buckwheat attracts this harmless wasp. The trichogramma wasp feeds on the eggs of over 100 species. The Peruvian Government has introduced this wasp to such effect that chemical spraying of the cotton crop is about to be banned by legislation. Everybody knows that ladybirds (ladybugs) eat aphids. Some organic gardeners build 'winter quarters' for these friendly insects

The large hover fly (*chalcide wasp*) devours about 50 greenfly an hour

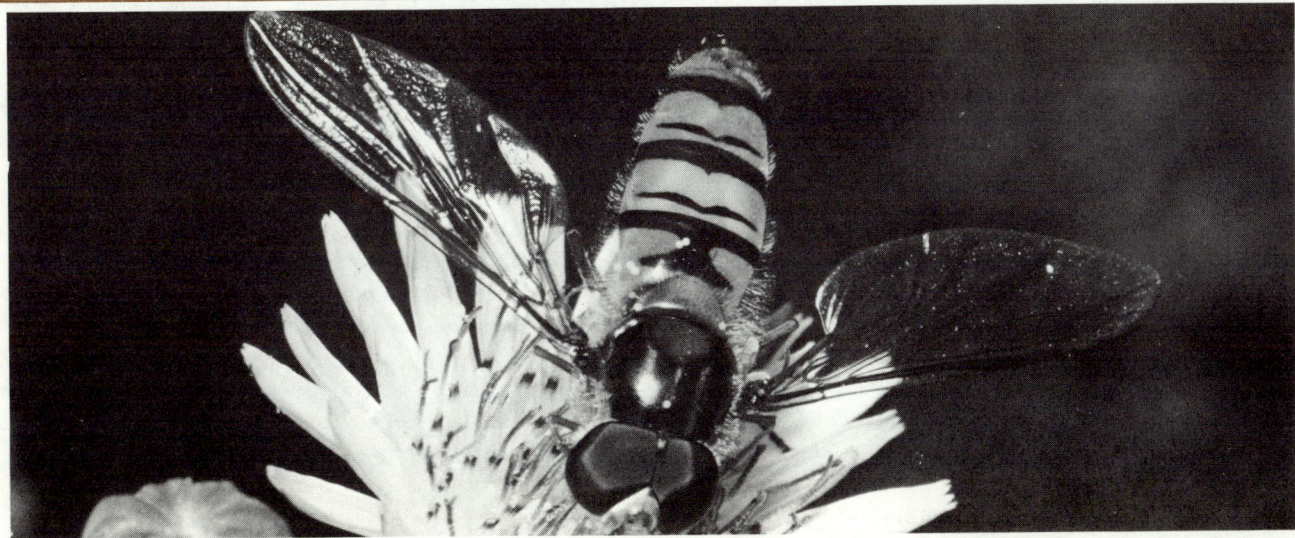

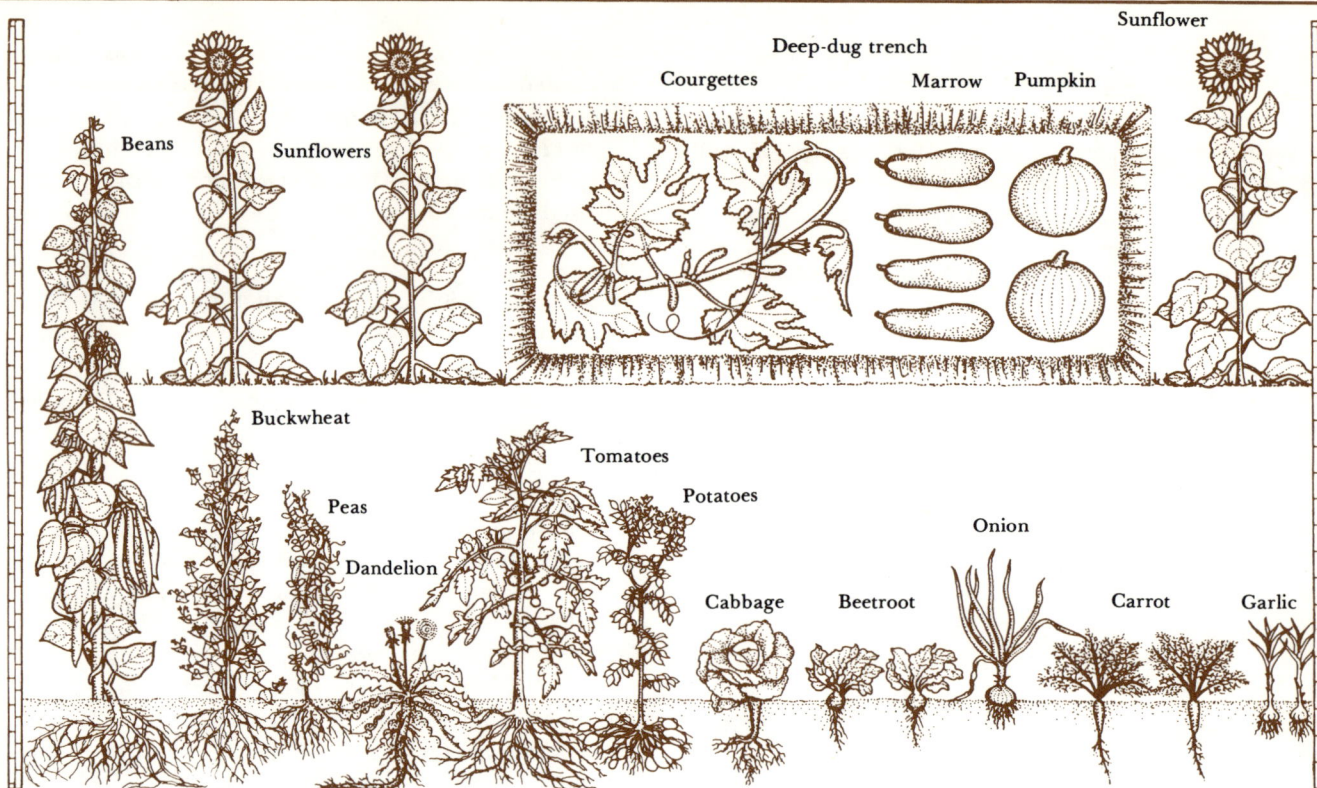

so that they can pass the cold months in safety.

At Arkley Manor, black fly is sprayed with a solution of oil of garlic. Garlic bulbs also are planted between rows of beans so that the sulphur smell can deter bugs. Other pests are sprayed with organic substances such as pyrethrum and derris.

Biological control is practised by encouraging predators such as the chalcide wasp (hover fly). The chalcide wasp loves BUCKWHEAT and rows of it are planted between vulnerable plants.

Companion planting

All plants exude secretions and the secretions of some species are antagonistic to certain insects. For example, the cabbage white butterfly is repelled by the tomato, onion and garlic repel carrot fly; the flowers of summer savory repel black fly. The root secretions of Tagetes-minuta appear to kill potato and other eelworms and also keep weeds down.

Increased yields through companion planting One fascinating aspect of this subject is that some plants really like each other and flourish side by side. Just like a human being, next to something it dislikes, a plant will mope and never be at its best. Many of the beliefs about plant loves and hates are based on years of observation by dedicated gardeners. Research is now going on to attempt to measure exactly how root secretions affect a neighbouring plant. The HDRA is at present testing the effects of: beetroot on the growth of onions; radishes on the growth of lettuce; celery on the growth of leeks; tomatoes and potatoes on the growth of cabbages and cauliflowers. This is something that every grower could prove for himself. If you keep notes of yields over several seasons, the Association would be interested to hear of it. (See ORGANIZATIONS page 150).

The good companions plot

The small organic plot illustrated above has been worked out with two ideas: first for 'good companion' planting, and second to include the plants particularly important in food values.

Buckwheat has been planted next to the runner beans to encourage the hover fly which devours black and green fly. The buckwheat can also be ground to make an excellent flour rich in rutin.

Any organic grower might care to include culinary dandelion whose flowerhead and leaves are rich in iron and vitamins A and C. The roots can also be ground into excellent coffee. (See BEVERAGES page 136). Both garlic and onions give protection from carrot fly. Beetroot and onions have an affinity with each other.

Sunflower seeds are a charming way to take in linoleic acid which is an essential body nutrient. The new hull-less pumpkins contain unhusked seeds which are rich in iron and contain a natural hormone.

Greedy feeders such as courgettes and pumpkins need a deep-dug trench. Some organic gardeners dig down two spades' depth and line the trench with layers of kitchen waste throughout the winter. Cover all waste with a good layer of soil to keep off vermin. The trench should then be ready for spring planting. Otherwise, the 'no-digging' method suits all other vegetables. Put down a layer of compost, plant the seeds, mulch if need be, and feed with liquid seaweed.

A-Z list of organizations

Alternative Society, 21 Union Street, Woodstock, Oxfordshire, U.K.
This group has an impressive list of patrons, including Yehudi Menuhin, Dr Magnus Pyke and the Rt Rev Hugh Montefiore, Bishop of Birmingham, and seeks to bring together people with a common interest in the earth and its resources. It is active in planning craft groups, seminars and instructional camps. The Society hopes to provide some of the answers for those who long to go back to the land, or come to terms with our urban society.

Beauty without Cruelty International, 1 Calverley Park, Tunbridge Wells, Kent, TN1 2SG, U.K. Tel: Tunbridge Wells 25587
The BWC was founded by Muriel Lady Dowding to investigate malpractices and cruelties to animals throughout the world. BWC observers have documented and crusaded against whale hunts, seal killings, and the many experiments on animals for cosmetics and drugs. It is one of the leaders in the wildlife preservation campaign. Executive director David Whiting travels extensively filming evidence of animal suffering and species near extinction. BWC owns shops that sell imitation fur and leather and other approved products and their celebrated cosmetics are mailed worldwide from the Tonbridge warehouse. (*See* WHERE TO BUY) New members are welcomed and provided with a journal '*Compassion*' twice a year plus full details of the campaign's activities.

Beauty without Cruelty U.S.A. Dr Ethel Thurston, 175 West 12th Street, New York, N.Y. 10011, Tel: 212 989 8073
Beauty without Cruelty Australia, *Melbourne:* Mrs Liesma Rek, Barbers Road, PO Kalorama, Victoria 3766. *Sydney:* Mrs Elizabeth Ahlston, PO Box 356, Broadway, Sydney, NSW 2007.
Beauty without Cruelty Canada: Mrs Gaile Campbell, 2370 Palmerston Avenue, West Vancouver, B.C., or Miss Edith Armstrong, 85 Bellwood Avenue, Ottawa, Ontario K1S 158.

The Bircher-Benner Clinic (Physio-dietetic and natural treatment), Keltenstrasse 48, CH-8044 Zurich, Switzerland. This world famous clinic was founded by Dr Bircher-Benner (see MUESLI) and is open all the year round.

The Country College, 11 Harmer Green Lane, Digswell, Welwyn, Hertfordshire AL6 BAY, U.K. Tel: Welwyn 6367.

The Country College was started by an enterprising journalist, Anthony Wigens. He has become an extra-mural teaching expert on self-sufficiency, and has written popular handbooks on *The Solar Household — a Consumer Guide to Solar-Heated Hot Water Systems, Wood Fuel, Using a Rotavator, Wholewheat Baking, The Wasteland Grower's Guide.*

Mr Wigens has also started a group called Resources which mainly reclaims and cultivates waste ground. His wood stove national exhibition was an instant success. The Country College's aim now is to meet the demand for information on self-sufficiency.

The Farm and Food Society, 4 Willifield Way, London NW11 7XT, U.K. Tel: 01-455 0634
This extremely active society is perhaps best known for its well publicized research into battery hens, and it also investigates every aspect of factory farming. It has special representatives in Australia, Germany, Hong Kong and Switzerland. Patrons include a number of leading scientists and politicians. The FAFS scheme gives a seal of approval to guaranteed free-range eggs.

The Society publishes many detailed and informative reports, such as an *Enquiry into the Uses of Antibiotics in Animal Husbandry* and *The Effects of Modern Livestock Production on the Environment.*

Members receive an annual report and a quarterly newsletter giving details of the Society's current activities, latest international developments in agribusiness and organic farming, book reviews, and conference reports.

The Society is not a registered charity because it wishes to be politically active if necessary and the underlying theme behind all its work is 'Do you believe that cruelty to animals and risks to your own health are too high a price for "cheap" food?' Members or donations welcome.

Friends of the Earth, 124 Spear Street, San Francisco, 94105, U.S.A. (Lisa Waag 415-495-4770)
The Friends of the Earth (FOE) is perhaps the leading international ecological organization and has very active offices in 12 countries. Its objectives are as follows:
'We intend to generate among all people a sense of personal responsibility for the environment in which we live.
We intend to campaign against specific projects which damage the environment or squander our resources, and fight for their correction with every legal means at our disposal.
We intend to make the crucial environmental issues the subject of widespread and well-informed public debate.

But above all we intend to campaign for the universal adoption of sustainable and equitable life styles.'

FOE has a good track record with many results. In the U.K., for example, the group played a major role in initiating debate about nuclear plans. FOE policies have had influence in bringing about the Endangered Species Act and legislation to protect the National Park in Snowdonia, Wales. It was the FOE who started to organize waste collection and recycling on a national level. Other campaigns include transport, and food and the use of land. Many pamphlets are issued in support of these objectives, such as *Getting Nowhere Fast* (transport), *Many Happy Returns* (Recycling), *Nuclear Prospects* and *Food Co-ops Manual.*

Local groups form the background of the international FOE. Each group is autonomous, with a co-ordinator who liaises with national headquarters. Members receive an introduction to local groups, a newsletter three times a year, and a reduced subscription rate to *Not Man Apart,* the magazine published twice a month by the FOE headquarters in California.

The FOE advisory council includes Jacques Cousteau, Lord Caradon, Paul Newman, Linus Pauling, Robert Redford, Pete Seegar, C.P. Snow, Harriet Van Horne, Joanne Woodward.

Friends of the Earth Australia, 51 Nicholson Street, Carlton, Melbourne 3053. (Co-ordinator Neil Barrett)

Friends of the Earth/Energy probe, 54-53 Queen Street, Ottawa, Canada K1P 5C5

Les Amis de la Terre, 117 Avenue de Choisy, Paris 75013, France. (Co-ordinator Brice Lalonde)

Freunde der Erde, Postfach 100221 — 2 Hamburg 1, Germany. (Co-ordinator Theda Strempe)

Friends of the Earth England, 9 Poland Street, London, W1V 3DG. Tel: 01 434 1694

Friends of the Earth New York, Loran Salzman, 22 Jane Street, 10014. Tel: 212 675 5911

The Good Gardeners' Association (International Association of Organic Gardeners), Dr W.E. Shewell-Cooper, (Director), Arkley Manor, Arkley, Nr. Barnet, Hertfordshire, U.K.
This was founded and is still led by Dr Shewell-Cooper, who is a leading figure in organic gardening and has written many widely respected books both in the fruit, vegetable and flower fields. He also trains several students each year.

Dr Shewell-Cooper is the leading expert in the no-digging method. (*See* GARDENING ON A HEALTHY SOIL)
The organization arranges lectures and demonstrations in support of their ideas. Arkley Manor itself is open seven days a week for those who wish to see the organic no-digging method in practice. New members and visitors are welcomed.

Henry Doubleday Research Association, Bocking, Braintree, Essex, U.K.
This is the largest organization of organic gardeners in the world, and conducts trials and research at the Bocking station. The aim is to involve members in the experiments and the results are published in the regular newsletter and information sheets, as well as in the first class booklets and pamphlets available to members and non-members, such as the following selection: *Dig for survival, Pest control without poisons, Slugs and the gardener.*

The Director, Lawrence D. Hills, is one of the most expert writers on organic gardening in the world and many of his books are available through retail bookshops.

HDRA specializes in research into COMFREY and will supply comfrey plants and comfrey products, such as flour, tea, tablets, and ointments by mail order. Many other organic products and aids are also available. (*See* WHERE TO BUY)
HDRA Australia
Henry Doubleday Research Association (NSW Group), June Fear (Secretary), Greggs Road, Kurrajong, NSW 2758
June Fear will give information on HDRA plus addresses of other Australian groups.

The Herb Society, 34 Boscobel Place, London SW1, U.K. Tel: 01 235 1530
The Herb Society follows a thoroughly twentieth-century approach to herbs and healing plants and under the leadership of its director, Dr Malcolm Stuart, it is setting up a huge computer programme to assess herb ingredients and their reactions in the body. This scientific approach is nicely blended with the practical experiences of the thousands of members organized regionally around the U.K.

The Herb Society organizes practical courses, lectures, outings and demonstrations. The official publication *The Herbal Review* is issued four times a year and contains excellent articles on herbal remedies, natural beauty aids, scientific research, history and every aspect of the subject. New members welcome.

International Federation of Organic Movements, Dr Hardy Vogtman (Secretary), Postfach, CH 4104 Oberwill/BL, Switzerland.
The IFOM is the authoritative body which co-ordinates the research done by the many organic organizations around the world. Dr Vogtman will also initiate and promote research, the results of which are then published in leading journals. IFOM also organizes conferences and symposiums to which delegates of affiliated groups are invited.

The McCarrison Society, Dr Barbara Latto (Secretary), Derby Road, Caversham, Reading, Berkshire, U.K.
This society was started by a group of doctors in 1966, who wanted to perpetuate and develop the ideas and teachings of the great pioneer Dr Robert McCarrison (*See page 7*)

Dr McCarrison carried out the original research into the Hunza tribe from 1904 until 1911. Later years as Director of Nutrition Research in India gave him a particular insight into the relationship between food and disease. The McCarrison Society is dedicated to persuading people to improve their eating habits. Members are active in lecturing, writing and broadcasting and the society is generous in making its findings available to interested bodies and individuals.

The National Conservation Corps, Zoological Gardens, Regents Park, London, NWL 4RY, U.K. Tel: 01 722 7112
The Corps is an organization of volunteers who are actively conserving Britain's countryside. Groups of people literally get out on the land and work with their hands or shovels as the case may be. Corps work bulletins are full of phrases such as: 'Worthington Pump House — plastering, painting, glazing,' or 'Blean Woods — power-chain saw operators needed.' Many young people are great enthusiasts and flock to volunteer and some tasks count towards the Duke of Edinburgh Award Scheme.

Natural Health Society of Australia, 131 York Street, Sydney 2000, NSW, Australia. Tel: 29 8656
The NHSA organizes regular meetings, symposiums and discussions on all aspects of the natural way of life and wholefoods. They welcome visitors or newcomers to the country to the above offices. Advice on health food shops, diet reform and restaurants is given to members and non-members alike.

Nutrition Education Center Inc (NEC), PO Box 303, Oyster Bay, Long Island, New York 11771, U.S.A.
This is a centre dedicated to the 'new nutrition' based on wholefoods and organic gardening. NEC organizes regular lively teach-ins and workshops on all aspects of food, vitamins and healthy living. One NEC meeting in 1977 was addressed by Dr Harry Sackren who spoke on nutrition and disease; Dr Robert Fand on the nutritional approach to psoriasis and skin disorders; Dr Juan Wilson on low blood sugar; and Irwin Burnstein on food and dental disease. All NEC lectures are on tape and available to other groups. Membership of the Center brings a regular newsletter full of health hints and recipes, and free admission to the ten monthly lectures. Non-members pay $1.50 (£0.80) for each session.

Organic Farmers & Growers, Martello House, 5 Station Rd, Stowmarket, Suffolk, U.K. Tel: 04492 2845
OFG provides a full range of services for the organic farmer or would-be farmer. It acts as a clearing house and retail outlet for organic produce, sells organic fertilizer, and acts as an agent for machinery and farm implements. Managing director David Stickland visits farms and gives advice on organic husbandry and growing. Members' farms range from 1-1200 acres.

The International Institute of Biological Husbandry has been founded by the directors of OFG to co-ordinate research into organic husbandry. It is affiliated to the International Federation of Organic Movements. Members include scientists, farmers, and members of the public interested in promoting these aims.

The Pye Research Centre, Mr Colin Fisher, Director, Walnut Tree Manor, Haughley, Stowmarket, Suffolk, U.K. Tel: Haughley 235
This is an academic organization which has taken over the original three farms owned by the SOIL ASSOCIATION. Pye continues the experiments on organic husbandry and farming in a highly scientific manner: one farm is completely organic, one organic supplemented with chemicals, and the third completely chemical. The Pye Research Centre is acknowledged as one of the leading investigatory bodies into organic gardening, and publishes its results in the main journals. (*See page 145*)

Rodale Press Inc. 33 East Minor Street, Emmaus, Pa 18049, U.S.A. Tel: 215 967 5171
Rodale Press are the publishers of the magazine *Prevention* and many excellent books on the organic way of life. They have lists of every organic gardening association in the U.S.A., together with up-to-date information on environment groups and organic food sources.

Small Farm Research Association (Mr Eliot Coleman), Greenwood Farm, Harbor Side, Maine, 04642, U.S.A.
An organic association which co-ordinates research and trials and organizes meetings, lectures, discussions on farming and husbandry. It is actively linked with other groups in the U.K. and Europe and arranges visits for members.

The Soil Association, Walnut Tree Manor, Haughley, Stowmarket, Suffolk, IP14 3RS, U.K.
The Soil Association (S.A.) is one of the most important organic organizations. It is based on the belief that:
Organic husbandry is the best means of building up soil fertility to produce better crops of high nutritional value leading to better health.

The Soil Association is concerned with health — of man, of animals, of plants, and therefore especially with the health and fertility of the top few inches of the soil on which all life depends.

The SA deserves a special mention in this book because it actually coined the word wholefood to describe natural unrefined, unprocessed foods. It will give advice to individuals or farmers or anyone interested in learning more about organic husbandry. Courses are run regularly throughout the country for members, plus conferences, lectures and exhibitions. The S.A. is supported by outstanding organic writers such as Lady Eve Balfour. Members also receive invitations to the many meetings and activities, as well as a regular magazine. The S.A. retail outlet is the 'Wholefood' shop, Baker Street, London W1. (*See* WHERE TO BUY)
The Soil Association Australia, H. W. Short (Secretary), 6 Brickham Court, Dernancort 5075, South Australia. In Canada: Citizens' Association to Save the Environment (CASE), 6002 West Saanich Road, Victoria RR7, British Columbia, Canada V8X 3X3

United States Government Printing Office,
Superintendent of Documents, Washington D.C. 20402, U.S.A. Tel: Washington 2752051
The U.S. Government Printing Office provides an outstanding range of informative leaflets and books (free list on request) ranging from *Feeding Young Children, Senate Select Committee on Human Needs,* to *The Nutritive Value of American Foods.* The information ranges from basic explanations to the highly technical, from how to choose beans and dry them to famine in the world today.

The Vegetarian Society of the U.K., Parkdale, Dunham Road, Altrincham, Cheshire, U.K.
Tel: 061 928 0793
The Vegetarian Society (VS) is a long established organization dedicated to the principles of food without the slaughter of animals. It attracts people of all beliefs and draws no distinction between members who wish to avoid all dairy produce and eggs (vegans). There is a healthy climate of free discussion. Views are aired at the regular meetings and discussions as well as in the monthly magazine *The New Vegetarian.*

The U.K. society is affiliated to the International Vegetarian Union which is co-ordinating some outstanding research into food and agriculture. In the U.K., the V.S. published its *Green Plan for Farming, Food and Land* in 1977 which set out a whole system of alternative agriculture and food production. It is also sponsoring a *Campaign for real bread,* which advocates making bread once more a major source of nutrients.

In line with the nutritional researches the V.S. issues some excellent booklets such as *Outline of Vegetarian Nutrition, World Food Production in the Balance,* as well as many sheets of dietary advice and recipes. The V.S. also has a research section which constantly investigates important aspects of the meat-free diet. It sponsors research at various universities, and has contributed greatly to the fibre-hypothesis by assessing vegetarian diets. Subscribers receive regular information sheets on the research.

The Society's motto is: 'Killing for food is unhealthy, uneconomic and unnecessary; a vegetarian diet offers a humane solution to the world food problem.'

Vegetarian speakers and cookery demonstrators travel nationwide and also organize cookery courses.

The Vegetarian Society of Australasia, 723 Glenhuntly Road, S. Caulfield, Victoria 3162, Australia.

Association Vegetarienne de France, 8 bis rue Campagne-Première, 75014 Paris, France. Tel: 663 43 25

Bund fur Lebenserneuerrung, e.V. (Herrn Rudolk Meyer), D 3000 Hannover, Munzeler, Strasse 18B, West Germany.

The American Vegetarian Union, Dr. Jesse Mercer Gehman (President), R.D. no 3, Duncannon, Penna 17021, U.S.A.

The American Vegan Society, Mrs F. Dinshah, (Secretary), Sun Crest, Malaga, New Jersey 08328, U.S.A.

Working Weekends on Organic Farms, 56 High Street, Lewes, Sussex EN7 1XE, U.K.
This is the co-ordinating body for organic farms throughout the U.K. It issues lists and details of those farms that welcome visitors for weekends or longer stays. Some farms specialize in actually teaching about organic methods. In such cases, visitors should be prepared to help.

Where to buy
Australia

Australia is in a different position regarding natural and wholefoods and mail order for two reasons:
It has a quite outstanding range of health food shops. Practically every small suburb or town has an excellent specialist store run either by the Sanitarium Health Food Company or the PDF (Producers, Distributors Federation). These shops supply wholefoods, vitamins, handmills and other aids. Commercial postage rates in Australia are higher than in the U.S.A. which means that mail order companies cannot compete with local shops. For details of health food shop addresses contact: The Sanitarium Health Food Company, 78 Old Canterbury Rd., Lewisham, N.S.W. 2049

Captain Distributing Co. Pty. Ltd., Bridge Road, Dandenong, Victoria 3175
Clearing outlet for many organic growers and beekeepers. Captain Distributing supply bulk honey, seeds, grains, flours, and legumes cash and carry.

Honey Corporation of Australia Ltd., 391 Archerfield Road, Darra, Queensland, 4076
Large honey specialists with a huge selection of blends and varieties. Many bulk sizes available, with price reductions for quality.

G.O. Jackel & Sons, 99-103 Williams Road, Wangaratta, Victoria 3677
Suppliers of basic wholefood staples, such as flours, grains, beans and peas, oils, and also limited supply of aids such as organic spray fertilizers.

P.D.S. Co-Operative Ltd., Quay and Valentine Street, Sydney, N.S.W. 2000 (P.O. Box k-403 Haymarket, Sydney, 2000)
P.D.S. is Australia's leading marketing and distributing co-operative. It deals with local and export markets and co-ordinates the sale of farm produce, stock feeds, and grains. P.D.S. organizes bulk sales of butter, honey, cheese, and other dairy produce from local suppliers. This large organization is generally helpful in supplying bulk buy details to groups.

Vitamin Supplies (Pty) Ltd., 51-55 Warrah St., East Chatswood, Sydney, N.S.W.
Australia's leading specialists in vitamins and health supplements. They will supply mail order. Vitamin Supplies are also the agents for many overseas companies.

South Africa

B. Ginsberg, Corner Strand and Railway Street, Woodstock, Cape Town, South Africa.
Ginsberg are the growers and distributors of Rooibosch tea. They will send small amounts of tea by mail-order worldwide, and also supply a list of retailers who stock Rooibosch.

United Kingdom

Beauty without Cruelty Ltd, Avebury Avenue, Tonbridge, Kent TN9 ITL. Tel: Tonbridge 365291
The entire range of Beauty Without Cruelty products is sent mail order from this warehouse. The cosmetics and toilet preparations are made entirely without animal products and tested on human beings, not animals. The organization has shops throughout the country which stock cosmetics, simulated fur coats and imitation leather handbags and shoes.

Beauty without Cruelty Shop (Martha Hill), 40-41 Marylebone High Street (1st floor), London W1. Tel: 01 486 2845 (also deals in mail order)

Cathay of Bournemouth Ltd, Dept VG, 32 Cleveland Road, Bournemouth, BH1 4QG, Dorset. Tel: Bournemouth 37178
Complete medicinal herb service from the largest retail herbalists in the U.K. Herbal remedies for catarrh, rheumatism, fatigue, psoriasis, and many other complaints. Send 20p for colour catalogue. Personal callers also welcome.

Chase Compost Seeds Ltd, Benhall, Saxmundham, Suffolk. Tel: Saxmundham 2149
Suppliers of organically produced seeds and herbs. A wide variety of vegetable and flower seeds, some guaranteed non-chemically dressed. Send SAE and 20p for catalogue.

Cranks Health Foods, Marshall Street, London W1 Tel: 01 437 2915
Cranks has become a byword in the wholefood world. It began in 1961 when Daphne Swan and David and Kay Canter opened a restaurant on vegetarian principles. The trio have succeeded in turning the term 'cranks' from one of abuse to praise. Cranks' food is served in an atmosphere meticulously detailed by David Canter to provide the right environment. The business is constantly growing and now includes health food shops throughout the U.K., a wholegrain shop, a craftwork shop, and an outside catering service. The principles behind Cranks are:
We reject the trend in modern food towards lifeless, devitalised, refined and chemicalized foods. We believe, along with a growing minority of the population, that the vast majority of mankind's disease is the direct product of this type of food.
Cranks' premises at Marshall Street include a large restaurant and health food shop which will send health food items by mail order on request.

Cranks Wholegrain Shop, 37 Marshall Street, London, W1 Tel: 01 439 1809
Sells a wide variety of beans, peas, grains, rice, flours, mueslis, and freshly baked wholemeal bread. There are reductions for larger quantities ordered and all goods, except bread, are sent mail order on request.

Craftwork Gallery (a subsidiary of Cranks), Newburgh Street, London W1 Tel: 01 439 3002
This shop specialises in craft jewellery, hand-woven garments, unusual toys and hand-blown glass. Mail order for the special convenience of customers.

Crystal Harvest Wholefoods, 28 London Road, St Albans, Hertfordshire. Tel: St Albans 30911
Specializes in mail-order wholefoods and stocks a very

wide variety. Beans, peas, seeds, grains, organic rice, wholefood pastas, unrefined cold pressed oils, cider vinegar, sea vegetables, wholemeal and unbleached flours, soya products, coffee and tea substitutes, honey, nuts, and dried fruits are sold in both small and bulk sizes. Discounts are given on larger sizes. Send SAE for price list. Callers welcome.

Culpeper Ltd, Hadstock Road, Linton, Cambridge, CB1 6NJ. Tel: Cambridge 891196
Culpeper is one of the truly outstanding herb suppliers in the world. The firm was founded in the seventeenth century by the great English herbalist,. Thomas Culpeper. The name Culpeper has a ring of authority that the modern company has done much to maintain. Regular customers in 46 countries from the U.S.A., Europe, Africa, Australia, and the Middle East deal direct with the mail-order headquarters in Cambridge. A very comprehensive selection of products is offered: herbal medicines and remedies, cosmetics, hair and bath preparations, herbs and spices for cooking, herbal beverages, vinegars, honeys, chutneys, pot pourris, lavender, pomanders, sleep cushions and sachets, books and cards.

Dietmart, 4 Fife Road, Kingston, Surrey. Tel: 01 546 2394
This is the mail-order section of Holland and Barrett, the leading health food chain in the U.K. It specializes in vitamins and herbs and offers a huge variety. Medicinal and healing herbs and vitamins from A to F, tonics and sprouting seeds are among the items on the mailing list. Its products are sent all over the world.

Elizabeth David, 46 Bourne Street, London SW1. Tel: 01 730 3123
This shop, founded by the famous cookery writer, Elizabeth David, supplies by mail order an exceptionally wide range of kitchen equipment and utensils, as well as traditional French cuisine terrines, bain-maries, casseroles and pans. Detailed catalogue on request.

Faith Products Natural Cosmetics, 17 Bellevue Crescent, Edinburgh EH3 6NE, Scotland. Tel: 031 556 0312
This is one of the great natural cosmetic companies recommended by the Herb Society with mail-order customers worldwide. Only the pure herbal extracts are used, and no mineral oil, harsh chemicals, or artificial colouring are present. The 'organic seaweed shampoo' is made from freshly gathered seaweed; the 'Marigold Sunshine Shampoo' combines pure marigold extract with carotene, rich in Vitamin A. A free list will be sent on request. It includes rosemary and camomile moisturizer, honey and almond moisturizer, sunflower and wheatgerm scrub, and oatmeal cleansing cream.

Harmony Foods, 1-9 Earl Cottages, Earl Road, London, SE1 Tel: 01 237 8396
Harmony foods are the distributors of high quality organic produce such as grains and cereals, beans and peas, sauces and spreads, oils, drinks, and specialities such as Umeboshi plums and Wakame. They will deal in bulk orders over £30 ($54) which must be collected from the above address. However, Harmony specializes in mail-order quality ginseng which is sent worldwide. They have a regular supply of the rare Red Chinese ginseng roots, plus American ginseng, both wild and cultivated.

Henry Doubleday Research Association, Bocking, Braintree, Essex.
This organic gardeners' association specializes in mail-order goods that are hard to find in ordinary retail outlets. They offer a very comprehensive range of organic sprays, fertilizers, weed killers, and approved compost bins. HDRA publishes an excellent range of booklets. (*See* ORGANIZATIONS)

Höfels Pure Foods, Woolpit, Bury St Edmunds, Suffolk, IP30 9QS Tel: 0359 40592
This is the company started by Dr Höfels to retail his garlic pearles. Höfels are still the leading garlic retailers, but they also deal in many other organic products: kibbled wheat, wheat grains, oatmeal, sesame salt, breadmaking kits, soya beans and soya flakes, wheatgerm oil, and rye flour. They are the distributors for the Belgian Lima Company which deals in high grade buckwheat, millet and grains.

R. Hunt & Co, Ltd, Atlas Works, Earls Colne, Colchester, Essex. Tel: Earls Colne 2032
Specialists in hand-grinding mills and stone buhrs and other types of equipment and organic aids. Free list available on request.

Jacksons of Piccadilly, 172 Piccadilly, London, W1 Tel: 01 235 9233
This famous London shop specializes in exotic food items which they will send to customers around the world. The wide and unusual herb selection is geared to gourmet cooking. Other items of interest to wholefood cooks include freshly pressed olive oils, rice vinegar, and green peppercorn mustard.

Lighthorne Herbs, Lighthorne Rough, Moreton Morrell, Warwickshire. Tel: Moreton Morrell 426
Specialists in growing and marketing a wide variety of decorative and culinary herbs with particularly good selections in mints and thymes. The plants are sent well-packed ready to plant. Special prices are given for named collections.

Pure Honey Supplies Co. Ltd, Mildon House, Cedar

Avenue, Enfield, Middlesex. Tel: 01 804 5506
The U.K. pure organic honey supplier who will send
mail order anywhere within the U.K. in sizes from 3 kg
(7 lb) upwards. Alternatively you can collect from their
warehouse. Excellent selection of honey, such as Pure
Australian, Light Amber, Hungarian Acacia, Jamaican
Logwood, Canadian White Clover, and Chilean Wild
Flower. This supplier also deals in pure demerara sugar
cane, Barbados sugar, black molasses, malt extract,
and bulk cider vinegar. Samples and lists available on
request.

Ranolan Health Foods Co. Ltd, Wargrave on
Thames, Berkshire. Tel: Wargrave 2735
Specializes in bulk honey and molasses by mail order
throughout the U.K. Ten varieties of honey available
(Australian Amber, Spanish, Tasmanian) in 3 kg (7 lb)
containers upwards, as well as black molasses.
Transport costs are included in the price. Samples and
price list on request.

Real Food, 37 Broughton Street, Edinburgh 1,
Scotland. Tel: 031 557 1911
The largest wholesaler in the U.K. who sends its large
range of goods by mail order throughout the U.K. Real
Food's motto is: 'The healthiest food at the lowest cost
per pound.' Special bulk price catalogue will be sent on
request. Real Food deals in millet, barley, wheatgerm,
wheatflakes, flour, beans, special sprouting beans, nuts,
dried fruit, cider vinegar, honey oils, TVP milk
powder, and many other wholefoods.

J.I. Rodale & Co. Ltd., Chestnut Close, Potten End,
Berkhamsted, Hertfordshire HP4 2BR. Tel: Tring 4166
The Rodale Company can be called the mouthpiece of
the organic world as it publishes a magazine and a
huge selection of books on health, nutrition, gardening,
beauty, and organic living generally. It also mail orders
The Natrodale range of vitamins from the above address,
as well as water filters, humidifiers, cheese kits, yoghurt
kits and culture, relaxator chair and organic seeds and
sprouting equipment.

Rutin Products Ltd., 82 High Street, Sandhurst,
Camberley, Surrey, GU17 8ED Tel: Yateley 879151
Rutin Products Ltd. specializes in natural products
high in rutic acid, such as green buckwheat tea. Pure
rutic acid, or rutin is sold as Rutivite tablets. Rutin
tablets are prescribed by homeopathic and
naturopathic doctors for many circulatory complaints,
hardening of the arteries, high blood pressure, and
varicose veins. Mail order worldwide.

Synpharma International Ltd., Castle House,
Norwich, NR2 IPJ, Norfolk.
Specialist firm for wheatgerm treated by the 'Keimdiat'
fermentation process to preserve freshness without

additives. Small introductory samples are available.
Send SAE for mail order details.

Thompson & Morgan (Ipswich) Ltd., Crane Hall,
London Road, Ipswich, Suffolk, 1P2 0BA Tel: Ipswich
214226
Thompson & Morgan offers a very wide range of
vegetable and flower seeds, some of them organically
grown, and are the leading innovators in the seed-
growing world. They offer the latest hybrids, strains
and crosses and often completely new varieties. It is
their policy to keep up with nutritional researches so
this is reflected in their catalogue. They promote low
oxalic acid spinach and hull-less pumpkin nuts, herbal
teas and remedies, ginseng, garlic and comfrey.

Other Thompson & Morgan specialities include
sprouting seeds, from alfalfa to triticale, fish farming,
and honey bees. The kitchen aids section includes
water filters, food dryers, yoghurt makers and icecream
and Chinese woks.

They will send mail order worldwide for orders
accompanied by international money orders and where
necessary, import permits. Send SAE for free catalogue
and advice.

Tumblers Bottom Herb Farm Ltd., Kilmersdon, Nr.
Radstock, Somerset. Tel: Radstock 3452

Nearly 300 varieties of culinary, medicinal and
aromatic herbs. A descriptive catalogue giving planting
and other details costs 20p.

Wholefood, 112 Baker Street, London W1
Tel: 01 935 3924
This is perhaps the premier wholefood shop in the
entire U.K. It was founded in conjunction with the Soil
Association to sell goods and fresh produce strictly in
accordance with organic principles, and consists of a
very well-stocked health food shop with a fresh fruit
and vegetable section, plus a comprehensive bookshop.
The staff are knowledgeable and helpful. The shop
stocks the whole range of organic foods such as free-
range eggs, freshly baked bread made from unsprayed
wheat, vitamin supplements, dairy produce, beverages,
baby foods and refrigerated wheatgerm. It also supplies
electric juicers, grain mills, water filters and seed
sprouters (*See* KITCHEN UTENSILS). The books cover a
wide range of food and health subjects. Wholefood will
send mail order by request.

Wholefood Butchers, 24 Paddington Street, London
W1 Tel: 01 486 1390
This is a most unusual butcher's shop run on the strict
organic principles of its sister shop, Wholefood, in
Baker Street around the corner. The meat is supplied
from animals reared without hormone injections or
artificial stimulants or factory farming methods and fed

155

non-sprayed food. The Wholefood Butchers has a delicatessen counter selling top quality pâté, brawn and cooked meats. Bulk prices can be negotiated with the head butcher.

Cash and Carry UK

Community Wholesale, 5 Prince of Wales Crescent, London NW1 Tel: 01 267 5845
Main suppliers of unpackaged wholefoods to co-ops and other retail outlets. Community Wholesale is run on a non-profit basis and all sales are cash and collect. Obviously the large quantities like 50 kg (112 lb) are much cheaper, and this is where food-buying groups score. Many products do come in smaller amounts such as 11 kg (25 lb) or 5 kg (12 lb) lots. Products include beans, peas, grains, rice, nuts, honey, juices, peanut butter, and oils.

Neals Yard, Wholefood Warehouse, 2 Neal's Yard, Covent Garden, London WC2 Tel: 01 240 1154
Cash and carry wholefood warehouse that deals in small amounts as well as bulk. For example, aduki beans can be bought in 1 kg (2 lb), 2 kg (5 lb), 5 kg (11 lb), 10 kg (22 lb) and 50 kg (110 lb) packs. This Warehouse stocks the complete range of dried, natural foods.

USA/Canada

Anderson's Organic Grains, Box 186, Lower Farm, Manitoba, Canada.
One of Canada's leading organic wholesalers and retailers who specialize in grains and cereals. They deal in bulk and also smaller packs of wheat, rye, and maize plus a wide variety of other grains. Many blends of flours are available.

Anvil Mineral Co., Bay Springs, Miss 39422, U.S.A.
Specialists in organic fertilizers offering a good selection of seaweeds, mineral compounds, barks, and manures.

Arrowhead Mills Inc., P.O. Box 866, Hereford, Texas 79045, U.S.A.
This is one of the most important mills in the U.S.A. Arrowhead specialise in the famous Deaf Smith County wheat which is commonly considered the best available. Bulk or smaller quantities are available mail order. They also deal in white and yellow cornmeal, and soya beans. Arrowhead are widely noted for their granolas, seven-grain cereals and Deaf Smith crunches which are packed in convenient small packs.

W. Atlee Burpee & Co., Philadelphia, Pa 19132, or Clinton, Iowa 52732, or Riverside, Ca 92502, U.S.A.
A major seed company mailing its catalogue automatically to 'Organic Gardening' subscribers. Fruit, vegetable, flower, and almost every possible seed available. Huge selection, all seeds untreated. Catalogue on request.

Bio-Control Co., R.2 Box 2394, Ladybird Drive, Auburn, Ca. 95603 U.S.A.
Leading biological control company which supplies ladybugs, praying mantis, and general non-toxic insecticides.

Biorganic Brands Inc., Long Beach, New York 11561, U.S.A.
Supplies a complete range of vitamins mail order, plus apple pectin, flora plus, bee pollen tablets, natural whey, lecithin, and amino acid tablets.

California-McCulloch Equipment Co., Box 3068, Torrance, Ca. 90510, U.S.A.
This company manufactures shredder-grinders which reduce stalky compost to fine shreds in minutes.

Clivus Multrum U.S.A., 14A Eliot Street, Cambridge, Mass. 02138, U.S.A.
A company specializing in the Swedish composting toilet invented by Rikard Lindstrom. The State of Maine has formally approved the use of the Multrum which returns human wastes to compost.

Community Market, P.O. Box 268, Deerfield, Mass. 01342, U.S.A.
Community Market is a clearing house for 36 groups throughout the country which practise cottage economy and community projects. A free catalogue will be sent on request. Products vary from hammocks to snowboots.

Dominion Herb Distributors Inc., 1447-51 St. Lawrence Boulevard, Montreal, Canada.
One of the largest herb dealers in Canada with a wide variety of medicinal and culinary herbs. Free list sent on request.

Gothard Inc., Box 370, Canutillo, Texas, 79835, U.S.A.
Biological control experts, and one of the few suppliers of the trichogramma wasp.

Harvest Health Inc., 1944 Eastern Ave. S.E. Grand Rapids, Michigan, 49507, U.S.A.
Harvest Health Inc. supplies an extensive list of dried herbs as well as healthy live plants. Details supplied on request.

Indiana Botanic Gardens, P.O. Box 5, Hammon, Indiana, U.S.A.
The unusual aspect of this mail order herb company lies in their scientific approach to botanical herbs.

They send a botanical catalogue for 25 cents and a herbalist almanac for 15 cents.

The Infinity Food Co., 171 Duane St., New York, N.Y. 10013, U.S.A.
Infinity send a free catalogue listing their extensive mail-order list of basic natural food staples, such as legumes, grains, and oils, plus their own stone-milled organic flour. Other items include homeopathic tissuesalts; snacks and beverages. Minimum order $50 (£28).

Insectivorous Botanical Gardens, 1918 Market St., Wilminton, N.C. 28401, U.S.A.
This company leads in another aspect of biological control, carniverous plants. IBG supplies descriptive free literature about their products.

International Yogurt Co., 628 North Doheny Drive, Los Angeles, Ca. 90069, U.S.A.
International Yogurt Co. is the leading company in this field. It specializes in yoghurt cultures, incubators, controllers, and many other related products.

Laurelbrook Foods, P.O. Box 47, Bel Air, Md. 21014, U.S.A.
Laurelbrook Foods provides organic foods in bulk and top quality. Grains, seeds, beans, peas, soya products, honey, fruits, lotions, and approved soaps are among the wide range. List on request. Minimum order $150 (£83).

R.C. Nichols, Box 113, Wilton, NH. 03086, U.S.A.
A company expert in biological control. Insect traps, predators and other items sent by mail order. List on request.

Nichols Garden Nursery, 1190 North Pacific Highway, Albany, Or. 97321, U.S.A.
Nichols Garden Nursery sells three varieties of the hard-to-find flour corn, including Black Aztec, and Indian corn.

Nu-Life Nutrition Ltd., 871 Beatty Street, Vancouver 3, B.C., Canada.
A top Canadian organic food company specializing in herbs and healing plants. A wide range of dried herbs available plus other organic foods. Free list on request.

The Other Way, P.O. Box 20, Grand Isle, Vermont, 05458, U.S.A.
Self-sufficiency suppliers of essential goods such as hand-powered mills and grinders and electric grain mills.

Pfeiffer Foundation Inc., Hungry Hollow Road, Spring Valley, N.Y. 10977, U.S.A.

This company specializes in the Pfeiffer Field Spray and Bacterial Starter developed according to bio-dynamic principles. Instructions and prices sent on request.

The Redwood City Seed Company, P.O. Box 361, Redwood City, Ca. 94064, U.S.A.
A company providing an interesting selection of vegetables, herbs, and fruit seeds. Unusual points include a barter programme in which seeds from private gardens or wild seeds are traded for Redwood seeds. Prices are generally lower than other companies. Informative catalogue on request.

Rocky Hollow Herb Farm, R.D.2, Box 215, Lake Wallkill Rd., Sussex, N.J. 07461, U.S.A.
This is a leading organic farm which specializes in herbs but also sells dried fruits, grains and cereals, and many other foods. They sell live seedlings as well as dried herbs. American ginseng is also under cultivation. Informative catalogue on request.

Stokes Seeds Inc., Box 548, Buffalo, N.Y. 14240, U.S.A.
Stokes Seeds Inc. present one of the largest selections of seeds available. They take pride in quick delivery even during the height of the growing season. Sources include Burpee seeds at generally lower prices. Seed packets also give extremely informative detail. Some treated seed is also available. Detailed catalogue on request.

Stone-Buhr Milling Co, 4052 28th Avenue S.W., Seattle, Washington 98126, U.S.A.
This organization guarantees stone-milled flours and kibbled grains and is one of the few 100% stoneground mills which produce organically approved products.

Stur-Dee Health Products Inc., Island Park, N.Y. 11558, U.S.A.
Stur-Dee Health Products deal in all the vitamin tablets, both chelated and ordinary presentation, plus protein powders, amino acid tablets, raw bran, papaya and peppermint tablets, acidophilus tablets, as well as cosmetic aids such as shampoos, sprays, and skin tablets.

Sudbury Laboratory Inc., Sudbury, Mass. 01776, U.S.A.
Sudbury are the leading dealers in soil kit analysis with prices ranging from $2-200 (£1-111). Sudbury guarantee a full refund of price if properly used test kits do not produce a better crop. They issue two booklets 'The Good Earth . . . Can Do You Dirt', and 'The Organic Supplement to Sudbury Soil Test Kit Manual'.

U.S. Health Club Inc., Yonkers, N.Y. 10702, U.S.A.
An organization supplying a huge range of vitamins and minerals including high potency supplements. Some free samples are sent. Each enquirer receives free copies of *'Health Watchers Daily Check List'*.

Whole Earth Truck Store, 558 Santa Cruz Street, Menlo Park, Ca. 94025, U.S.A.
This company now deals in many aids to the organic way of life, in particular hand-powered and electric mills. They still have some back copies of the famous Whole Earth Cktalogues. Details on request.

World Wide Herbs Ltd., 11 St. Catherine St. East, Montreal 129, Canada.
Whole Earth Catalogues. Details on request. comprehensive catalogue anywhere in the world. As the name suggests, this company will send their herbs mail order anywhere, plus other products light enough to be packaged. They have an outstanding selection of dried herbs and spices, a long list of essential oils, also ginseng and other roots. World Wide specialize in unusual items such as cubeb, nerolis, petitgrain and other items rarely found in ordinary herb dealers.

Cash and Carry USA/Canada

Erewhon Trading Company Inc., 342 Newbury Street, Boston, Mass. 02115, or 8003 Beverly Boulevard, Los Angeles, Ca. 90048.
Good source for the complete range of natural foods. Free brochure on request. Erewhon does not use mail order, but sends goods UPS or by truck. Bulk orders get good wholesale prices.

Mutual Trading Co., 431 Crocker Street, L.A. Ca. 90013
Cash and carry wholesale goods, especially Koda Brothers brown rice. Send for complete list.

Get bulk prices locally
Check the yellow pages for your local Feed Dealer or Seed Dealer. He will have information about farmers' co-ops and other outlets. Many dealers will sell you rice, beans, and flour at prices far below the supermarket.

Organic bulk buys
The Small Farmers' Research Association have lists of members specializing in organic growing. (*See* ORGANIZATIONS)

Acknowledgments

Drawings by
Lindsay Blow: 121-133, Cheryl Clarke: 35, Ingrid Jacob: 16-17, 23-4, 30-1, 44, 59, 61, 64, 67-80, 84-5, 89-91, 93-100, 106, 109-110, 112, 148, Angela Lewer: 26, 34, 37, 39, 40-3, 47-9, 51, 53, 55-7, 105, 146

Picture sources
The producers of the book would like to thank the following who have given permission for pictures to be reproduced:

Christopher Algar: 147, Allinson Flour Millers: 10, Australian Information Service: 54, 63, Heather Angel: 60, 64, 101, 107, 111 (*bottom*), Anglo-Chinese Educational Institute: 105, A-Z Botanical Collection Limited: 46, 91 (*top and bottom*), 94 (*top*), 145, The Bircher-Benner Clinic, Zurich: 86, Anne Bolt: 38, 92, 108, The British Egg Information Service: 42, 43 (*bottom*), Bulmer's Cider: 25, Camera Press Limited: 104, Canadian High Commission: 58 (*top and bottom*), Faber and Faber Limited: 35, Bryan Furner: 1, 72, 94 (*bottom*), 111 (*top*), Robert Harding Associates: 80, 120, George Hyde: 61, The Mansell Collection: 28, 113 (*left*), Mary Evans Picture Library: 50, 102, 113, (*right*), 139, Radio Times Hulton Picture Library: 53, United States Department of Agriculture: 81, The Wellcome Museum of Medical Science: 28

We would also like to thank the following: Geoff Goode (photography), Chris Sorrell (illustrated boxes), Ellen Crampton (index), Michael van Straten (who read the text), Wholefood and Elizabeth David (who kindly supplied us with specialist items for the photography), Rob Matheson (Muesli photograph), the Flour Advisory Board, Paxton & Whitfield Ltd. (who kindly allowed us to do the cheese photography on their premises), and Penguin Books Ltd. for permission to reprint the basic recipe for *Tagliatelle* from Elizabeth David's *Italian Food* (1976 reprint) pp. 97-8, Copyright © Elizabeth David 1954, 1965, 1969.

Book sources
Ackroyd W. and Doughty J. *Legumes in Human Nutrition* United Nations Food and Agricultural Organization, Rome 1964

Borsook H. *Vitamins — What they are and how they can benefit you* Pyramid Publications, New York 1970

Bumgarner M.A. *The Book of Whole Grains* St. Martin's Press, New York 1976

Colimore and Colimore *Nutrition and your Body* Phoenix House, California 1974

Davis A. *Let's Eat Right to Keep Fit* Harcourt Brace Jovanovich Inc., New York revised edition 1970

Hills Lawrence D. *Fertility without Fertilizers* Henry Doubleday Research Association, London 1976; Universe Books, New York 1977

Jarvis D.C. *Folk Medicine* White Lion Publishers, London 1973; Fawcett World, New York 1973

Lucas R. *Nature's Medicines* Universal Publishing and Distributing Corp., New York 1968

Mackarness Dr R. *Not all in the Mind* Pan, London 1976

Shute Dr W.E. and Taub H. *Vitamin E for ailing and healthy Hearts* Pyramid Publications, New York 1972

Stanway Dr A. *Taking the rough with the smooth* Pan, London 1976

Trum Hunter B. *Fact Book on Food Additives and your Health* Keats Publishing Inc., Connecticut 1972

U.S. Dept. of Agriculture *Composition of Foods — raw, processed, prepared* Washington 1975

U.S. Dept. of Agriculture *Nutritive Value of American Foods in Common Units* Washington 1975

Index

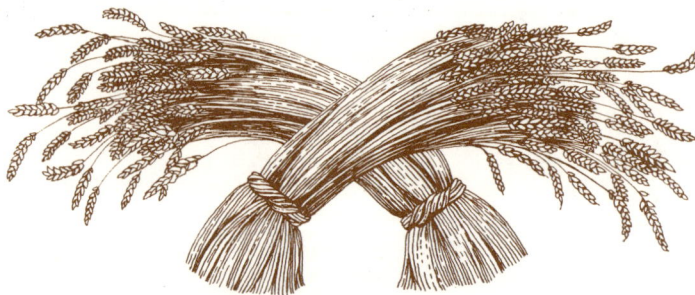